THE ANATOMY OF A HYBRID

THE ANATOMY OF A HYBRID

A Study in
Church-State Relationships

by
LEONARD VERDUIN

William B. Eerdmans Publishing Company

Copyright © 1976 by Wm. B. Eerdmans Publishing Co.
255 Jefferson Ave. S.E., Grand Rapids, Mich. 49502
All rights reserved
Printed in the United States of America

Library of Congress Cataloging in Publication Data
Verduin, Leonard.
   The anatomy of a hybrid.
   Bibliography: p. 261.
   Includes index.
   1. Church and state — History.   2. Religious liberty — History.   I. Title.
BV630.2.V47   261.7   76-3654
ISBN 0-8028-1615-0

CONTENTS

	Introduction	7
One	"THE DAUGHTERS OF MEN"	11
Two	"SONS OF GOD"	41
Three	"THE BIRTH OF THE HYBRID"	91
Four	"AND ALSO AFTERWARD"	155
	Episode One	155
	Episode Two	212
	Postscript	253
	Appendix	257
	Bibliographical Notes	261
	Index	268

INTRODUCTION

During the past half-century the world has witnessed the rise of totalitarian governments and monolithic societies, that is, societies in which all are expected to share in the same ultimate loyalty. These are societies in which there is no room for diversity of conviction. I view this development with alarm. My conviction is that for a person to be his proper self he must live in the presence of genuine options, must be able to exercise choice, must, in a word, be free to enjoy a measure of sovereignty. In order to be fully human, a person must be part of a composite society.

Moreover, it is my conviction that the composite society is to a large extent the product (albeit a by-product) of the world-view of authentic Christianity. Authentic Christianity is firmly committed to the idea of nonsameness, to the idea that people are never to be thought of as all being in the same category in the matter of ultimate convictions. Authentic Christianity sees human society as composite, that is, consisting of people of diverse ways of thinking. It does not expect to encounter unanimity in human society; it expects to find some men stumbling at the very same cross in which other men glory. Totalitarian systems, on the other hand, view all members of a given society as basically unanimous; such systems can thus arise only in a climate in which authentic Christianity has either lapsed or has never been. If this is correct, authentic Christianity is the only viable alternative to totalitarianism.

A word of explanation is necessary concerning the expression "authentic Christianity" as it is used in this study.

By it I mean Christianity that is true to the blueprints laid down in the New Testament. "Historic Christianity" is not the same as "authentic Christianity"; indeed, "historic Christianity" is often a mixture in which the Christian world-view is mingled with non-Christian systems of thought. As a consequence of such mingling, history is the story of a constant fluctuation between a faith that feeds on compositism and a faith that fights it. This book renders an account of that fluctuation.

A word is in order concerning the schematization of the argument. A quaint old story, occurring in the book of Genesis, has supplied the literary framework into which I have cast the argument. In this story we read: "And it came to pass, when men began to multiply on the face of the earth, and daughters were born unto them, that the sons of God saw the daughters of men that they were fair; and they took them wives of all which they chose. And the Lord said, My spirit shall not always strive with man, for that he also is flesh; yet his days shall be an hundred and twenty years. There were giants in the earth in those days; and also after that, when the sons of God came in unto the daughters of men, and they bare children to them, the same became mighty men which were of old, men of renown" (Gen. 6:1-4 KJV).

I shall let this ancient story of the birth of the "giants" serve as a sort of literary framework for the study I am about to undertake. Under the heading of "daughters of men" I will discuss that structuring of society which one encounters in every ethnic situation ("ethnic" I define, with Webster's Collegiate Dictionary, as "neither Jewish nor Christian; pagan" — meaning thereby anything that is either pre-Christian or post-Christian). The heading "sons of God" will set forth that new and different structuring of human society which evolved under the pressures of Judaeo-Christian insights. Under "giants" I will discuss the hybrid that was born when, in the fourth century of our era, the "sons of God" and the "daughters of men" came together and became "one flesh," out of which cohabitation a "giant" was born, a large and rugged hybrid. The section entitled "and also afterward" (which will introduce the largest part of the book) will relate the fact that, as in the Genesis story, the two parties of such illicit commingling came back for more of the same, again and again, with the result that each time another hybrid ca-

INTRODUCTION

vorted, first on one side of the Atlantic and then on the other.

Within the text, footnotes that appear in numerical sequence refer to bibliographical information and appear at the end of the book. Those that appear in alphabetical sequence provide additional information germane to the subject, and they appear at the bottom of the page so that the reader can conveniently consult them as he reads. Translations of foreign language quotations, unless otherwise noted, are by the author.

A word, finally, concerning the timing of this study. Part Four, Episode II, takes the reader to the American scene, where it is now two centuries since the blueprints were drawn up for a new structuring of human society. This book traces the genesis of this new structuring, known also as "the American experiment." It is probably fair to say that no feature of this "American experiment" has been quoted more frequently or examined more carefully than what is known as the First Amendment of the Federal Constitution of the United States, the amendment that reads: "Congress shall make no laws touching the establishment of religion nor prohibiting the free exercise thereof." Since this book is essentially a setting forth of the evolution of that amendment, it comes at an opportune time — the bicentennial year 1976. The author cherishes the fond hope that this study will contribute to a better understanding of the thought system that led to the "American experiment." May this book give many Americans a new awareness of the heritage that is theirs and a greater gratitude for it.

Part One

"THE DAUGHTERS OF MEN"

Let us begin this study with the assertion that pre-Christian societies are *sacral,* meaning — as Webster defines the word — "of or for religious rites." A sacral society has a single religiosity at its heart, an ultimate loyalty of soul, which, it is assumed, is common to each member of that society. In a sacral society one's religion is a matter of course, determined by one's inclusion in the societal unit. A sacral society is held together by sacrament. It has a shrine to which each member of that society is oriented, and it has a specified deportment before that shrine, deportment that is essentially sacramental in character. In fact, it may be said that the basic function of sacrament in such a sacral society is the tying together of the societal unit. Sacrament properly understood is a device whereby an already existing togetherness allegedly becomes a religious togetherness. As a mere glance at the words indicates, sacrament, sacred, sacral, and sacrifice are related words. It may thus be said that a sacral society is a society held together by the sacred, the sacred encapsulated in sacrament and expressed in sacrifice.

In a sacral society there is unanimity on the religious plane, the plane on which man's deepest loyalties lie. What Cicero said of the Rome of his day is true of all sacral societies, of all pre-Christian societies: "Every commonwealth has its religion and we have ours."[1] It follows that in a sacral society it makes no sense to speak of "church" and "state"; these institutions are as yet undifferentiated. To be sure, there may be a king and a priest, each with his own function; but the two offices may also be combined in one person: the king (*rex*) may also be the priest (*sacerdos*). But whether they be one or two, the "parish" is one: the king rules over the same populace for which the priest officiates at the altar. There is no "church" that is distinguishable from the "state," and there is no "state" that can be distinguished from the "church." Sacral society precludes the idea of a "non-confessing state"; its "state" has the same commitment to ultimates that is the heritage of each of its citizens. Their gods are its gods; their mysteries are its mysteries; their faith is its faith.

What Hendrik Berkhof has said about the religion of ancient Rome — that it was a *Groepsverbandgodsdienst*[2] — can be said of all pre-Christian religions, namely, that they have as their primary purpose the tying together in religion that which is already tied together by other considerations. A few examples may serve to support and illustrate our contention that pre-Christian religion serves this purpose. The Babylon depicted in Chapter Three of the book of Daniel is such an example. Babylon operated on the assumption that all who dwelt within its jurisdiction should, could, and would, fall down in worship before an image (whether erected by the king or the priest is not pertinent — it would be an anachronism to ask). The Babylon of those days was big and varied (we read of "satraps, princes, governors, captains, judges, treasurers, counselors, sheriffs, and all the rulers of the provinces" assembled for the dedication of the image that Nebuchadnezzar had set up); but the assumption was that all who were under Babylon's rule would bow as one man in an unbroken unison. Here we see a classic example of the sacral society. To be of Babylon implies genuflection before Babylon's object of worship.[A]

Another example is the Nineveh of which we read in the book of Jonah. It was a sacral city-state, and as such it had a

---

[A]It is worth noting that the whole ceremony was staged because of a reported threat to the sacral structuring of Babylonian society. Rumor had it that three young men, members of a vanquished race, who by way of unusual diligence had insinuated themselves into the affairs of state, were worshipping in secret at *another*, a *non-public* shrine. The king and his advisors saw in this slight threat to the sacral order a danger so great as to warrant the great lengths to which they went to neutralize it. They were convinced, as are all sacralists, that to allow even a modicum of pluralism on the plane of religion is to invite chaos. The king and his court were adamantly committed to the sacralist postulate that the health, indeed the very existence, of ordered society depends on unanimity at the shrine.

publicly espoused religion. When the rulers of Nineveh, impressed by the preaching of the prophet from afar, came to the conviction that fasting in sackcloth and ashes was in order, they published a decree calling all Nineveh to a mass ceremony of contrition. Every Ninevite was expected to participate; every throat was to join in a grand ensemble — without exception. There was no one who elected not to join in the massive demonstration, no one who chose to participate in another litany of compunction. Here again we see a typically sacral society in action.

Or we may glance at an example recorded in the New Testament: the city of Ephesus as shown in Acts 19 is typical of the sacral society. Here a whole city chants the religious phrase "Great is Diana of the Ephesians!" in endless repetition, until the chant falls in step with itself so that, like the purr of a tractor in a valley, it pushes the sound ahead of itself. For three whole hours the Ephesians chanted the phrase that their Diana was illustrious. No Ephesian so much as thought of staying indoors — much less of substituting one syllable in the chant of adulation. Ephesus too was sacral; all Ephesians shared in the same religion, in which Diana was the favorite deity.[B]

Or we may select an example not drawn from the Christian scriptures and not belonging to ancient times. In the society of the Navajo Indians of our great Southwest prior to the coming of Christian missionaries (we say "prior" because, since their coming, it is no longer typical of the sacral society), every Navajo's religion was a foregone conclusion; his Navajoness determined that. When the Navajo medicine man went through his religious ritual, carefully guarded and executed with minute attention to detail, every member of the tribe looked on in unanimous involvement. There were no non-participating ones, no dissenters, none oriented toward any *other* religiosity. Navajo society, in those early days, was sacral.

The same is true of the Navajo's long-time neighbors, the

[B] Once more it is important to notice that what brought the Ephesians out that day was that it had come to their attention that there was a man in the city who posed a threat to its religious homogeneity. He was gaining converts to *another* ultimate loyalty. The lone preacher had come but recently, and there was every indication that he would be on his way before long. Nor had he made any large number of converts. Nevertheless, the threat to the sacral order, small though that threat was, was enough to bring sacral Ephesus into turmoil and its usual activities to a standstill.

Zuni Indians. When they performed their rain dances (we use the past tense, for among them also, due to the influence of the Christian missionary, that erstwhile homogeneity has made way for a composite situation), every member of the pueblo felt himself to be involved in it. He was present as a matter of course; he had never had occasion to evaluate an alternative because he had never been confronted with one. His religion had come down to him in much the same way as the color of his eyes, the texture of his hair, his diet, his language, or whatever else characterized the population group whose genes he carried. The Zuni pueblo was likewise structured as all pre-Christian society is structured: it was sacral.

Having given examples of sacral societies, ancient and contemporary, we go on to point out that sacral societies are not necessarily monotheistic. Indeed, they can be, and usually are, decidedly polytheistic. For example, the society of pagan Rome had a veritable college of deities. This was Rome's boast. Each time she vanquished a people, she admitted to her already large inventory of recognized deities, with pomp and ceremony, the god or gods of the newly subjugated people. The religion of the conquered tribe was thenceforth a legitimate note in the chorus of Rome's chant vis-à-vis the divine; from that moment on, the subdued people's deity was in the yellow pages of Rome's religious directory.

This policy of inclusiveness was assumed to be good politics. In the *Octavius* by Minucius Felix, a near contemporary testimony, we read that "the Romans serve all gods. That is why the power and the authority of the Romans has embraced the whole world. . . . Having stormed the ramparts, even in the first frenzy of victory, they respected the divinities of the conquered, seeking everywhere for strange gods and adopting them as Rome's own, even setting up altars to unknown powers and the shades of the dead. Thus, by adopting the rites of all nations they of Rome became entitled to rule over them." For political reasons the deity or deities of a newly conquered nation were admitted into Rome's college of deities, and from that moment on the religion of the conquered tribe was a legitimate note in the chorus of Rome's overture to deity. One could at any time and in any place be partial to the deity of his choice — in much the same way that the medieval Christian could be partial to his patron saint. Rome's college of deities was a federation brought about by annexation, just as the Roman state was a federation achieved by annexation.

Not one of the constitutive units had been monotheistic; at best they had been henotheistic (that is, partial to their own tribal god while granting that the gods of other tribes were just as real as their own). It was hence quite easy for such vanquished peoples to go along with the policy of Rome; they had always thought of their tribal deity as *primus inter pares* (the first among equals), and they could continue to think that way even after they had been annexed by Rome. The changeover was therefore not traumatic.

There were, however, two restrictions, two points at which Rome's seemingly liberal policy stopped short. The restrictions were these: first, that no one's favored deity was to push the rest of the gods out of the god-pool; second, that no one was to do homage to a deity not listed in Rome's inventory of deities. Neither of these two courses of conduct could be tolerated, because each posed a threat to the sacral pattern: the former estranged those elements of the population who were unwilling to tolerate the elbowing out of their object of worship; the latter introduced into society a nonpublic cult, a cult that was behind the back of the rest of the citizenry.

It was on both of these counts that the early Christians ran into trouble, trouble that resulted in the persecutions. The Christians were stark monotheists; they could not, for that reason, allow the object of their worship to be ushered into a god-pool — not even as first among equals. Their God was the God that ends all gods: where he entered all others had to get out. Had the early Christians been able to let their God be added to the list, there would have been no difficulty. Rome would have been quite ready and willing to let these Christians be as partial to the object of their worship as they pleased — just so the worship of other deities was left uncensured. The early Christians could not go along with this inclusiveness. They therefore walked in the path that was intolerable in the eyes of sacral Roman society: they practiced a nonpublic cult.

It was this that drew the wrath of contemporary Roman society. How severe this wrath was may be gathered from the following accusation, hurled at the Christians in the aforementioned *Octavius*:

> At their nocturnal gatherings, their solemn fasts and barbarous meals, the bond of union is not any sacred rite but crime. It is a people that lurks in darkness and shuns the light, that is silent in public but talkative in caves . . . . Ill weeds grow

apace, and these vicious habits are spreading by the day; these abominable secret haunts where these impious wretches hold their meetings are increasing in number all over the world. These execrable conspirators must be utterly rooted out . . . . Why do they make such effort to hide and conceal whatever it is that they worship? Honorable acts always welcome publicity; only crime delights in secrecy. Why have they no altars, no temples, no well-known images? Why do they never speak in public, never meet freely, unless it be that the hidden object of their worship is either criminal or disgraceful?[3]

There are two things in this quotation to which we call special attention, both of them matters to which we shall refer repeatedly in the course of this book. One is the underlying assumption that religion is essentially a matter of "sacred rite," of solemn act, of *sacrament,* if you will. The other matter is the idea that religious rite practiced anywhere save in the public eye and under public auspices is undesirable, behavior that makes the participant culpable. These two matters are definitive features of the sacral view of things. We shall encounter them again and again in the course of this study.

That the early Christians met in secret, that is, off by themselves, was a fact. It is usually assumed that this was because it was dangerous to do otherwise. Although there is no doubt that it was dangerous, it must be pointed out that the holding of nonpublic gatherings was done for reasons of *principle* rather than of *practicality;* there was no other course open to the early Christians because of certain items in the Christian creed. One of these was the doctrinal item that although the God of the Christians was held to be the creator and sustainer of all men, he was nevertheless the Father in a redemptive sense of only a percentage, the percentage that had been metamorphosed from the modality of being lost to the modality of being saved. The fruit of this doctrinal item made the early Christians very obnoxious to sacral Rome, with its sacralist notion that there must be unanimity at the shrine if there is to be tranquillity on the square. In the sacralist view, any citizen who does not see eye to eye with other citizens in things pertaining to primary loyalties is by definition seditious, intolerably so. In a word, it was the early Christians' break with sacralist tenets that made them engage in a nonpublic cult, which in turn resulted in the persecutions they endured.

A quick glance at Athenian society will reveal that in this matter Athens was an exact duplicate of Rome. Athens too was sacral, albeit polytheistic. Athens had its publicly espoused religion, its altars displayed in public places and erected at public expense. It also had its list of officially recognized objects of worship, the kind and the not so kind. Athens too was always ready to add names to its list of recognized deities. Like Rome, it had gone the second mile in a magnanimous effort not to exclude any existing deity. To make sure no object of worship was being slighted, it had even raised up an altar to "The Unknown God." One could pick and choose in Athens. But here too, as in Rome, the seemingly liberal policy was actually very intolerant. Athens also frowned on the idea of a God who demands the whole stage; and it too suppressed the nonpublic cult. No object was to monopolize the stage, and no object was to be worshiped in a nonpublic way. Athenian society was sacral, and — as we said — a sacral society cannot permit either the one or the other; to allow either would be to allow a disintegrating solvent to be applied to the consensus at the shrine, the consensus which men of a sacral bent of mind say they must have.

The situation we have delineated puts the activity and the experience of Paul in Athens (as recorded in Acts 17) in their proper light. Paul was firmly committed to the idea of a God who ends all gods. He knew full well that Athenian society was in no mood to tolerate this idea. He himself was even less in a mood to let the God of the Christians become a member, even if it was the leading member, of the Athenian pantheon. What to do in this dilemma? To fall in line with Athenian sacralism was to fall out with his sender, and to walk in step with his sender meant to break step with Athenian sacralism. Paul was up early that morning to plan the strategy of a day that promised to be difficult. He planned as he walked; and as he passed the shrine to "The Unknown God," it gave him an idea. He would introduce his object under this label, thus avoiding the charge of introducing an object not already on the approved list. He would work within the letter of the law even as he ran against the spirit of it; his conscience did not permit him to do otherwise. But, though Paul's clever device worked for a brief while, the Athenians were not so dull that they did not realize that he was after all introducing a new and unlisted object. They fastened on the words *Iēsus* and *Anastasis* ("Jesus" and "Resurrection"), and on the strength of these noncurrent names they hustled Paul off — not gently we may assume — to Mars Hill, the place where such infractions were customarily broached and punishment pronounced. Paul did get enough of his message across so that "some men joined him and believed." One of them was Dionysius of Mars Hill. Athens had become composite, with those who were witnessing and those who were witnessed to.

So far we have urged that ethnic society is sacral, offering some examples. We have also pointed out that a sacral society is not necessarily monotheistic, but is in fact regularly polytheistic. It remains to call attention to a few other outstanding features of the sacral situation.

* * * * *

Let us observe then, in the first place, that in a sacral society there is no kerygma, no body of doctrine that is preached. In a sacral situation, religion does not revolve around a body of teachings; it revolves around cultal act, ritual, and liturgy. In a sacral situation, deviation does not consist of nonconformity in the matter of *doctrine;* it consists of departure from, or nonparticipation in, the publicly approved *cult*. It is early Christianity's refusal to involve itself in the approved cult that occasioned the persecutions, not this or that doctrinal item in the Christian creed. Roman intolerance was not directed against a teaching; not belief but cultus was the ground of the offense, and at this point the demand was stringent: he who refused was executed.

Because the prime concern in a sacral situation is participation in cultal act, coercion is altogether reasonable there. Participation in an act can be forced. He who refuses has no excuse; the thing asked of him anyone can give, and he is simply obstinate. He must therefore be brought to his knees for refusing to comply with orders. He must be made to conform — or be destroyed. It is thus no mere coincidence that a sacramental religion is always intolerant. It has act at its heart; therefore, it proceeds automatically to attempted coercion. Sacramentalism generates intolerance because noncompliance has a meaning in a sacramental religion that it does not have in a nonsacramental one.

In authentic Christianity, the essence of religion is believing response to kerygma, response in faith and love. These are things that cannot be forced. It is by nature impossible to force a man to the act of faith, as it is impossible to force him to the stance of love. For this reason, coercion makes no sense in the frame of authentic Christianity. The difference lies in the fact that cultal act is central in the one system, whereas believing response to kerygma is central in the other.c In a sacral society there is no pressing for decision: there are no alternatives and hence no need, or even possibility, for decision-making. The spectacle in Athens which we described above repeats itself every time the Christian kerygma is heard, namely, that some "believe" and some "disbelieve," some begin to glory in the cross and some begin to stumble over it. Such alternatives simply do not present themselves in a sacral situation. In it there is consensus, unanimity, agreement: what is done for one is done for all.

We do not mean to say that in a sacral situation all is act, with no words spoken. There can be, and usually is, such a thing as a recital in troubadour style of a series of heroic deeds performed by the gods or god-like men (called *gesta dei*), the Paul Bunyan feats of the tribe's past. But these recitals, or recountings, are things in which the whole society is involved, every member of it in the same way. The heroic deeds that are sung are the deeds of representatives of the total society. Such recitals do not call for decision on the part of the listeners; there is no for and against. Such recitals of heroic deeds are wholly sacral in character and quite unlike the Christian kerygma.

Another outstanding feature of the sacral situation, one that results from the foregoing ones, is that there is no mission — neither *ad intra* nor *ad extra*. There is no mission *ad intra* (toward those within the same tribe or social or cultural group to which the missionary belongs) because all who are a part of the socio-political unit are assumed to be already in the same category in the matter of ultimate loyalty. How can there be mission in such a situation? Nor is there mission *ad extra* (toward those outside the missionary's tribe or social group). Sacral societies do not, even if they live in close

cWe use the expression "authentic Christianity" because Christianity has also been presented in other forms. "Christianity" has coerced and it has persecuted — but not until it had been made over into a sacramental system. When such a "Christianity" persecuted, it was again not for deviation in kerygma but for an imagined threat to the sacral society, a threat contained in the "heretics" who refused to participate in the cultal act. Whenever and wherever "Christianity" persecuted, it was because of a "heresy" that did not consist of ideas held.

proximity (as do the Navajo and Zuni, for example), engage in mission vis-à-vis each other. All they ask is that each society be allowed to go its own way, unmolested by the other. A sacral society does not seek to infuse its religion into another society with which it comes in contact — unless it has political annexation plans. In that case, a representative of the *regnum* (we use this word henceforth to denote the "civil power") of the aggressing society, accompanied by a representative of its *sacerdotium* (this word henceforth denotes the "ecclesiastical authority") invade the territory of the object of their aggression. For example, in New Spain a conquistador and a padre stepped ashore, the former to plant the flag of the *regnum* of Spain and the latter to place a crucifix in the name of its *sacerdotium*. This sort of behavior, even though it has been called mission, is nothing of the kind. It is a genuinely and typically pre-Christian way of operating.[D]

The urge to engage in mission *ad extra* does not occur in a heart not convinced of the need for mission *ad intra*. People who see no need for evangelizing within the society of which they themselves are members do not evince any urge to evangelize those belonging to another society. As long as a people do not envision the possibility that some in their own societal unit may be "lost," it does not occur to them that some in a neighboring societal unit may be "saved." It speaks volumes that Paul's urge to go to the heathen with the gospel came up in his soul simultaneously with the realization that "not all is Israel that is called Israel." Paul felt no urge for mission *ad extra* until he had felt an urge for mission *ad intra*. The two urges are genetically related. We see this in the thinking of Jesus, who spoke of "children of the kingdom cast out" precisely at the moment when he saw an "outsider" coming in; his statement "many shall come from the east and

---

[D]The alert reader will think to detect here an inconsistency in our argument. We were saying that in a sacral society there is no mission, and we point to Spain, a "Christian" land, by way of illustration. How can we say that such a "Christian" land's way of operating is "genuinely and typically sacral"? The reader is asked to hold this question in abeyance for broader treatment at later junctures in this book. Suffice it here to say that *historic* Christianity is not necessarily *authentic* Christianity. What is done under the sponsorship of "Christendom" is not necessarily done in line with authentic Christianity. For this reason we have put the word "Christendom" in quotation marks, to indicate that the word is something of an anomaly. It is the burden of this book to show that "Christendom" is Christianity after it has been thrust into the cast-off clothes of sacralism.

from the west" was the correlative of "children of the kingdom cast out." The one is dependent upon the other. That explains why sacral societies are not missionary societies. No sacral society is likely to develop a theory and a practice of mission. To this day a sense of mission is found only among persons and groups that have repudiated sacralism. All who still include on their membership rolls all who are part of the tribe are regularly nonchalant concerning missionary activity. They have even been known to be definitely hostile toward it.

We point to yet another feature of sacralism, one that results from the others. We have in mind the heavy accent on sacrament. The word "sacrament" connotes a religious act or gesture whereby a togetherness already existing on some secular level allegedly becomes a togetherness on the religious level. The function of sacrament is to bind together on the religious level that which is already bound on such other levels as tribal consanguinity, political homogeneity, national solidarity, and linguistic similarity. This is the meaning the word "sacrament" had in the pre-Christian world; it is the meaning that it had when it entered the Christian vocabulary. It is therefore the only historically defensible meaning of the word, and it must be said that authentic Christianity is averse to sacrament thus defined. It is averse to the idea that inclusion in any such prevenient togetherness is a help (and exclusion from it a hindrance) toward that new togetherness that Christ came to establish. It is not by chance that the very word "sacrament" is not to be found in the Christian scriptures. It is a word that is at home in a sacral situation and in no other place.

We mentioned above that in a sacral situation there is no kerygma; in its place stands solemn performance, ritualistic act, sacramental manipulation. In the sacral situation religion revolves around ritual; in fact, religion *is* ritual. It is in regard to the ritual of sacramental act that the priest is expected to be proficient. He must know what stuff to take in hand and what to do with it, what contortions of the body to engage in, what clapping of hands, what stampings of the feet, what writhings of the torso. Upon such acts the tribe, every member of it, gazes en masse. This is the total "service." If and when these sacramental acts have been performed, the kernels of corn correctly placed, the beads properly put in line, the bits of meat rightly proffered, and the oblation orthodoxly poured — all carefully executed according to the procedures handed down over the generations — then the tribe's religion has been adequately practiced. Each individual member has been caught up in the sacramental act, and in this ceremony the tribe's inner cohesion is assured. The essence of religion in a sacral situation is not something said, heard, and responded to; its essence is act or gesticulation done and seen.

We should perhaps interject at this point that in a sacral situation religious act is nevertheless sometimes accompanied by speech. The priest not only acts, he also utters — for instance, in the oracle at Delphi. But we hasten to point out that such speech is purposely incoherent mumbo jumbo, mummery consisting of disjunct syllables, intentionally repetitive and deliberately ambiguous. The "audience" does not hear speech; it hears only rhythmic sound, usually accompanied by rhythmic movement. The oracle in a pre-Christian setting is purposely ambiguous and uninforming. That which is uttered in a sacral situation is muttered — intentionally so. To perceive how little information the sounds attending sacramental act can impart, one need only recall that the *Hoc est enim corpus meum* ("For this is my body") of the medieval mass reached the ear of the auditor as "hocus-pocus." All the participant who knew no Latin heard was what seemed to be some vague and thoroughly mysterious reverberation that seemed to fall into a cadence, a cadence he reproduced back on the street as the alliterative "hocus-pocus." Subsequently, he used the expression "hocus-pocus" for any mysterious goings on.[E]

We must focus on yet another trait of sacralism: the place, or rather the absence of place, assigned to private devotions. In view of the sacral situation, in which religion and the cult of religion serve primarily as a cement to hold the societal group together, it follows that nonpublic devotions are at best meaningless and without purpose, and at worst decidedly undesirable and evil. They are said to defeat the very end for which religion exists; for the nonpublic practice of religion tends to fragment society. The nonpublic cult

[E]The observant reader will here detect once more what must seem to him a lapse of logic on our part: a "Christian" institution taken to illustrate pre-Christian sacralism. We must ask the patient reader once more to hold his fire as we remind him again that *historic* Christianity is not necessarily *authentic* Christianity, and that "Christendom" and Christianity are not the same thing.

draws men away from the societal totality. Private devotions feed diversity rather than uniformity. For this reason the theoreticians of the pre-Christian faiths have regularly advised against any religious activity that is not wholesale, not engaged in by all members of the society.

A classic example of a sacral society's aversion to the nonpublic practice of religion is to be found in Plato's *Laws*. Here we read:

> Let this then be the language of the law: no one is to possess shrines of the gods in private homes, and he who is found to possess such, and perform any sacred rite not publicly authorized . . . shall be informed against by him who is acquainted with the fact, which shall be announced by him to the guardians of the law; and let them issue orders that he or she is to carry away his or her private rites to the public temples, and if they fail to persuade them, then let them inflict a penalty on them until they do comply. And if a person be proven guilty . . . whether he have sacrificed publicly or privately to any gods, let him be punished with death.[F]

It should be noted that in a sacral situation religion and the practice of religion is not *individual*. It has been asserted with a great deal of truth that pre-Christian society does not know the concept of the individual, that it knows only the concept of the group. For this reason pre-Christian society does not know the concept of private property and individual possession. Therefore, it does not know the concept of private or individual morality, private or individual responsibility, or private religiosity. Pre-Christian man knows himself only as an ant knows itself, simply as one of the group. It is for this reason that sacral society frowns on anything that would tend to compromise the group quality of religion. That is why Plato wanted all religious activity that was not group activity suppressed by publicly enacted statute. It is by no means a mere coincidence that the emphasis on the group rather than the individual is a characteristic of every pre-Christian society,

---

[F]This passage from Plato requires a brief analysis. "Whether he have sacrificed publicly or privately to any gods" must not be taken to be a plea for atheism; that would be quite out of harmony with Plato's well-known convictions. Rather, it is to be taken as a prohibition against two things: 1) worshipping in private, 2) worshipping at the public shrine of "any god," whether recognized and having a place in the pantheon or not. It comes as no surprise that the early Christians experienced persecution: they did precisely what Plato's *Laws* forbade.

as it is of all post-Christian society. Nor is it a mere coincidence that emphasis on the individual is a characteristic of societies that have been influenced by authentic Christianity.

Moreover, it is a characteristic of a sacral society that in it there are no heretics. The words "heretic" and "heresy" are derived from the Greek verb *hairein,* which means "to stand before alternatives and make a choice between them."[G] However, in a sacral situation there are no options on the level of one's highest loyalty, no choice, no two or more contestants for that loyalty. For this reason it is correct to say that in the pre-Christian situation there are no heretics — because there is no choice.

It should also be pointed out that in a sacral situation there is no diversity of life-style: the life-style is the same for all. The virtues and vices that come to expression in a sacral society are spread evenly over that entire society. Sacral society has a latitudinarian posture with regard to behavior patterns: it tends to discourage any polarization in the matter of conduct. This posture was for good reason: such polarization would tend to divide society and make it composite, create two camps within it, the camp of the "sinners" and the camp of the "saints." Should such differentiation in life-style begin to develop in a sacral society (which is quite unlikely), it would be slapped down immediately because of its allegedly harmful implications — the erosion of the oneness.

Finally, we must also point out that in a sacral society there are no martyrs, that is, no persons who suffer because of a religious commitment that sets them off from their fellows. In a sacral society there is a "right" religion, and all members of that society adhere to it. How could anyone suffer for his religion? How could one be a martyr? In a sacral situation persecution for one's faith is unthinkable.

* * * * *

At this point we take a step forward in our argument, a step that to some will seem intolerable. We turn our attention to the earliest days of the Old Testament and point out that

---

[G]This explains how and why the seventy scholars who translated the Old Testament into Greek rendered the "free-will offering" of the Hebrew Old Testament as "the heretical offering." These offerings were optional: one could bring them or not bring them. People had to make a choice in regard to them.

here too we witness a sacral situation. In the oldest deposits of the Old Testament the sacral situation does not differ much, if indeed it differs at all, from the world in the midst of which the Old Testament took shape.[H] For our present purpose this means that the redemptive enterprise of God begins on the level of things as they are. Whatever the later divinely triggered development may be (as we shall have occasion to point out in some detail, that development is considerable), it all *begins* on the level of things as they are. We must not be surprised, therefore, to find the movement from the sacral pattern to something other and higher to be a transition, a passing from one stage of development to the other. There is a gradualness in the passing from the pre-Christian structuring of society to the Christian structuring, something of process — of progress.

The Old Testament begins on a level very close to that of the pre-Christian world. To begin with, the worship of Jahveh was culture-wide: all who were of the tribe were oriented toward the shrine of the tribe, the worship of Jahveh. Any given Israelite had come to worship Jahveh by the very same route that led a member of a neighboring tribe to the shrine of its god. Hebrews came into a relationship with Jahveh in very much the same way that Philistines came into a relationship with Dagon. Every Hebrew man, woman, or child "belonged" — by virtue of his or her inclusion in a specific population group. No one else did. It was as inconceivable for a Hebrew to worship Dagon as it was unthinkable for a Philistine to worship Jahveh.

The similarity between the typically sacral situation and the situation in the earliest moments of the Old Testament is indeed extensive. We saw earlier that in the sacral situation

[H]One will have difficulty taking this step only if he is not aware, or not sufficiently aware, that *process* (evolution, if you will) is of the very essence of the authentic Christian vision. Of all the world's religions, authentic Christianity is the only one geared to historic process. Only authentic Christianity honestly takes God into history: only it operates with the concept of "the fullness of time"; only it has the dimension of early and late; only it has a calendar. The incarnation is perhaps Christianity's most definitive feature; it makes God a fellow traveler through "this bourne of time and place" and in so doing divides history into B.C. and A.D. The incarnation is simultaneously intemporation. Authentic Christianity, it may be said, is in the idiom of "first the blade and then the ear and then the full corn in the ear." Christianity ignores the distinction of early and late at tremendous cost to itself.

one's involvement in that which takes place at the shrine does not result from personal choice; the same was true of Israel in its earliest days. In the case of early Israel, a person's participation in the religious cult was without the exercise of option, without a decision based on choice. It was without that act of the human soul which the Germans call *Entscheidung*.[1]

We saw earlier that in the typically sacral society the king and the priest are colleagues. The *regnum* and the *sacerdotium* are one entity — looked at from two different vantage points. This was likewise the case in the early days of the Old Testament. Here civil ruler and religious pontiff were in league with each other; they could even be the same person. This differed in no way from the typically sacral society of the times. Such was eminently the case in the days when the judges ruled, although it did not extend very far beyond those days, as we shall see. In the early days of the Old Testament experiment, "church" and "state" were as yet undifferentiated. The king was every Hebrew's king and the priest was every Hebrew's priest.

We also mentioned that in a sacral society there is no kerygma, no body of proclaimed truth; also in this matter things were not very different in the early days of Israel. As is common to all sacral societies, there were sagas and recitals of the deeds of God and of the deeds of the tribe's heroes. But there was no systematic presentation of a body of truth, no credal recital of a rounded-out body of dogma, nothing to which one could say yes or no, nothing to believe or disbelieve. Such sagas were kept alive by oral tradition, in song and chant. The peregrinations of Abraham, Isaac, and Jacob were a favorite theme. The predominant element in all of this — as in every sacral situation — was a recital of happenings, of the vicissitudes of the tribe, and especially of its victories. But there was no kerygma that challenged the hearer to acceptance or rejection.

The society of the Old Testament was at first also similar to the typically sacral society in that it had no sense of mission. Israel did have dealings with neighboring tribes — Moabites and Ammonites, Hittites and Philistines, Egyptians

[1] This German word combines the ideas of choice and decision. *Entscheidung* implies a certain amount of foregoing existential tension, antecedent pull in opposing directions: it is that sense in which we will use the word "decision" in this study. *Entscheidung* is also climactic: it stands at the end of a contest for loyalty.

and Midianites, and many others. With these tribes Israel bartered; it fought against them and made alliances with them. But there was no urge and no recognized command to carry out any mission among them, no tendency to gain converts among them and so bring into being an "indigenous church" among them. Israel seemed quite happy to be and remain the "chosen" people and to allow the rest to be and remain the "unchosen" *goyim*. This lack of missionary attitude becomes more noteworthy when it is recalled that there was virtually no language barrier, no biological disparity worth mentioning, and no color barrier. The prevailing conviction was that all Israel was "God's people"; and this went hand in hand (as it regularly does) with the conviction that no other people was, not even in candidate form. There was as little thought about the possibility of a Hebrew's being "lost" as about the possibility of a non-Hebrew's being "saved." It did not enter the mind of the common man in Israel at this stage of development that "many shall come from east and west to sit down with Abraham, Isaac, and Jacob, while children of the kingdom are cast out into outer darkness." Both projections would have been dismissed as wild and revolutionary ravings — as indeed they were dismissed when the greatest revolutionary of all times uttered them many centuries later. Israel was a stranger to the concept of mission, save for the voice of the prophet who stationed himself in a distant future. (For example, the bard who composed the 87th Psalm spoke of "Rahab and Babylon . . . Philistia and Tyre with Ethiopia" being "born" in Zion.)

It is true that Israel did take in slaves (young persons of other tribal antecedents) and processed them so that they too were henceforth of the tribe; these were also circumcised. But this was not yet mission, if for no other reason than that the membership thus implied was without choice or decision. The motive behind such amalgamation with the tribe was not missionary; much more probably the motive was the sacralism-nurtured desire to preserve the religious unanimity that marks the sacral society, the consensus to which pockets of slaves who were devotees of some other god would pose a threat. These circumcisions, in which the slaves had no choice, served to keep the sacral formula viable: Israel could not as yet afford the luxury, so to speak, of a composite society and that is why it circumcised those bought with money.

The heavy emphasis on sacramental manipulation, which characterizes the sacral society, was also evident in the early Old Testament situation. Very prominent in these manipulations were the gestures associated with the Passover — striking the blood on the lintels, eating the unleavened bread, partaking the paschal lamb, etc. The blowing of the ram's horn on the great day of atonement may be listed as another ritualistic and sacramental act, as well as the building of the booths and the other ceremonies connected with the Feast of the Booths. Very important was the involved ritualistic act performed in connection with the scapegoat and the many acts of lustration. The service of the Tabernacle was, in fact, an elaborately executed sacramental act — with the blood, the showbread, the lavers, and the candlesticks. Most important of all was the sacramental act of circumcision (far more than a bit of surgery) with its potential for serving sacralism. Circumcision was for Israel a practice that provided solidarity; it served to bind all Israel together, a sign of a league with one's fellow tribesmen. Circumcision had high political value in that it cemented the tribe together. Therefore, the king was as much concerned with the circumcision of his people as was the priest.

In the matter of life-style, the situation in ancient Israel was also very similar to that of the typically sacral society. Although Israel had a tribal morality that contrasted favorably with that of surrounding tribes, there was in ancient Israelite society no group of saints that was differentiated from a group of sinners. All Israel was said to be "saint," and all other tribal entities were held to be "sinners"; all Israel was of a piece in the matter of conduct patterns. We do see the idea of specialization in conduct within the group coming to expression quite early — in the Nazarites, for example. These Nazarites had a moral code that set them off from the rest of Hebrew society. Abstinence from strong drink was a central feature of Nazarite sainthood, and they were also conspicuous because of a unique tonsure. As such, they may thus be looked upon as a kind of pilot development, an adumbration of a future day when differentiation of conduct would be developed, as it did develop in New Testament Christianity. It is significant, however, that the rest of the Israelite society went out of its way to suppress the rising conduct differentiation that accompanied the Nazarites: we read in the book of Amos that men made it a point to try to get the Nazarites to conform to the rest of society by "making them to drink wine." Israel was not yet ready for the composite society, and this implied that it was not yet ready for polarization in the matter of life-style. No sacral society tolerates such polarization, and Israel was at this stage still too much like any other sacral society to allow the Nazarite experiment to be very successful. As we shall see, deviations from authentic Christianity regularly seek to squelch all forming of separate groups in the matter of life-style.

Early Israel was also like any other sacral society in that it had no martyrs, no dissenters who experienced difficulty because of their divergence from the norm. The assumption was that the religious loyalty of the one was identical with the religious loyalty of the other, and this yielded a climate in which martyrdom was unthinkable.

* * * * *

However, the many similarities between Israel and the "nations," which were apparent in the earliest deposits of the Old Testament, must not blind us to the fact that very early there was also a forward movement, a movement toward differentiation. Israel did begin the journey to a new and different structuring of human society. At no point is this more apparent than in the relationship of king and priest. In the course of time, the king began to have his domain, a domain into which the priest was not allowed to intrude; and the priest began to have his domain, a domain into which the king must not transgress. We must trace this development in some detail, for it heralds a new order. It points to an eventual separation of *regnum* and *sacerdotium,* and such a separation is a necessary step if a composite society is to come into being. For, if a society is to be composite, it must have a loyalty *common* to all (loyalty to that body of which the king is the symbol) plus a loyalty *not common* to all (loyalty to that body of which the priest is the symbol). If all loyalties are the same for all, the result is a sacral society; if no loyalties are the same for all, the result is chaos. For this reason the separation of functions, of which we are speaking, was a very significant development.

It is highly significant that although the God of Israel in the days of the judges had no objection to the idea of the same person officiating as both king and priest, he became extremely sensitive in the matter a little later. It is also highly significant that this sensitivity began to appear just at the time when Israel was clamoring for "a king such as other nations have." The account has it that Jahveh went along, albeit rather reluctantly, in the installation of "a king such as the other nations have." He even bestowed considerable favor upon Saul, the first Israelite king. But before it was all over, King Saul was in complete disfavor with the God of Israel, and the exact point at which Saul's decline begins (which is spelled out to us) speaks volumes.

Saul's disgrace (as recorded in I Samuel 13) began when he as king, irked by the tardiness of the priest (whose job it was), "offered the burnt offering" — thus invading the domain of the priest. The moment the priest (Samuel) arrived on the scene, he asked the king, with rebuke in his voice, "What have you done?" To this incriminating question, King Saul replied defensively: "When I saw that the people were scattering from me, and that you did not come within the days appointed . . . I forced myself, and offered the burnt offering." It should be noted that Saul needed religion because "scattering" was taking place; and it should also be recalled that in a sacral situation the prime function of religion is to counteract scattering by means of a sacrament. A more sacral mental climate and an act more strongly dictated by sacralism than that of Saul can scarcely be imagined. To Saul's feeble apology for his course of action (which he knew to be out of order — for he contended that he had "forced" himself to it) the priest replied: "You have done foolishly; you have not kept the commandment of the Lord your God, which he commanded you. . . ." From that moment on, King Saul was under the frown of God, a frown that was not lifted again; it only grew darker as the months and years went by.

The exact content of the "commandment" to which Samuel refers here is not known to us, but it is quite apparent that it was an order issued with the coming of the first king of Israel and clearly known by king and priest alike. This "commandment" was therefore a part of the divine accommodation to the innovation that had brought in the "king such as the other nations have." It is as if Jahveh had declared something like this: "Very well, have your king as the other nations have, but I must then insist that he confine himself to the things that pertain to the *regnum*, that he leave the functions of the priest to a different kind of servant of mine." Manifestly, something new and different was in the making, something that no longer fit into the old sacralist pattern.

The change of which we speak here, as well as the profound importance the matter had in the eyes of God, may be examined further in the story of King Uzziah recorded in II Chronicles 26. Here we make the acquaintance of a good king of Judah, an exceptional man, so good in the sight of God that he was "marvelously helped" of God. Everything to which he put his hand was a success. But he died in disgrace nonetheless, "excluded from the house of the Lord." He was deprived of his scepter, and a regent took over his regal functions. Later, after he had died, they buried him not in the royal burial place but in "the burial field which belonged to the kings." What had gone wrong? Why the demotion? It was occasioned by one rash act: Uzziah the king went into the holy place to perform the functions of the priest; the king had once again invaded the province of the priest. That did it. Nor was it done by him in ignorance, for his rash deed set the whole sanctuary in an uproar, the horrified priests remonstrating: "It is not for you, Uzziah, to burn incense to the Lord, but for the priests. . . . Go out of the sanctuary; for you have done wrong, and it will bring you no honor from the Lord God" (II Chron. 26:18). This, we are told, only made the king more unruly: such finickiness — didn't these priests know that he was, after all, the king! As he gesticulated with the priest's censer, leprosy "broke out on his forehead" and, seeing that, the priests hustled him out of the sanctuary, he running and they pushing.

Plainly, the sin of Uzziah was that he ignored completely the divine instruction in the matter (that there had been such instruction is wholly apparent from the fact that the assembled priests were to a man horrified at the spectacle). He refused to move along with the division of labor that God had instituted with the coming of the first Israelite king. Uzziah preferred to continue along the lines of the older epoch, in which the man who swung the scepter was also considered competent to swing the censer — or, to put it in our terms, when the *regnum* and the *sacerdotium* were as yet undifferentiated.

No one can read the sad tale of King Uzziah and his demotion (nor that of King Saul and his earlier demotion for the same infraction) without being amazed, and probably perplexed, at the rigor and severity of the God who is portrayed in these accounts. Can we hope to see through such scrupulousness, such sternness, in a matter that must seem quite trivial to us? Is there perhaps the inculcation here of so important a piece of truth as to render understandable the seemingly unreasonable punctiliousness of the Being not known for trifling with men? Is the Spirit of God perhaps wrestling with the spirit of man in these admittedly strange events? Is he trying to get something across to men, a matter of such far-reaching importance as to warrant the rigor of the pedagogical method used in this lesson?

We submit that such is indeed the case. Because of its pivotal importance in the present study, we do well to try to put in words that piece of truth which the revealing Spirit was trying to get across to men in the rigors practiced with King Saul and King Uzziah. Until better terminology presents itself, we shall call that piece of truth the *theology of progressive grace,* that is, the theology that there is a progression in God's gracious dealings with a world in rebellion, an early and a later gracious interference with the downward plunge of fallen man. We shall call every theology that fails to reckon with this early and late view a "flat" theology. We can make plain what we mean by "flat" by taking an example from the world of photography. Ordinary photography records two dimensions, the vertical and the horizontal. But there is a more sophisticated photography (known as stereo-photography) in which a camera with two lenses, placed as far apart as human eyes, takes two pictures simultaneously — each from its slightly different vantage point. When the pictures are developed and the human eyes are each trained on the corresponding picture, a third dimension becomes perceptible — the dimension of far and near. Such stereo-photography is not "flat," like ordinary photography; it is three-dimensional. Transferring this terminology to the present subject, we speak of three-dimensional theology, meaning thereby a theology in which early and late are essential ingredients. Such three-dimensional theology has an eye for the progressive quality of God's gracious dealings with a fallen world. Traditional theologies have all too frequently been flat, ignoring the progressive quality of God's gracious dealings with a world in sin. By failing to see the third dimension, traditional theology has made things unnecessarily hard for itself. Perspective is an important thing in all representation, and flat theology tends to be deficient in regard to perspective. It is time for theologians to recognize the stereo quality of God's grace; it is time for men to learn the lesson God was apparently trying to teach in the demotion of Saul and Uzziah.

One of the leading theologians of our times, G. C. Berkouwer of the theological faculty of the Free University in

Amsterdam, leads us to at least see the problem with which every flat theology is burdened, when he says: "This problem, the problem of the relation of nature and grace (which problem is better stated as the problem of the relationship between human existence as created and sustained by God and the grace of God), this problem comes up constantly in the history of Church and theology."[4] The problem in question is the problem of an early grace and a later grace: a grace that comes to expression in the Creator-creature relationship in which sin is *curbed,* and a grace that comes to expression in the Redeemer-redeemed relationship in which sin is *vanquished.* It was this distinction which was the burden of God's ways in the case of Saul and Uzziah.

It is quite true, of course, that even in an otherwise flat theology scholars have found it necessary to make certain distinctions within the concept of grace. They have spoken of "common grace" and of "special grace." To tie down the distinction between them, Dr. Abraham Kuyper, one of the greatest theologians of the last hundred years, used a Dutch word of Latin origin (*gratie*) for the former "grace" and a word of Germanic origin (*genade*) for the latter "grace." This was at the least a step in the right direction and evidenced a feeling for the third dimension. Regrettably, this distinction could not be carried over into discussions in the English language since English does not have two distinct words for "grace." However, the distinction between "common" and "special" has proved to be far from satisfactory: the terms were inadequate. Consequently, these distinctions within the concept of grace have tended to disappear in recent years. The good beginning Kuyper made has been lost again, by and large. This leads us to believe that what is needed is better terminology as we discuss the distinctions that must be recognized within the concept of grace.

Fortunately, better terminology has already been offered and is already current, at least to a certain extent. We find that the late Emil Brunner speaks of the grace that has given us the civil power: "Doubtless we have to do here not with an institution of redemptive but of conserving grace, common grace, called common because it, like rain and sunshine, reaches all people, also those who have no knowledge of Jesus Christ or of special grace."[5] Brunner's distinction of "conserving grace" and "redeeming grace" has much to commend it. One thing is still lacking, however. It is the idea of early and late. If we now inject this early and late concept into Brunner's terms, if we incorporate into them the idea that "conserving" grace is *preliminary,* and "redeeming" grace *subsequent,* then we have terminology with which the idea of the progressive quality of God's gracious dealings can be set forth. Therefore, we shall henceforth in this discussion speak at times of "conserving grace" (alias "common grace") as "preliminary grace" and of "redeeming grace" (alias "special grace") as "subsequent grace."

Along with Brunner, and in keeping with a Reformed tradition of long standing, we must look upon the civil power (which is vested in what we today call the "state") as the creature of this preliminary grace, seeing that it is the creature of a grace that swung into action before redemptive grace went to its assignment. The *state* results from the first thing the Almighty did with a world that was in rebellion. Something had to be done at once: the drift toward chaos had to be checked first of all, and it had to be done among men who were still in the modality of fallenness. Preliminary grace therefore seeks contact with fallen man at the point of those "remnants of original righteousness" of which the Belgic Confession speaks (Art. 14), tattered ends of an original rectitude allowed by God's grace to be still present in fallen man. This preliminary grace, therefore, utilizes resources that are residual, or backward-looking; in this respect it differs significantly from subsequent grace, which utilizes resources that are anticipatory or forward-looking. In every sense, grace is a stance of God with reference to man in sin; but the stance assumed by God in preliminary grace is not the same as his stance in subsequent grace. As God moves from the posture of conserving grace to the posture of redeeming grace he does an about-face.

Flat theology has been unable to develop an acceptable doctrine of the entity we call the state. The Belgic Confession of the Reformed churches says correctly, in reference to "the Civil Magistrate," that "our good God, because of the depravity of mankind, has instituted kings, princes, magistrates, it being his will that the world should be governed by their laws and policies, to the end that the dissoluteness of men might be restrained." This confession sees the state as a postlapsarian (after the Fall) thing, something called into being as a preliminary device for the curtailment of the drift toward chaos inherent in the Fall, a grace that does not go about curing the illness of sin but controlling and suppressing somewhat the symptoms of that illness. So says this surprising confession. Unfortunately, however, it goes on to say that the state so conceived has an assignment — a sword assignment — in the realm of redemptive grace! Small wonder that the Reformed churches have found it necessary to take this creed in hand at this point and perform major surgery on it.

We said that a flat theology cannot develop a suitable doctrine of the state. It must either picture the state as an entity that lies outside the grace of God —and is thus essentially demonic — or it must subsume the state under the program of redemptive grace. Either of these alternatives, however, leads to wholly unacceptable conclusions. The New Testament teaches in the plainest of terms that the state (reference is to the Roman state of the days of the persecutions) is "of God"; this makes the former alternative totally unacceptable. But the latter alternative — of subsuming the "civil magistrate" under the program of redemptive grace — is just as unacceptable. For if we do so, one of two things follows: we must then either make the sword a tool to be used in the program of redemption (as the Belgic Confession held, before men in our time performed surgery on it); or we must divest the "civil ruler" of his sword and instruct him to govern according to the Sermon on the Mount. However, an officer of the law cannot and may not "turn the other cheek," as men are told to do in the program of redemption; a state that instructs its policemen to "turn the other cheek" is no longer a state as authentic Christianity conceives it. The sword of steel is a requirement in the program of conserving grace, but it is contraband in the program of redemptive grace. A swordless *regnum* is a contradiction in terms; but the sword function is contraband in the affairs of the *sacerdotium*.

All this implies that the state is not subject to redemption. Being itself a counter measure, it is not a candidate for redeeming grace. For to qualify as a candidate for redeeming grace an entity has to be part of the original blueprint. Wherever redeeming grace has performed its mission, the "sword" (to borrow an old term for the civil power) has become obsolete. The state continues to function in this age only because the completion of the program of redeeming grace still waits. In the New Jerusalem there will be no king and no *regnum,* no sword, no police power: these institutions will no longer be necessary. The state is therefore purely temporal and strictly secular — secular in the etymological sense of the word, of this age *(saecula)*, for the here and now. For this reason the state was not meant to come under the water of baptism. It is not salvable; it does not "go to heaven."

This implies that there cannot be such a thing as a "Christian state." For a given state to qualify for the adjective "Christian," all its subjects would have to be believing men and women, a prospect whose realization is not promised in the New Testament. In the New Testament vision, society is not unanimous, not homogeneous, neither in its entirety nor in its components. It is seen as existing at all times and in all places as a composite of widely diverse and divergent elements in the area in which men's ultimate loyalty lies. The New Testament does not anticipate a state in which it is unnecessary for one man to say to another man, "Know the Lord" because "all already know him, from the least to the greatest." The New Testament does anticipate a church thus unanimous, but not a *regnum* thus unanimous.

This, we hasten to add with considerable emphasis, does not imply that the state cannot be influenced for good by God's program of redemptive grace. It can — most assuredly. In fact, one of the duties of each believer and of believers corporately is so to influence the state for good, primarily in the matter of justice between man and man (which is at the heart of the assignment God has given to the state). Christians must seek to make the state a justice-providing institution, and they must do so in the firm conviction that these efforts will not be barren. It so happens, thanks to God's common grace, that there remain in fallen man vestiges, residual particles *("traces"* in the language of the Belgic Confession), of an original righteousness and awareness of justice. It is out of these resources that the state is fashioned, and the state can be influenced by an appeal to these resources. Part of the Christian's task is to do all he can to have these resources fully exploited in the society of which he is a part.

This is to be done through what has been called "the percolation method," a kind of spiritual osmosis. Christians are called to influence public opinion in word and deed, because public opinion plays an important part in the life of every state. They are to do this in matters that concern justice. Whether Christians are to perform this task as individuals in existing organizations (to which people of other ultimate loyalties also belong) or through organizations brought into being for that purpose is a matter that has often been debated.

It is sufficient to mention here that the very idea of the composite society seems to imply that confessing folk and nonconfessing folk must, at least at the higher levels, meet around the same table, so that believers and nonbelievers look each other in the eye. It would seem that if such meetings are possible and fruitful on the higher levels, similar meeting of minds on lower levels is not out of the question. It is to be remembered as this problem is pondered that there are primary loyalties (which the Christian cannot and may not compromise) and secondary loyalties (which he can share with those who do not share in his ultimate loyalty). In the area of preliminary grace there are commonalities not to be found on the level of subsequent grace.

* * * * *

It appears then that the punctiliousness that came to expression in the demotion of Saul and Uzziah finds its explanation and justification in the divine travail accompanying the birth of a new and higher concept than that of sacralism. If Saul and Uzziah had not been stopped, the idea of progressive grace would have died in the birth canal. With that the new structuring of society would have been thwarted. Consider what such a successful negation of the forward movement would have entailed: it would have made the separation of church and state impossible; the idea of a primary loyalty and secondary loyalties would have been precluded; the concept of limited government would have been stifled, and along with it the concept that led to the formula, "Render to Caesar the things that are Caesar's and to God the things that are God's." Freedom of conscience could never have come about.

Flat theology, as we noted above, has never been able to "think" the separation of church and state. It has never been able to abandon the idea that the state must be a "confessing" institution. It is the position held to this day by Roman Catholics and the Reformed Presbyterian Church. But with this as a requirement, we are back in the times when king and priest had their heads in one sack, each scratching the other's back. In such a situation it becomes quite unthinkable for the church to do anything but rubber-stamp whatever the state does.[J] One

---

[J] An outstanding example of such rubber-stamping may be seen in the policies of the Reformed churches of South Africa in our time. South African society is still an essentially sacral society, a society in which

may say without fear of successful contradiction that the "confessing" state has a way of becoming demonic; when a given *regnum* is seduced to underwrite the "right" religion, it will presently be persecuting God's dearest children. The state that takes sides in essentially religious issues always ends up not on the side of the angels but on the side of the adversary. There are, so history seems to teach, no exceptions to this rule. All the bloody persecutions from time immemorial were undertaken by states that had been taught by adherents of a flat theology that their primary duty was to see the "right" religion through to victory. In so doing they suppressed and put to death their subjects who found it impossible (usually because they stood too close to the New Testament) to make their peace with this "right" religion. From the bloody butcheries of the Christians in Nero's Rome to the Crusades' frightful massacres, to the mass liquidations of Albigensians and Waldensians, to the burning of Servetus and the extermination of many thousands of Anabaptists in Reformation times — the story is the same. It is a fearful one. Probably the most deplorable aspect of the whole grisly mess is the fact that in it all the church was kept from being what it was intended to be.

There is a feature in the collision that began in the days of Saul and Uzziah and reached into later times that must not escape us: whenever the revealing Spirit seeks to move men forward they have a way of resisting. The division of labor was something for which that Spirit had to fight. It came into being in spite of the people among whom it was launched because, in the language of Paul, it is "not of man." The Christian kerygma came into being in spite of the people among whom it was introduced. One of the greatest blunders in the history of men's thinking is the assumption that the Judaeo-Christian faith was "in keeping with a kind," endemic to certain people and their native culture — that in the Judaeo-Christian faith we have simply the religiosity of an ancient people. Nothing could be further from the truth. Throughout ancient Israel it was the "false prophet" who was ethnically endemic. Always at right angles and at loggerheads with the false prophets was the prophet of Jahveh. Israel was related to

---

regnum and *sacerdotium* fit together as warp and woof. What this does to the church is easily surmised: the state says that it is immoral for a white person to marry a black or a colored person, and the church cannot bring itself to say that this law is immoral.

the false prophets as all sacral societies were and are related to their prophets; but Israel was unique in having in its midst a second kind of prophet, one carried in from the beyond. Jerusalem, far from being a place that produced the prophets of Jahveh, was a city that killed them. There is something passing strange about these prophets of Jahveh, these lonely men from the deserts. Israel, like any other sacral society, coddled its ordinary prophets, let them eat at the king's table. But Israel was notorious for the way it treated the prophets of Jahveh. The emergence of the prophet who was not endemic to the culture is the outstanding feature of the Old Testament and perhaps the greatest novelty in the religious history of mankind. Without this development the Christian religion would be simply unthinkable. The idea of a prophet sent from God rather than put forward by the culture runs through the Christian vision from start to finish. When we read (in Amos 7) of the conflict between "Amaziah, the priest of Bethel," and Amos, the former "herdsman of Tekoa," we see on the one hand a "king such as other nations have" sustained by a prophet such as other nations have; on the other hand we see the nonendemic prophet of Jahveh — more than likely at right angles with such a king. This is typical of the entire vision of authentic Christianity, and it all began with the division of labor that sent the king and the priest each to his own assignment. The concept of the nonendemic prophet finds its classic and ultimate expression in Jesus of Nazareth, the prophet of God who was the furthest of all from being ethnically indigenous.

The naive but very dogmatic assumption that the Judaeo-Christian tradition was culturally endemic is of course as common as daylight. But it is a grand mistake, one that has bedeviled almost all of contemporary theological construction. This uncritical assumption makes it quite impossible, from the outset, to see through the nature of that faith. One can understand the genesis of Saul of Tarsus, for this Saul can be factored out of the givens of the cultural heritage; he was completely endemic to his culture. But how shall one understand and factor out of the cultural givens the Paul of the Damascus road? The concept of mystery runs through the story of the genesis of Paul, as it runs through the authentic version of the Christian faith throughout — "mystery" being the name given in authentic Christianity to the immediate, that which is done without recourse to a human go-between.

The length to which Paul — and all those through whom

"God spoke of old to our fathers by the prophets" (Heb. 1:1) — was willing to go to insure and secure the mystery dimension (i.e., the *immediate* dimension) of their message is astounding. We see Paul take out his diary, as it were, as he writes to the Galatian church and from that diary gives an account of every moment spent in the presence of persons from whom, it could be argued, he had derived his message; but Paul swears an oath that he did not derive his message from any go-between. All this resulted from his conviction that there had been immediate contact between the revealing Spirit and himself. Paul's absolute insistence on the immediacy of the message should not surprise us; for it is on the concept of immediacy that the idea of the nonendemic dimension of authentic Christianity depends. For if Paul had derived his message "from men" or from any given third party, the question would naturally follow from whom that third party had received it, and so forth, a formula whereby the nonendemic quality of the Christian kerygma would evaporate and disappear.

It was through such a mystery that among an early people the *regnum* and the *sacerdotium* were instructed to go each its own way, were each sent to a unique assignment, the former to an assignment resulting from God's preliminary grace and the latter to an assignment flowing from his subsequent grace. To a further unfolding of that mystery we shall turn now, to the rise of that structuring of human society to which we have attached the metaphorical label "the sons of God."

Part Two

"SONS OF GOD"

Very early in the evolution of the Judaeo-Christian tradition, not very far into the Old Testament, the erstwhile saga in which the deeds of God were recited began to make way for kerygma: a body of theology came to be enunciated, a system of doctrine that was to be believed. The heritage of sacrament began to meet competition from a heritage of message — oral message — done in propositions. Israel had been started on the road that leads to the New Testament, with its concept of an evangel to be preached and responded to. This was indeed a mighty forward movement. There was also a significant forward movement with regard to mission. As we have already intimated, the bards of Israel were already talking anticipatingly (and that quite early) of a day when "Tyre, Philistia, and Cush" would be caught up in the redemptive enterprise of God. The oracle of God also spoke, again quite early and prophetically, of a day when "in thee and in thy seed shall all families of the earth be blest." But this is in the future tense, this is prediction; no one thought of seeing this prediction come true — until New Testament times. We have no evidence that these prognostications were fulfilled until a long time afterward — in New Testament days.

It is true, there was in Old Testament times some movement in the direction of mission, in the rise of proselytism, which played a most important part in the development of the new structuring of society. But to make and incorporate proselytes is still far short of engaging in mission. The word "proselyte" means "one brought to," whereas a missionary is "one sent to." The proselyter is an "importer," whereas the missionary is an "exporter." The Old Testament church never attained missionary activity, although the emergence of the proselyte was a step in that direction, in that by it the Old Testament church became multiracial.

Not only did ancient Israel stop short of being a missionary society, but every prompting to go beyond the tribe met with stiff resistance. The prevailing assumption was that since Israel was the "chosen" race, God's beneficent concern did not reach beyond its borders. Needless to say, this allowed the individual Israelite to be unconcerned with "outsiders" also (whom the Israelites called the *goyim*). Such a mental climate not only precluded the rise of mission but made men resist any gesture in the direction of mission. Even a prophet of Jahveh, Jonah, the son of Amittai, was unable to break free of the antimissionary attitude common to sacral societies and thus present in Israel. When called to go to Nineveh on a preaching mission, Jonah flatly refused, choosing rather to go to sea on a tramp freighter. That Jonah went to sea rather than to some hide-out in the desert is itself a revelation of the man's antimissionary frame of mind. In the Old Testament the sea is symbolic of the mass of mankind outside the "promise"; it symbolizes the *goyim*. Something of this survives, incidentally, in the expression "the sea of humanity." Because the sea stood for the *goyim* and Israel had a negative attitude toward the *goyim*, Israel had a dislike for the sea, a dislike that shines through in many a Psalm. For example, Psalm 98:7 reads: "Let the sea roar, and all that fills it; the world and those who dwell in it! . . . for [the Lord] comes to judge . . . the world with righteousness, and the peoples with equity." Jonah's flight to the literal sea must therefore be seen as an alternative for the projected trip to the figurative sea, of which Nineveh was an important center. It was as though Jonah wanted to say that he would rather go to the literal sea than to the figurative one. Did he perhaps think that he was going to "pull the wool over the eyes" of Jahveh by substituting sea for "sea"?

The thing Jonah didn't like in the orders Jahveh had given him was contained in one phrase in the assignment, something in fine print as it were. It was the phrase "after forty days." This was intended to leave the way open for conversion on the part of the Ninevites and for consequent cancellation of the message of doom. It was this phrase, providing forty days of grace, that made Jonah balk. We have this from his own lips: "Is not this what I said when I was yet in my country? That is why I made haste to flee to Tarshish, for I knew that thou art a gracious God and merciful, slow to anger, and abounding in steadfast love, and repentest of evil" (Jon. 4:2).

Surely this Jonah is very reluctant indeed to undertake mission. He is not only not in favor of a mission to Nineveh; he hates the mission's success when it comes, moping and pouting on a hilltop that overlooks the now penitent city. God stages the gourd scene in order to show the prophet how far afield he is. When the gourd dies as suddenly as it has sprung up, the prophet grumbles. And then Jahveh has the chance to preach, the chance for which he has caused the gourd to come up: "You pity the plant, for which you did not labor, nor did you make it grow, which came into being in a night, and perished in a night. And should not I pity Nineveh, that great city, in which there are more than a hundred and twenty thousand persons who do not know their right hand from their left, and also much cattle?" (Jon. 4:10-11). In this preachment Jahveh tries to get Jonah to realize that the divine concern does not restrict itself to the "chosen" people, something men would have to learn if ever there was to be mission. At that, it seems that the message contained in this book of Jonah failed to convince the Israel for whom it was intended; God met with plenty of resistance as he pressed to move his people to a new level in the matter of mission. We shall see at a later juncture in this study that resistance to the forward movement did not end with Jonah. It was frequently evident many years later and in diverse places and times.

During the Old Testament dispensation a development took place that was to be of incalculable importance in the centuries that followed. This was the rise of the distinction between "Israel after the flesh" and "Israel after the spirit." The same refinement also presents itself in the formulas "circumcised in the flesh" and "circumcised of heart." Through this distinction we see an *ecclesiola in ecclesia* (a little church within the great church), a "people of God" in a narrow sense sandwiched in among the "people of God" in a wide sense. They are concentric circles, the larger circle enclosing the whole tribe and the smaller circle encompassing only those who have undergone an inner change, have made a personal commitment. Before long we hear of "seven thousand who have not bowed the knee to Baal" embedded in the folds of an entity that is "God's people" in a different and altogether preliminary way.

One of the most tragic consequences of flat theology, which ignores the forward movement because it has no eye for process and progress, was the assumption that the *ecclesiola in ecclesia* situation was intended to be a timeless feature, something descriptive of the church of all ages. Staged by the God of history as a means to get men ready for the idea of a church not coextensive with any tribe or socio-political unit, it was afterwards looked upon as a permanent phenomenon. Out of this failure to understand the transitional meaning of *ecclesiola in ecclesia* have come a great many of the later church's faults and failures. This failure to understand continues to evince itself in the distinction, heard to this day, of "church visible" and "church invisible." This too is terminology that finds no support in the New Testament: the concept of an "invisible" church is as foreign to the New Testament as is the concept of an "invisible" Christian. If the latter can be known by their "fruit" (as Jesus said was the case), then how does it happen that when they are grouped together in the church, that group becomes "invisible"?

* * * * *

Since the so-called intertestamentary period (roughly the four centuries that lie between the last days of the Old Testament and the first days of the New) belongs really to the Old Testament regime, we must give some account of it here, especially since some extremely important developments took place during this period, developments that have everything to do with the new departure of which we are speaking in this section.

The subjugation of the Israelite state and its mass deportation to a foreign country was an indescribably traumatic experience. The trauma was not simply due to the inconvenience and hardship naturally attending such dislocation and resettlement of an entire people in a strange and foreign land, although these were no doubt bitter enough. What hurt much more deeply was the religious implication of the exile. Because of it, the people of God lost their *regnum;* only the *sacerdotium* remained to them. No longer could Israel be what other tribal groups were and what it had been in the distant past — an entity in which "church" and "state" were partners. Because of the captivity, Israel was forced to live under a *regnum* that was not aligned with its *sacerdotium*. Israel had to learn to live under a king who was not circumcised, while it continued to worship under a priest who was. This created a situation unlike that of any other nation under the sun. It virtually forced the Israelites in captivity to develop a three-dimensional theology of early and late grace.

That Israel survived this traumatic experience is one of the mysteries of history. Ordinarily, people exposed to such a challenge break down before it: they are absorbed into the situation in which they find themselves, submit in the end to its *regnum*, and allow themselves presently to be served by its *sacerdotium*. This is precisely what happened to the ten tribes as such: they simply became a part of the sacral society in the midst of which it was their lot to live. That this did not happen to all of Israel is quite inexplicable — except to the man who believes that God works in history. God was not only keeping Israel in existence but he was taking it on a field trip in the direction of the idea of progressive grace.

It must be pointed out, however, that even though Israel in captivity was obliged to live with a *regnum* not committed to the worship of the Jahveh to which its *sacerdotium* was committed, it was slow to adopt progressive grace theology. Its flat theology made it consider the nonconfessing *regnum* as evil, as not-of-Jahveh and thus demonic. It was because of this flat theology that Israel's nonvoluntary experimentation with a new formula in regard to *regnum* and *sacerdotium* did not go smoothly. The prevailing attitude was one of sullen resentment: captive Israel looked upon the uncircumcised *regnum* as a demonic order. The doctrine of a preliminary grace was as yet far from dominant in Israel's religious thinking; for that reason Israel knew only of a terrain where redemptive grace was operative, plus a terrain (the remainder) that was under divine displeasure, unrelieved by any kindly divine disposition. Hence the captive Israelite had a wholly negative attitude toward the *regnum* under which he was obliged to live. In vain did the prophet of Jahveh advise: "Bring your necks under the yoke of the king of Babylon, and serve him and his people, and live" (Jer. 27:12). These words of Jahveh's prophet fell on deaf ears, and so did the following: "But seek the welfare of the city where I have sent you into exile, and pray to the Lord on its behalf, for in its welfare you will find your welfare" (Jer. 29:7). Israel still adhered to a two-dimensional view of God's grace, and this made any kind of cooperation or collaboration with the occupying power unthinkable. No one knew better than the men of that *regnum* what surly and intransigent subjects were these Jews, whose flat theology made them what they were.

There is no evidence that Israel in captivity sensed the theological implications of the prophets' instruction that they pray for the nonconfessing state. The instruction plainly implied that this state was *of God* if prayer was to be made for it. The plain implication was that the nonconfessing state is not a demonic thing, not an invention of the devil, not a thing over which God's people are to breathe an anathema. But the progressive grace implications of the prophets' word went largely unnoticed. Judging from the attitude of the Jews in captivity, not many prayers were uttered in behalf of the nonconfessing *regnum*. It was during this time, and as a result of this negative attitude toward a secular *regnum,* that the hope of a "return" came up. In the idea of return was the prospect of some day going forward by going back to the promised land. It was this hope of return that gave to captive Israel the will to live. After Israel had suffered enough, so ran the dream, the people of God would find their way back to the promised land, where a biological descendant of the house of David would then once more hold the scepter. Then the *regnum* and the *sacerdotium* would once more coalesce — so it was hoped, dreamed, believed, expected.

It was in those days that a child was born to Isaiah, one of Jahveh's prophets, who received the outlandish name of Shear-jashub (Is. 7:3). The meaning of *shear-jashub* is ambiguous, perhaps intentionally so: it can be rendered "a remnant shall return"; but it can also be translated "a portion shall convert." Naturally, Israel in captivity was predisposed to take it in the former sense: this rendering fit and fed Israel's fond hope of some day going forward by going back — when a descendant of David would once more give Israel a *regnum* in the signature of its *sacerdotium*. Two other infants were born in those agony-filled days — to Hosea, another prophet of Jahveh. They were likewise given oracular names: the older of the two, a girl, was named Lo-ruhamah (meaning "not pitied"); the other, a boy, received the name Lo-ammi (meaning "not my people"). Both these odd names (Hos. 1:6-9) were full of pathos at the plight of Israel. God had apparently ceased having compassion and had seemingly dismissed "his people" from his mind. But then Isaiah, the father of Shear-jashub,

takes up the theme of the "return": when "they shall go up
. . . great shall be the day." Hosea, the father of the other
two children so oracularly named, breaking into metric speech,
begins to speak enthusiastically of a time when the negative
lo of Lo-ruhamah and Lo-ammi will be dropped, when "not
pitied" will make way for "compassion," and "not my people"
will become "my people."

Israel did return — a fragment of it, and after a fashion.
It happened in the days of Cyrus the Persian, under Ezra and
Nehemiah. In great elevation of spirit, with much rejoicing
at what seemed to be the fulfillment of an ancient aspiration,
the leaders pulled together some straggling remainders and
marched back the many weary miles. There, with a pathetic
fervor, they sifted rubble and found some still usable stones
with which to resurrect the "good old days," days in which the
regnum had been closely allied with the *sacerdotium*. But the
building didn't amount to much: four walls, a roof, a hut of
sorts. So thin and feeble was it, so utterly prosaic and plain,
that those who still had some memory of what once had been,
sobbed out their disappointment, while the jeers of the in-
habitants of the land tore their souls apart with mockery:
"What are these feeble Jews doing? Will they restore things?
Will they sacrifice? Will they finish up in a day? Will they
revive the stones out of the heaps of rubbish, and burned ones
at that?" (Neh. 4:2). An equally disdainful Tobiah the Ammonite supplied the answer: "Yes, what they are building —
if a fox goes up on it he will break down their stone wall!"
(4:3). Neither the onlookers nor those Israelites who were in
the know were greatly impressed with the reversion to the past.
And in this they were right. The whole thing had great difficulty getting off the ground; the walls and the buildings were
a laugh. It was a colossal anachronism. The heart of Jahveh
didn't seem to be in it, certainly not with much enthusiasm.

Worst of all was the fact that the *regnum* remained in
heathen hands. The relation between the *regnum* and the
sacerdotium remained what it had been since the day the
exiles had first sat down by the river Chebar. Israel was permitted to build a sanctuary, such as it was, and to perform the
religious cult behind its poorly pointed walls. But the *regnum*
did not slide back into the palm of some scion of David; an
uncircumcised man ruled the land and continued to do so
right into New Testament times. The abortive character of the
whole enterprise did not escape Israel's leaders. Even the

seemingly dauntless Nehemiah had his moments of deep disillusionment, as when he lamented: "Behold, we are slaves this day; in the land that thou gavest to our fathers to enjoy its fruit and its good gifts, behold, we are slaves. And its rich yield goes to the kings whom thou hast set over us because of our sins; they have power also over our bodies . . . and we are in great distress" (Neh. 9:36-37).

If the return, such as it was, was Jahveh's doing — as it is reported to have been — then his ideas concerning it were not of a piece with those of the people who so gleefully involved themselves in it. In any event, he did not encourage the philosophy of going forward by going back. He did mean to convey an idea through the strange names of those children of the prophets, but it was not the idea which the overly eager captives read into them.

If we may take the New Testament's word for it, the *shear-jashub* prophecy reached its fulfillment not in the return under Ezra and Nehemiah but in the conversion of the Gentiles in New Testament times (Jahveh had evidently favored the translation "a portion shall convert"). Nor did the *lo-ruhamah* that became *ruhamah* and the *lo-ammi* that became *ammi* refer to the return; these too found their fulfillment in the conversion of the Gentiles which took place under the eyes of Paul. Do we not read that the inspired apostle sees in the conversion of the Gentiles the fulfillment of the *lo-ammi* oracle and the *lo-ruhamah* prophecy, as well as the fulfillment of the *shear-jashub* prophecy (Rom. 9:25-27)? The same idea is advanced in I Peter, where the changes of *lo-ammi* and *lo-ruhamah* are seen to take place with the conversion of non-Jews.

Those who in the days of the return under Ezra and Nehemiah had invested so heavily in the idea of going forward by going backward, who were so greatly disillusioned by the nonrestoration of the ancient coalition of *regnum* and *sacerdotium,* met frustration in still another direction: their abortive attempt to undo the "evil" of racial mixing. There had been quite a bit of this mixing in the days of the captivity — as was to be expected. What was even worse was that those who returned began at once to take up relationships with the native population. We read that even the Levites (the men of the *sacerdotium*) "have not separated themselves from the peoples of the lands with their abominations, from the Canaanites, the Hittites, the Perizzites, the Jebusites, the Ammonites, the Moabites, the Egyptians, and the Amorites. For they have taken some of their daughters to be wives for themselves and for their sons. . . . And in this faithlessness the hand of the officials and chief men has been foremost" (Ezra 9:1-2). However, the attempt to undo this evil was by no means a rousing success. No matter how much Ezra tore first at his mantle and then at his beard, he was unable to win the people back to that idea of racial purity that had been so much a feature of their essentially sacral system of long ago. The little that he could accomplish in the matter was confined to the Levites, and even there the degree of success was limited. It was manifestly impossible to reintroduce the idea of a tribally delineated people of God. The notion that "racial purity" has something to do with religious rectitude had evidently had its day.[A]

An extremely important development in the intertestamentary period was the rise of the synagogue. This institution is very important in the evolution we are tracing because it is the direct antecedent of the New Testament church. The synagogue was "free" — free in the sense that it was not espoused by the *regnum,* neither assisted nor opposed by the civil ruler. No doubt there were civil laws that had a bearing on synagogue affairs (such as fire precautions, safety requirements), but the *regnum* left the synagogue as such pretty much to its own devices. This was, of course, a compromise with the *regnum's* own sacral assumptions, which tended to require unanimity at the shrine. How this compromise was effected is something of a problem. He who believes that God is in history will be inclined to see the hand of God in it; at the least, it taught the world the error of the sacral premise that all must worship at the same shrine if there is to be civil tranquillity. The synagogue taught the world the formula of societal compositism. However, its members may receive no credit for this

---

[A]The idea that racial purity is part of religious rectitude survives to this day in the churches of South Africa, where it survives partly because a flat theology still prevails in these churches. It is foreign to the thinking of these churches that the Spirit of God, as he brings into being the church of Jesus Christ, is as insensitive to the boundaries of any given *regnum* and any race as migrating geese are insensitive to the boundary line that separates the United States from Canada, or as the meadowlark that flies singingly out of Montana into Alberta and back again. The churches in South Africa have not to this day made their peace with the idea of worship services attended by people of different races. Leaning on the Old Testament, they still hold that "keeping the race pure" earns men favor in the sight of God.

lesson, for they of the synagogue hated and opposed the very idea to which the synagogue was giving birth.

An extremely important development in the forward movement of which we are all the while speaking was the emergence in the synagogue of a new kind of member — the proselyte. Though it is difficult to explain, non-Jews were attracted to what transpired in the synagogue. No doubt the breakthrough occurred first and foremost among the agents of the *regnum* whose duties brought them in contact with the synagogue. This would explain why a large percentage of the proselytes in New Testament times were what we today would call "government people." That they fell in love with what they saw and heard in the synagogue is noteworthy. No doubt the shabby depths to which the Romans' ancestral faith had fallen contrasted to the much loftier quality of religion in the synagogue had a good deal to do with it. They asked permission to join, a request that must have caused the rulers of the synagogue considerable embarrassment. The number of such applications for membership must have been large, for an elaborate ritual was devised to handle the requests, a ritual whereby the non-Jew could become a full-fledged member of the "people of God." Although the date of the rise of proselytism as well as the details of the induction procedures are disputed, it is certain that they began long before New Testament times and that the controlling idea was spiritual metamorphosis. The proselyte had to break with his erstwhile mode of existence and adopt a new mode; this metamorphosis was symbolized by baptism.

The influx of proselytes gave the synagogue a new kind of member, so that now there were two kinds: those who belonged by an exercise of choice, members by decision, in addition to those who belonged by the happenstance of birth within the tribe. The latter were the sort of members one encounters in any sacral situation; the former were a novel kind of member. The emergence of the proselyte members (also known by the alternative name "God-fearers," by which they are designated as they cross the stage in the New Testament) brought into the synagogue a new and different attitude toward the nonconfessing *regnum*. Those whose membership in the synagogue was the concomitant of racial and cultural grouping had a decidedly negative attitude toward the nonconfessing *regnum;* the new proselyte could not and did not share in this negative attitude. Many of them were employed by that *regnum* and thus cooperated with it daily in the affairs of state. They had assumed a loyalty toward the Jewish *sacerdotium* without thereby repudiating or lessening their loyalty to the Roman *regnum*. Both were good in their eyes — each on its own level. The proselytes were thus predisposed to the theology of progressive grace, at least to the intuitive practice of that theology. Their mode of existence was a living departure from sacral presuppositions and the monism implied in them. That such widely divergent points of view were able to exist side by side in the synagogue is most remarkable. However, they did continue to exist far into New Testament times. It was doubtless in the presence of these two diverging synagogue groups that the question of "whether it is lawful to give tribute to Caesar" came to be debated.

The proselytes then were men of two loyalties whose philosophy of life could be well expressed in Jesus' formula: "Render to Caesar the things that are Caesar's and to God the things that are God's." That is, do the proper thing vis-à-vis the creature of conserving grace as well as vis-à-vis the creature of redeeming grace. It is very significant that, although the synagogue community produced wave upon wave of Maccabean rebellion against the nonconfessing *regnum*, none of these rebellions was propelled by the proselyte faction. The mentality of the more ancient kind of synagogue member engendered and nurtured the Maccabean spirit, which can best be understood as the expressed frustration at the lack of success of the program of going forward by going backward. The Maccabean uprisings were the direct result of the atavistic conviction that a *regnum* that does not compare notes with its *sacerdotium* is by definition demonic and must be destroyed — in a religious war if necessary. The Maccabean Wars were "holy" wars if ever there were any, wars fought by a people still committed to the sacral formula. These rebellions were the outcome of a theology then already obsolescent, the theology of sacralism; they were fought by men who refused to follow the forward movement of history and of history's God, by men who remained strangers to the concept of progressive grace.

The Maccabean rebellions were also a pathetic failure: no good was achieved by them, and they only made a reasonably tolerable situation intolerable. If the mind of God may ever be determined by an examination of history (a procedure fraught with grave theological peril), one must conclude that the heart of God was not in the Maccabean rebellions. These wars were fought — with unspeakable human anguish and loss — to regain the confessing state and the erstwhile synthesis of the *regnum* and the *sacerdotium*. They were an anachronism and hence an abysmal failure. And it must be emphasized that the Maccabean revolt was not the work of these adherents of the synagogue who were members by decision; it was carried on by those who were members by birth.

So different was the new kind of synagogue member that many intuitively felt the need for a new badge of belonging to signify solidarity with the family that worshiped Jahveh. Although the proselyte was circumcised, that was held to be inadequate. From the beginning, circumcision had been associated with the "loins of Abraham" (in our day we would say "the genes and chromosomes of Abraham"); it had always been associated with a biological link, with pigmentation of skin and texture of hair, with the profile of nose and chin, and with a "mother tongue." Circumcision was therefore something of a misfit when applied to men who had come out of other "loins." The new *mode* of belonging (by decision) called for a new *badge* of belonging. In the search for such a badge, men's eyes fell on the rite of baptism, a rite already in use among some of the religious cults of the day (as had been the case with circumcision when it was appropriated earlier), where it had the same kind of symbolism. It is at this point — the emergence of the proselyte — that baptism as a badge of belonging entered the Hebrew-Christian tradition. It is wise to remember baptism's first connotation (that of membership by decision) for, as we shall see below, baptism was often stripped of this erstwhile and authentic connotation in later times.

The leaders of the synagogue had probably considered other potential badges indicative of belonging by decision. We are led to ask why the badge of the pierced ear was passed by. The pierced ear was already an old institution in Israel when the first proselyte was being admitted into the synagogue. From earliest times, it was a mutilation that marked a slave who had opted to stay with his master even when, in the year of jubilee, he was free to go (Ex. 21:5). If such a slave chose to stay with his master, the latter would thrust an awl through the lobe of the servant's ear, and the mark was henceforth a sign of perpetual but voluntary service.[B] That this venerable

[B] The idea of the pierced ear returns in the New Testament, in Heb. 10:5, where Ps. 40:6 is translated rather freely and applied to Christ, whose whole earthly life was one of obedience freely rendered.

institution was passed by is more noteworthy when one considers how its symbolism of service by choice fit the situation so admirably. Perhaps the reason for not appropriating it was that the pierced ear was a visible mark, whereas the revealing Spirit manifestly wanted an invisible one, one that would leave no outward trace. In this matter baptism is quite unlike the marks by which tribes, socio-political groupings, and cultural collectives are ordinarily denoted. A new people of God was coming into being, one marked by an invisible quality, a fellowship not helped by the affinities or hampered by the antagonisms characteristic of other groupings and their visible signs and markings. Did the Redeemer God for that reason lead men to choose a badge of belonging that was likewise invisible? If so, baptism served that purpose very well indeed.

* * * * *

We have now come to the eve of the New Testament era. Those who realize that God works in an evolutionary manner, that is, by way of process, will not expect outright innovation in the New Testament era. Nothing wholly novel is broached there. What we do see in the New Testament is the emerging adult form of certain things that were present in embryonic form earlier. Strictly speaking, the New Testament era began with Pentecost. Thus, John the Baptist, as well as Jesus himself, actually lived and worked within the Old Testament framework. This admittedly unusual representation explains how Jesus could say and have as his policy during his ministry, "Go nowhere among the Gentiles, and enter no town of the Samaritans" (Matt. 10:5) and "I was sent only to the lost sheep of the house of Israel" (Matt. 15:24). And after that ministry was concluded, he could say, with a look to the future, "Go therefore and make disciples of all nations" (Matt. 28:19). This seemingly irreconcilable contradiction in the attitudes and words of Christ is an insoluble matter in any theology that is blind to early and late; however, it becomes quite manageable in a three-dimensional theology. Salvation had to be set up among the people of the promise; only after it was set up were its emissaries to fan out in all directions. Christ's earlier command came *before* his crucifixion and resurrection; the later command came *after*.

We must begin with John the Baptist, the forerunner

who "prepared the way" for Christ. John's baptism was a continuation of proselyte baptism. It was as though the forerunner had gone into the synagogue, observed the two kinds of members that were present there, and had decided to gather together a communion in which only the proselyte variety was acceptable, for whom baptism had been appropriated. John concentrated on the member by decision, and he served notice that any other kind of applicant was unacceptable — in terms that could not be misunderstood. Did he not speak gruffly to those who offered to belong in a sacral sense? Did he not rebuff those whose would-be qualification was tribal consanguinity? Did he not declare that they were not welcome or acceptable? John left no doubt: "And do not presume to say to yourselves, 'We have Abraham as our father'; for I tell you, God is able from these stones to raise up children to Abraham" (Matt. 3:9). And then he enlarged on this theme, so radical and in contemporary eyes quite blasphemous: an axe, said he, was already laid at the root of the tree (the tree of Abraham!) to cut off and haul to the burning every branch of the tree that does not bear fruit, the fruit of repentance. And he said that a fan has been taken to purge the threshing floor (the threshing floor of Abraham!) of all that is chaff. It is no wonder he came to be known as the Baptist, for all he had to say was contained in the word and the practice of the kind of baptism that had been appropriated earlier as a badge of belonging by decision. Had there been no proselytes, it seems safe to say, there would have been no John the Baptist. And may we also say that if there had been no John the Baptist, Jesus and his career as we know it would have been impossible? In any event, Jesus manifestly needed a way-preparer; and that way-preparer was the link between the segment of the synagogue community that held membership by decision and the little band of decision members that followed Jesus.

As is well known, Jesus had a very high regard for John the Baptist and his program, saying that of all who had been born of woman he was the greatest. No doubt this high evaluation was due to John's pioneering in the matter of a people of God held together by decision-making. With John the Baptist begins a people of God not coextensive with any already existing togetherness; with him evolves the format of the New Testament church. With John begins the idea of a composite society. He was indeed great!

Proselytes were converted people, and it is little wonder that John the Baptist — who had manifestly fallen in love with their type — preached repentance, which is substantially the same as conversion. The keynote of John's preaching was "repent ye," that is, "be converted." The Greek original has the word *metanoia*, a word that has been abused more regularly by translators and theologians than any other word in the catalogue. We must take a fresh look at it, especially because of the important role it played in the development we are tracing. The first part of the word is the Greek preposition *meta*, which in the Greek of the common man had come to mean "from . . . to." The second part of *metanoia* is related to the Greek *nous*, a word signifying the core of one's being. The combination of *meta* and *nous*, therefore, indicates a "from . . . to" movement in the inner man, a metamorphosis that takes place in one's "heart" or "soul." In John's theology such a "from . . . to" movement was an absolute prerequisite of discipleship; one could not qualify without it. For that reason John went over all applicants for a place in his following with a fine-toothed comb. If an applicant gave evidence of *metanoia*, John baptized him; if he did not, John sent him back — like a student who fails in the entrance exam.

With the band of the forerunner's followers a peculiar and distinguishing life-style comes to expression as the necessary feature for all who would belong. For "fruits worthy of repentance" is the equivalent of manifest *metanoia*, a change of heart that comes to expression in a contrasting way of life. One's being converted is expressed when a man who has two coats imparts one of them to a person who has none, when a publican "exacts no more than is appointed," when a soldier "does no violence to any man nor accuses any falsely," and considers his legitimate wage to be enough, etc. (Lk. 3:10-14). John the Baptist had no room in his following for persons whose life-style was like that of everyone else. He had room only for persons who evinced a life-style that contrasted with the environment. This requirement always remained a feature of authentic Christianity, although it was often abandoned in the times that followed. Whenever it was abandoned, the authentic meaning of *metanoia* was of course an embarrassment. For this reason the word was all too commonly misinterpreted and mistranslated in later times, when it was equated with doing penance — performing disagreeable religious chores, such as going on a pilgrimage.[c] This mistranslation of *metanoia* has served to accentuate the pardon aspect of salvation and to suppress the renewal aspect, thus creating an imbalance between pardon and the adoption of a new life-style. This in turn has had much to do with the humbling failure of Christianity to make much of a difference, certainly not enough of a difference, in the life-style of its adherents.

We must also call attention to the down-to-earth quality of John the Baptist's "fruits bespeaking *metanoia*." They are not the "good works" of later times, when men thought that the distinguishing marks of the Christian were masses, paternosters, Ave Marias, pilgrimages, fasts, candle-burning, rosary-telling, and genuflections. John's good works were not some specified conduct in connection with "sacrament" or some kind of ritual consisting of prayers and songs. Although there is no evidence that John disapproved of these or minimized them, it is noteworthy that his good works do not smell of incense. They are much earthier, homelier, and grander in that they are simply human conduct cleared of the dimension of fallenness, soldier conduct stripped of soldier sin, publican conduct cleansed of publican fault, etc. It is also noteworthy that in John's way of thinking one's convertedness manifests itself in his deportment toward his fellow men. This does not mean that John's theology does not know the vertical relationship, but that it puts the accent on the horizontal. His is the piety of the market place rather than of the sanctuary. It is geared toward the Master's portrayal of the Last Judgment, where things done and left undone on the horizontal plane are the acid test. It is certain that the so-called Christian world would be in a far better witnessing position today if the emphases of John the Baptist and his greater follower had prevailed, if their emphasis on the horizontal had not gone into eclipse. If that were the case, one would hear less in our times of Christianity's "irrelevance."

The Baptist dreaded any mass movement like the plague — any wholesale coming, anything that would lay the groundwork for another sacral society. When he saw the multitudes

---

[c]Even the translation "repent" is still far from satisfactory, if for no other reason than that repenting doesn't commit one to "do better from now on." The idea of the beginning of a better way of life is not necessarily present in the concept of repenting — although it is very prominent in *metanoia*.

coming to his baptism in whole population units, he stretched a net across the path, a net with mesh so fine that it would screen out the "snakes' young" — as he called those without *metanoia* (Matt. 3:1-12). Gone was the old ethnic idea of a "church" embracing a total society; if there was one thing John the Baptist did not encourage it was the concept of a visible church, a church embracing a whole society in a sort of preliminary membership by baptism. Gone too was the idea of an *ecclesiola in ecclesia*, a little church of converted people in the folds of the big church embracing a whole society. For John the *ecclesiola* is the *ecclesia*. The Baptist became almost violent when he contemplated the previous way of "belonging"; he demolished without mercy the old idea of a church that embraces a total language group. His words must have sounded like a mockery of what was holy when he said, "Say not 'We are Abraham's children.'" What is this but a passionate declaration that the old-line members of the synagogue were *candidates* for the real thing and no more, a status in which cobblestones could share! John thought in terms of a witnessing group and a witnessed to group; and these two groups, when thrown together, make up the societal unit. Consistent societal compositism begins with John the Baptist: with him the sacral system comes to an end and a new system begins.

Although the Baptist's conception of the church runs through the whole New Testament, it stands out most ruggedly in the book of Hebrews. Nor is this surprising: where would one expect to find as great an awareness of the mighty changes that had taken place, the immense surge forward, as in this book written by a converted Hebrew to converted Hebrews? In this book of the Bible we are told that the Old Testament prophecies have been fulfilled with the emergence of a "people" that has the law of God in their minds and on their hearts rather than on tables of stone. This is a "church" in which "they shall not teach every one his fellow or every one his brother, saying, 'Know the Lord,' for all shall know me, from the least of them to the greatest" (Heb. 8:11). Here there is no *ecclesiola in ecclesia* any longer. Here is a church consisting wholly of members by decision. No one could sense more strongly than a "Hebrew" what a tremendously changed situation this was. It is thus no wonder that the new dispensation's being bigger and better is the theme of the whole epistle to the Hebrews. In it the writer says without inhibition: "In speaking of a new covenant he treats the first as obsolete. And what is becoming obsolete and growing old is ready to vanish away" (8:13). It may indeed be said that the book of Hebrews is to the idea of early and late what the *Institutes* are to the theology of John Calvin.

Since John's baptism was one of *metanoia,* the coming of Jesus to his baptism posed a problem. Here was the "mightier" one, the one whose shoelaces John, in spite of his *metanoia-* born moral austerity, felt himself unworthy to untie. He was the "Lamb of God" who by his life of perfect obedience was to "take away the sins of the world." What was John to do when such a one asked for baptism, one for whom *metanoia* was unthinkable since he had no depraved mode of existence to turn away from? John knew how to deal with converted ones, and he knew how to handle the unconverted; but he did not know what to do in the case of a sinless one. In his embarrassment he offered to trade roles, to let Jesus do the baptizing, and he himself would be the receiver of the act. However, Jesus would not hear of this: there was a "righteousness," or rightness, that said John must baptize Jesus. The body of people bound together by a baptism signifying their *metanoia* must have a head similarly marked. And so to meet the requirements of correctness, "to fulfill all righteousness," John did as he was told: he baptized Jesus.

We do not know much about the political slant of John's preaching. He seems to have said little or nothing about the secular *regnum.* We do know that he rebuked a king for his unconverted life and for living in an adulterous relationship; and we know that this faithfulness to his calling cost John his life. But this does not add up to the negative attitude toward the secular *regnum* that characterized the old-line members of the synagogue. There is no evidence that John thought of the Roman state as a demonic thing. He was all for converting rulers, but there is no evidence that he envisioned a "converted" *regnum.* Not that the idea of a converted *regnum* was unknown in his day. It was altogether prevalent and available to him. The fact is that John had to fight it off. Although Maccabeanism had become a thing of the past, there was current in John's day a new and virulent form of Jewish nationalism, called Zealotry. It was born of the old conviction that *regnum* and *sacerdotium* must have their heads in one sack, and it held that since the existing *regnum* was not in the signature of the Jahveh-faith, it deserved to be shaken off and destroyed. Zealotry was the contemporary expression of the ancient hope of going forward some day by going backward.

That John the Baptist did not get involved in this Zealotry is noteworthy. Outwardly, he was very much like these Zealots (several of whom, as we shall see, entered Jesus' company). The desert, scene of John's activities, was full of hiding places from which Zealot guerillas made commando raids and to which they returned for hiding. John's refusal to get involved in their activities can no doubt be explained by his divergent appraisal of the secular *regnum*: John had adopted the proselytes' appraisal and their positive stance toward it, which precluded involvement in Zealotry. Moreover, John had appropriated the progressive grace concept of the proselyte, whose baptism he had also appropriated.

Furthermore, John seems to have had little interest in Jerusalem, its temple, and the cult connected with it: he did not "go up" to Jerusalem and did not talk about what went on there. It is as if Jerusalem lay outside the sphere of his interests. This is significant, for Jerusalem was the center of a tribal religion, the capital of an ancient sacral society. Jerusalem's "church" was a *Volkskirche,* the church of a total people. But John was not only not interested in such a *Volkskirche* but vehemently opposed to it. His dismissal of the concept of a "confessing" *regnum* implied the repudiation of an all-embracing and "confessing" society, tribe, or socio-political entity. The Baptist's inspiration did not come from the temple; it came from the synagogue, more particularly from the proselyte segment of the synagogue. These people and their baptism dominated the vision of the forerunner.

We do not know whether John the Baptist gathered those who had made a decision (whom he had therefore baptized) into a "congregation." He probably did; but if he did, their gatherings were surely of a type quite different from the format of the Temple congregation. The only kind of religious assembly John could have supported was the kind known later as the conventicle — the religious gathering where believers are members by decision. A conventicle is the kind of religious assembly that can take form after sacralism has been rejected, after the pre-Christian structuring of society has been repudiated. The synagogue had been the halfway house between the temple gathering and the conventicle, for it had elements of both. The conventicle type of gathering that became so important in the history of the Christian faith begins with John the Baptist. It is a gathering for religious purposes but definitely not under the auspices of the *regnum*. It is the kind of religious convening of believers that goes with non-public devotions. The conventicle is a subtle repudiation of sacralism because it presupposes a composite society and cancels out the unanimous society.

* * * * *

This then was the course of the way-maker, the forerunner. We find in his follower, as was to be expected, a continuation of the policies and practices of the Baptist. Jesus also gathered around himself a band of persons who had changed direction, followers by decision, men of *metanoia*. Although he often spoke to large gatherings, he always maintained a clear-cut distinction between the masses of listeners and his group of disciples. The former he dealt with as candidates — mere candidates — for the position already occupied by the latter. It is a fact far too commonly ignored that as Jesus spoke he constantly and consistently played in two registers, as does a musician on an organ with two manuals. One can divide Jesus' sayings into two columns, one consisting of sayings to those who were already of the company, the other of expressions to those who were but candidates for inclusion in that company. His formula is contained in the declaration made to his disciples: "To you it has been given to know the secrets of the kingdom of God; but for others they are in parables, so that . . . hearing they may not understand" (Luke 8:10).[D]

Jesus' attitude toward the temple and what transpired there was likewise in keeping with the attitude of the man who had prepared the way for him. Whenever Jesus came near the temple, a storm was likely to brew in his soul. Some of

---

[D]Failure to observe and respect Jesus' policy of playing in two registers has done untold theological damage: it has, for example, led people to attribute to human beings in general what Jesus predicated of believers and of them exclusively. A good example of this is the "Our Father" of the Lord's Prayer: "our" does not here refer to humanity as a whole but to that band of followers by decision who had asked the Master to teach them how they should pray.

the negative miracles he performed (e.g., the cursing of the fig tree so that it withered) were a reflection of his attitude toward the temple and the concept of which it was the rallying point. The only "flaw" unsympathetic critics have said they can find in Jesus' deportment — the lashing of people with an improvised scourge — occurred *inside the temple.* Jesus' real temple — as it had been with John the Baptist — was the desert. When by-standers (noting Jesus' evident lack of enthusiasm for the building that housed the culture-religion) prodded Jesus with expressions like, "Rabbi, what stones and what a structure!" he responded gloomily enough: "Truly, I say to you, there will not be left here one stone upon another, that will not be thrown down" (Matt. 24:2). When the woman at the well of Jacob gave Jesus the chance to endorse the Jews' high esteem of Jerusalem as the seat of a sacral society, he made no use of it. Instead he said to the woman: "The hour is coming when neither on this mountain nor in Jerusalem will you worship the Father" (John 4:21).

It is significant that, although Jesus predicted the total demolition of the temple at Jerusalem, he did not promise a subsequent restoration, as prophets before him had. There was no *shear-jashub* on his horizon. Jerusalem would be destroyed and with it the last landmark of a sacral order, the last vestige of a *regnum-sacerdotium* combination; it would be the final dashing of the forlorn hope of going forward by going backward. The fact that he did not feed this ancient hope had everything to do with his being rejected by a society that refused to move forward with him because it remained bound to the past and its structures. The issue was that of flat theology versus the theology of progressive grace, with the Jewish leaders fighting for the status quo and Jesus agonizing for a forward movement.

It should be noted that although Jesus kindled little hope for a *regnum* committed to the faith of which he was to be the center, his attitude toward the nonconfessing *regnum* under which he lived was not the negative attitude of the synagogue old-timers with their flat theology. He did not look upon the secular *regnum* as demonic by definition. In this matter Jesus stood once more — as John had — with the proselyte. Although his main concern was with the "kingdom of heaven" (his own designation of the realm in which redemptive grace is operative), he nevertheless called the *regnum* a thing that was "from above" (a realm in which preliminary grace was operative). It is significant that he spoke well of the *regnum* at the very moment it was about to crucify him (misled as it was by the Jewish *sacerdotium*). In Jesus' way of thinking, the malfeasance on the part of the *regnum* was attributable to the agency that had taken a matter belonging to the realm of the *sacerdotium* and had thrown it into the lap of the *regnum*.[E] Jesus had no quarrel with a *regnum* that goes its way without being subservient to the *sacerdotium;* his quarrel was with a *sacerdotium* that called in the *regnum* to perform a service for which it was not intended.

There is perhaps no passage in the New Testament that throws more light on Jesus' attitude toward the secular state than the account of the *didrachma* recorded in Matthew 17:24-27. This *didrachma* (a half shekel) was an ancient institution, first mentioned in Exodus 30, which required that every adult male in Israel pay a set fee toward the maintenance of the sanctuary. After falling into disuse during the hectic days of the captivity, it was revived at the return from exile (Neh. 10:32). According to the context, its revival then was a part of the large-scale attempt to re-establish a sacral order. There were some irregularities in the handling of these collected moneys (Neh. 13:10). Whether it was the questionable management or the threat this mode of raising moneys carried in itself (it provided a handy and unobtrusive way to gather funds for the support of seditious undertakings) is a question that need not detain us here. The fact is that by Jesus' time the Roman government had adopted the policy of picking up these contributions and then footing the bill for such repairs or improvements as these moneys warranted. We read in Matthew 17 that someone asked Peter whether his master was in the habit of paying the *didrachma* (literally "the two drams," as the temple tax had come to be called). No doubt what prompted this prying question was the presumption

[E] Jesus' complaint was that an unwarranted change of venue was taking place, that betrayal was occurring, that a traitor was at work. The Greek word in the original is *paradous* (the Latin equivalent is *traditor*, from which derives the English word "traitor"), a word that literally means "one who hands over," and the reference is to the act of handing over to the court of the *regnum* a case that belonged in the court of the *sacerdotium*. In Jesus' words, those who had engineered the unwarranted change of venue were guilty of the greater sin: "He who delivered me to you has the greater sin" (John 19:11).

that ardent flat grace religionists (as the questioner took Jesus to be) usually had scruples against paying the tax to an "uncircumcised" agency, which by its very handling of the money rendered it unfit for the "holy place." Peter, somewhat embarrassed by the unexpected question, hesitatingly answered in the affirmative. The matter would no doubt have ended there had not Jesus deliberately reopened it: "What do you think, Simon? From whom do kings of the earth take toll or tribute? From their sons or from others?" Peter replies that it is "from others," that is, from Jews, whom the Roman government knew as unamalgamated ones, "strangers," or "sojourners." The "sons," that is, the native Romans, were not asked to pay it. Thereupon Jesus summarized that if it was a tax exacted from sojourners, then the children, the native sons, ought not to be billed for it. Then he added, most significantly: "However, not to give offense, go to the sea and cast a hook, and take the first fish that comes up, and when you open its mouth you will find a shekel [a four-*drachma* piece]; take that and give it to them for me and for yourself" (Matt. 17:27).

The astounding thing in this incident is that Jesus put himself and his disciples in the category of "sons" rather than "sojourners," indicating that in the matter of his and their relationship to the existing *regnum* Jesus identified with the Roman citizen rather than with the Jew. We see in this identification the mentality of the proselyte members of the synagogue: he had distanced himself from the older element of the synagogue congregation and its negative attitude toward the nonconfessing *regnum*. In not objecting to identification as a "son" of the secular *regnum* of his day — a "son" rather than a sacral "sojourner" — Jesus clearly was committed to the theology of progressive grace. What he said in this incident throws an illuminating ray on his statement "Render to Caesar the things that are Caesar's and to God the things that are God's." Oscar Cullmann has said that this utterance can only be understood if seen "in connection with the Zealot movement."[1]

We come now to a consideration of Jesus' attitude toward the Zealot ideology as such. This is important: it is impossible to understand the career of Jesus Christ unless we see it in the context of the tensions caused by the Zealot mentality and movement. Zealotry was essentially a resurgence of Maccabeanism, and it was fed and sustained by a flat theology's appraisal of the nonconfessing *regnum*. The Zealots not only refused to cooperate with the Roman government but opposed it and sought to sabotage it at every turn — all in the name of religion. Since this *regnum* was manifestly not involved in the enterprise of redemptive grace, it was thus in the Zealots' eyes demonic. And so they treated it as such: instead of praying for it, they plotted against it. It had not occurred to them that there is such a thing as a preliminary grace, which seeks to conserve, and that the *regnum* is its agency. Their flat theology made the Zealots seek to destroy the secular *regnum*, to go forward by going backward, to restore the ancient but essentially pre-Christian sacral order.

Jesus had every possible opportunity to become involved in the Zealot philosophy, program, and practice; he had only to refrain from resisting it to be drawn along with it. However, that he did resist it is written large in the New Testament. Christ's whole life, in fact, was a grand victory over the Zealot ambition. From the slaughter of the innocents by King Herod (inspired by fear of a Zealot coup) to the *INRI* affixed to the Savior's cross (the initials of the Latin words meaning "Jesus of Nazareth, King of the Jews"), his life — and especially his death — reflected a policy *other* than that of Zealotry. We do well to look at this life and death rather closely in this study, particularly since the rejection of Zealotry and the substitution of another program for it are indicative of the forward movement toward a composite society which we are here discussing.

Consider the temptation in the desert, as recorded in Matthew 4 and Luke 4. In the devil's third proposition, in which his real objective becomes nakedly apparent (the first two being preliminary attempts, intended to "soften up" the Savior), "all the kingdoms of the world" are dangled before Jesus' eyes, the *regnum* in its worldwide scope his for the taking. He will allow Jesus to be king of it all, so says the devil, with the slight provision that Jesus bow to him, thus acknowledging Satan to be the final king. Jesus is here face to face with what has been called his master temptation, the temptation to go the way of the Zealots and in so doing evade the cross. With a resolute "Get thee hence, Satan!" he chooses the way of the cross. Upon this rebuff the tempter leaves Jesus — for a season, or as some translate it, "until another time." That "other time" comes when the apostle Peter tries again to deflect Jesus from his course of the cross, with the words:

"God forbid, Lord! This shall never happen to you" (Matt. 16:22). Again Jesus finds himself assailed by the master temptation; again we hear from his lips, "Get behind me, Satan! For you are not on the side of God, but of men" (Mark 8:33).

It was not merely the speech of Peter that smacked of Zealot ambitions; the speaker himself may have reminded Jesus of the Zealot alternative to the way that was for him the right way. Indeed, Peter may very well have been a rather poorly converted Zealot at the time. He was known as *Barjona*, a name that has been taken to mean "son of Jonah"; but it is quite probable that it was intended to mean "Zealot." As has been pointed out by G. Dalman,[2] *barjona* is in all probability a word borrowed from Akkadian, meaning "terrorist" or "freedom fighter" — virtual synonyms for "Zealot."[F] Peter's readiness to hack and hew with the sword at the time of Jesus' arrest could very well be a vestige of a Zealot past. Jesus' rejoinder was: "Put your sword back into its place; for all who take the sword will perish by the sword. Do you think that I cannot appeal to my Father, and he will at once send me more than twelve legions of angels? But how then should the scriptures be fulfilled, that it must be so?" (Matt. 26:52-54). This sounds very much like a reproof intended for a man with Zealot ideals. In this light Jesus' words, spoken much later, take on a new meaning and pathos: "Simon, *barjona*, lovest thou me?" It becomes a question that asks whether the old *barjona*, the old terrorist, has learned new ways, the ways of Jesus' love.

If some question remains as to whether Peter was a

[F] *Barjona* seems to have been a common noun rather than a proper noun. We read in the Talmud[3] that when some Jewish leaders recommended cooperation with the Romans, it was due to *barjona* pressures that this advice was not followed. We read of a certain Abba Sikara, who was "head of the *barjona* at Jerusalem." We read that when Jochanan ben Zakkai was unable to keep an appointment with a government person of the time, it was "because the *barjona* among us permitted it not." Clearly, *barjona* connoted people who, as was the case with the Zealots, were against détente with the Roman rulers and in favor of a fight to the finish to overthrow that rule and reinstitute the sacral society of the Old Testament. Peter may very well have been such a *barjona*. It is true that Peter is called "Son of John" (John 21:15) or "Son of Johannes" (which is closer to the Greek original); and it has been assumed that *barjona* is simply the Hebrew equivalent of "Son of Johannes." But this interpretation loses certainty when we consider that nowhere does "Jona" appear as a shortened form of "Johannes."

former Zealot, there is no question that at least one of Jesus' disciples was: it was the other Simon, known as "Simon Zelotes" (Luke 6:15; Acts 1:13). He is no doubt the individual referred to as "Simon the Cananaean" in Matthew 10:4. "Cananaean" has been translated "the Canaanite," but this is surely erroneous: "Cananaean" is derived from the Aramaic noun *kana* (meaning zeal), so that "Zealot" is simply the Greek equivalent of the Aramaic "Cananaean." Oscar Cullmann has pointed out that "*Cananaean* has nothing whatever to do with the land of Canaan; it is simply a transcription of the Aramaic designation of the Zealot. . . ."[4] Very probably Simon had been converted from his Zealot convictions and ambitions, but it is significant that he continued to be known as "the Zealot."

In addition, there were James and John, the two "sons of thunder" (*Boanerges*) as Jesus called them (a nickname that would fit any Zealot handsomely). The request they made — "Let us sit at your right hand and your left when this kingdom idea of yours materializes" (cf. Mark 10:35) — smacks strongly of Zealot ambitions. So does their quarreling about rank in the *regnum* they expected Jesus to set up, as well as their desire that fire be called down from heaven on people unwilling to serve in the program (Luke 9:54). Jesus' rebuke, "You do not know what manner of spirit you are of" (Luke 9:55, RSV margin) then takes on the sense of, "You don't seem to trace back the remarks you make to their proper source, that is, to the Zealot dream."

Then there was Judas Iscariot, a man who in all likelihood was a Zealot activist when he fell in with Jesus. The name "Iscariot" has been taken to refer to Judas' supposed place of origin, "Kerioth," that is, "man from Kerioth" (*ish* being the Hebrew word for "man"). However, this interpretation is quite certainly in error. To begin with, there is the fact that "we know of no place by that name."[5] And there is a much more plausible explanation: Cullmann thinks it "certain"[6] that "Iscariot" is derived from *sikarios*, a word that was synonymous with "Zealot."[G] The accuracy of identifying "Iscar-

---

[G] We read of fanatics who "took to themselves the name of Zealots, called *sikarii* by some people" (Hengel, *Die Zeloten*, p. 73). The two words seem interchangeable: Josephus refers to the four thousand *sikarioon*, as they are called in the NT (Acts 21:38), as the "four thousand Zealots" (*The Jewish Wars*, II, 13:5; see also *The Antiquities*, XX, 8:6). Here in Acts 21:38, the word "assassins" is an attempt to translate *sikarioon*; it has also

iot" with "Zealot" is borne out in some manuscripts of the New Testament (notably the *Codex Bezae*), where the name appears as "Judas Skarioth," as well as in a group of Latin manuscripts (the so-called *Itala*), where he is referred to as "Judas the Zealot."

It appears then that Jesus worked in a political climate heavily impregnated with Zealotism, that the temptation to go along with it was strong in his life, and that escape from Zealotism and substitution of another program for it was a major victory in his life. In this light it becomes significant that Barabbas, whom Pilate offered to set free as a gesture of good will to the Jews who had brought Jesus to his court, was very likely arrested for Zealot activities. Zealots were often called *lēstai*,[7] a Greek word meaning "looters" and "thieves" (as well as "insurrectionists") since looting was permitted in the Zealot program. Barabbas was no doubt a *lēstēs* (John 18:40) who had been apprehended in connection with an "insurrection" (Mark 15:7; Luke 23:19).[8] Pilate's sop thrown to the Jews turns out then to be an offer to execute a bona fide Zealot instead of one who was beginning to look very much like a phony. And the Jews' conscious refusal to agree to it becomes the more significant. Also, the two "malefactors" in whose company Jesus was crucified were surely two such *lēstai;* crucifixion was the prescribed form of execution for Zealot terrorists. That Pilate grouped the three together shows again how in the public mind Jesus' program was of a piece with Zealotism.[9]

Now that we know Judas Iscariot for what he was — a cryptic Zealot — a new light falls on his course of conduct. We can now answer some very important questions about him:

---

been translated as "murderers." The Latin form, *sicarii*, literally means "spear-hurlers." Although the apostle Paul seems never to have been involved in the Zealot program, it is significant that he was suspected of having been the leader of these notorious "four thousand assassins," because it indicates that his contemporaries attributed to followers of Jesus a sympathy for the Zealot cause. The Roman officials' conclusion that Paul's embroilment with the Jews implied his involvement in Zealot activities shows that severe polarities among the Jews concerning approval of the Zealot program were not unusual. And since the two polarized elements had existed for some time in the synagogue — one supporting Zealotism and the other opposed to it — it is not surprising that the friction which had produced the question whether "it is lawful to give tribute to Caesar" was well known to the Romans.

why he betrayed Jesus, and why he committed suicide. If we keep in mind exactly where the New Testament accounts place these two events, we will be well on our way to the answers. At the same time, a great deal of light falls on the development of the forward movement which we are tracing in this section of the book.

Judas decided to hand Jesus over immediately after the woman had poured an alabaster cruse of ointment over Jesus' head and he had uttered the little homily about anointing his "body beforehand for the burying" (Mark 14:3-9). Both Matthew (26:14-16) and Mark (14:10-11) report that it was at this precise point that Judas slipped over to the men of the Jewish Sanhedrin with the offer to hand Jesus over. Both the anointing and the homily were enough to turn the stomach of any Zealot, for neither of these could in any way serve the revolutionary cause. Judas had hitherto hoped that Jesus would develop into the kind of messiah the Zealot cause awaited, one who would "deliver" Israel by unseating the Roman *regnum* and restoring to Israel its own king. His expectation was not uncommon, even to Peter and the sons of Zebedee. In these disciples it was undergoing a radical change during their association with Jesus; however, in Judas it remained dominant. The anointing and the accompanying homily made Judas give up on this "savior," and because he was now all through with Jesus, he offered to do his part in clearing the deck for another "deliverer." That is why he decided to hand Jesus over. Of course, it is true that he gave another reason for his disgust with the anointing, one less patently Zealot-flavored. He knew by this time how Jesus would react to the real reason for his disgust, so that he felt he had to invent another reason for it; hence his pious speech about wasting an amount of money the poor could use so well. However, this speech was so out of character that one reporter (John 12:6) suggests that it was intended theft that inspired it. It seems most likely that Judas' disgust and subsequent offer to betray was born of a dashed ambition in his Zealot bosom.

But the answer to the question of why Judas betrayed Jesus is more involved. Judas offered to hand Jesus over because he wanted him to feel the bite of the sword of the nonconfessing *regnum,* which he was evidently not planning to unseat. This was also a part of the motive behind the betrayal. Because Judas could no longer hope that Jesus was the answer to the old dream of going forward some day by going backward, and because he was sick and tired of this phony messiah, he offered to take the initiative in getting rid of him — by delivering him into the ruling hands of the detested *regnum*. We should bear in mind that Judas confidently expected the *sacerdotium,* known to him as the Sanhedrin, to haul Jesus before the *regnum's* court and there have him tried and sentenced. However, it soon seemed that this expectation was not going to be realized: it looked as though the case was going to end in the court of the *sacerdotium* and not go to the *regnum* at all. Judas had seen Jesus go into the court of the Sanhedrin and had heard the verdict of guilty, with death as the penalty. When Judas saw his plan thus miscarrying, his thoughts turned to self-destruction. It is surely significant that Matthew (the only Gospel-writer to record Judas' suicide) interrupts the story of Jesus' trial at this very point to tell us of the suicide, before moving on to record that Jesus is tried before the court of the *regnum* after all (27:3-14). Matthew apparently wished to point out that it was because Judas' plot, hatched in his Zealot's dissatisfaction with Jesus, had failed, that life became unbearable for him. When it seemed to Judas that Jesus would die at the hands of the *sacerdotium* for matters lying on the plane of religion, a great dread came over him. Recall that it was precisely when Jesus had been put under oath to testify whether he was indeed the Christ, and he had said, "I swear," that the sentence of death had fallen. Here was an area to which Judas was a stranger and yet not a stranger — the area of redemptive grace. Here was a "messiah" who was going to die for things Judas had seen from afar, and yet had not perceived; and the thought of it made death seem better than life. Little did he think as he took his own life that on the next day the case would go to the court of the *regnum* after all.[H]

The next morning, after Judas had been buried, Jesus' case went to the court of the *regnum*. At this point a third

[H]We are told that "when he saw that he was condemned," Judas broke down and went to pieces (Matt. 27:3). This has sometimes been taken to mean that when Judas realized he had done a dastardly deed he felt very guilty, threw the thirty pieces of silver across the temple floor, and went and hanged himself. But it is quite certain that the antecedent of the latter "he" is not Judas but Jesus: when Judas saw that he (Jesus) was condemned to death (already, before he had been before the court of the *regnum*) then he (Judas) went and hanged himself.

thought-provoking question presents itself: why this change of venue? It has sometimes been said that the transfer was a matter of course since the Jews did not have the right of the sword and hence the case simply had to go to Pilate. This is a mistake. The truth of the matter is that the question of the right of the sword was very much up in the air at this moment in Jewish history: did they or did they not have the right to put anyone to death? We see this in the conflicting opinion concerning the matter: Pontius Pilate proposes that the Jews execute Jesus, and the Jews say that the law does not allow them to do so (John 18:31). That Pilate does not contradict this assertion of the illegality to punish capitally has been taken to prove that the Jews did not currently have the right of the sword; but it is more likely that Pilate was merely being tactful in handling a potentially explosive situation. To contradict the Jews at that point would only have made them very bitter. As a matter of fact, at this very time Sejanus, a Jew-hater high in the Roman government, was agitating — quite successfully — to have the right of the sword taken away from the Jews. Thus, the historic situation was just right for Judas to assume that Jesus' case would go to the court of the *regnum* for disposition; just right for Judas later to get the impression that it was *not* going there; just right for Pilate to suggest that the *sacerdotium* do the executing; just right for the Jews to complain that the right of the sword had been taken away from them; and just right for Pilate to shy away from the issue.[10]

The early church wrote into its creed "crucified under Pontius Pilate" not simply to give the matter a date that showed when in history Jesus was put to death; it wrote "crucified under Pontius Pilate" as a matter with a pistic dimension. The early church saw God's hand in Jesus' trial and sentencing in the secular court for alleged infractions in the area of religion. Jesus died at the hand of that institution which God's preliminary grace had called into being, the victim of the very sword-power that God had given to bring some sort of order out of otherwise inevitable chaos. That very sword-power was given (says the Belgic Confession) to "punish the bad and to sustain the good," as if to show the world once and for all that if the problem of man's fallenness were ever to be solved it would take more than the *preliminary* grace of God to do it. "Crucified under Pontius Pilate," therefore, has revelatory value, brings into sharp focus the need for a grace of God that transcends "common" grace.

Jesus himself had considered the matter of the change of venue so important — this handing over to the *regnum* a case pertaining to the *sacerdotium* — that he had mentioned it in a prophetic utterance long before it happened. The change of venue fulfilled a statement he had made at the beginning of his career "to show by what death he was to die" (John 18:32). He had spoken then about being "lifted up" (John 3:14); and John now informs us that the Jews' statement, "It is not lawful for us to put any man to death," brings to fulfillment this earlier prophecy about being "lifted up." For to die by "being lifted up" is just another way of saying "at the hands of the *regnum*." The *sacerdotium* executed by stoning, whereas the Roman *regnum* did it by "lifting up," that is, by crucifixion. Jesus had considered the change of venue of such importance that he had become oracular about it. He who had come to put an end to flat theology died a victim of flat theology; he who had come to give to human society a new structuring died a victim of the old structuring. The mode of Christ's death expressed in a nonverbal way one of the truths he had come to show mankind.

The deeper significance of "crucified under Pontius Pilate" dawned on Christ's disciples after Pentecost, when they were heard to say: "This Jesus, delivered up according to the definite plan and foreknowledge of God, you crucified and killed by the hands of lawless men" (Acts 2:23). "Lawless men" is a reference to the men of the *regnum*, not because they were lawless in the sense of "wicked," but "lawless" in the Jewish sense — "without the law." (The Jews prided themselves on being the law-havers, the only people to whom God had given his law; this put all the rest in the "lawless" category.) The point then is that the *sacerdotium* had disposed of Jesus by means of the *regnum*: they had killed him by making the Gentiles, the without-the-law people of the *regnum*, their tool.

If indeed this is the pistic dimension of the phrase "crucified under Pontius Pilate," if indeed the Spirit of God was struggling to teach men in the matter, then we must not be surprised to find men slow to learn and quick to forget, likely to slip back into sacralism. That they did slip back repeatedly is part of the story we are relating in this book. Often in later times, conduct that put a man at variance with the *sacerdotium* automatically put him at variance with the *regnum,* precisely as had been the practice before the Spirit of God had showed men a better way. Time and again, doctrinal "heresy" was said to imply political sedition.

It will serve our purpose to follow Jesus' trial before Pilate rather closely. It was a hopelessly mixed-up affair: the accusation went from sedition to blasphemy and from blasphemy back to sedition — all in the idiom of sacralism. In the court of the Sanhedrin it had been blasphemy; in the court of Pilate it was sedition. The sacral tradition and its flat theology made this seesaw possible. To get Pilate to put the case involving Jesus on his docket was the first problem for the Jews. Man of the law that he was, Pilate opened the court with the customary question: "What is the charge against the prisoner?" To answer this question honestly, the Jews would have to say that they didn't like Jesus' theology; but that would no doubt make Pilate throw the case out of court. It is thus no wonder that the Jews resented the question. They tried to detour it by saying something like: "Can't you take our word for it? If this man were not a evildoer, we would not have handed him over to you." Pilate sees the trap and tries to escape from it: if the sentence is to be on the strength of the *sacerdotium*'s findings, then let the *sacerdotium* see the matter through. He says: "Then take him and judge him according to your findings." But the Jews want to see Jesus taken in hand by the *regnum;* hence their contention that the power of the sword is not (or no longer) theirs. Pilate is caught. He agrees to try the case. This marks victory number one for the Jews: by getting the *regnum* to put Jesus out of the way their enemy will be destroyed while their own robes remain unstained by his blood.[1]

The trial of Jesus revolves around his claim to kingship. This is certain to be a complicated affair, for the discussion will pass from the claim to kingship on the level of preliminary grace to a claim to kingship on the level of redeeming grace, and from the latter back to the former — in a most bewildering way. The flat theology of the Jews not only made it possible for them to be party to this kind of jugglery, but also made it

[1] One of the iniquities inherent in a flat theology is that it provides the formula whereby the *sacerdotium* is able to liquidate unwanted persons and still keep its garments clean. This legalized passing the buck was in vogue all through ensuing ages. It is inescapable in a sacral society.

impossible for them to sense the enormity of their behavior, much less to have any qualms of conscience about it. And all the while Pilate, a product of sacral thinking, stands by, completely bewildered.

Pilate opens the case with the question, "Are you the King of the Jews?" (John 18:33). It should not surprise us that Jesus finds it impossible to answer this question with either a yes or a no: his was a progressive grace theology, a theology that made him speak of kingship on two levels, one deriving from preliminary grace and the other from subsequent grace. The former, he says, is "of this world," the latter "not of this world" (John 18:36). Hence Jesus' inability to answer Pilate's question in either the affirmative or negative. Jesus says in effect: "Not such a king as the Zealots try for, certainly not one who seeks to unseat the *regnum's* king. Did not I give my followers the slip when I saw that they were about to make me into that kind of king? And didn't I have a standing practice of forbidding my disciples to publish me as the Jews' kind of messiah, because I knew so well their pitiful Zealot propensity to think of the Messiah as a king? But if you are asking whether I am a king on the redemptive level, then the answer is a firm and determined yes. Will you therefore say whether you ask this from your own conception of kingship, or whether you are asking the question from the reports you have heard about me and my claims to kingship? Do you utter this question of your own accord or did others say these things to you about me?" (cf. John 18:34).

Pilate had been brought up in the sacral tradition. His theology, insofar as he has one, is too flat to grasp Jesus' reference to two kinds of kingship. He therefore barks back at Jesus: "Am I a Jew? Your own nation and the chief priests have handed you over to me; what have you done?" Jesus' theology of grace on two levels is clearly much too subtle for him. He draws back from water he knows is too deep for him. And not knowing what else to do, he goes back into his corner of the room and asks the only question that makes sense to his legal mind: "What have you done?" (John 18:35).

But Jesus is not so easily deflected from the theme of two kinds of kingship. His idea of kingship is too dear to him, lies too heavy on his soul, to let it be swept under the rug as flippantly as Pilate proposes to do. Therefore, he ignores the question "What have you done?" to pursue the matter of kingship further: "My kingship is not of this world; if my kingship were of this world, my servants would fight, that I might not be handed over to the Jews; but my kingship is not from this world" (John 18:36). Jesus is here saying that his kingdom is not a *regnum* (which has soldiers and which goes with conserving grace); if it were, his soldiers would come to keep him out of the hands of the Jews. As it is, that is out of the question. To this the mystified Pilate can only say: "So you are a king then, after all?" Jesus replies: "You say that I am a king. For this I was born, and for this I have come into the world, to bear witness to the truth. Everyone who is of the truth hears my voice" (John 18:37). Pilate's response, "What is truth?" indicates that it is completely beyond him that there could be a kingship concerned with the question of "truth." He figures that Jesus, whatever his claim to kingship, is not a person for him or any Roman ruler to fear. If this is another Zealot, then he is a new and harmless variety. Pilate therefore concludes, "I find no crime in him" (John 18:38).

Convinced as he is that Jesus has done nothing wrong, Pilate imagines that the Jews can be persuaded to drop the charges. They have heard Jesus' perfectly harmless speech; perhaps they are ready to back down. It is worth a try. So Pilate broaches a neat way to end the whole annoying case. It is near Passover, time for the release of one prisoner. Pilate wonders whether they want him to release this "King of the Jews." But in making this suggestion Pilate shows that he doesn't yet know his Jews, nor the depth of their dislike for this swordless "king." Instead of using the escape hatch Pilate has so adroitly opened, the Jews say they want him to release Barabbas, the convicted Zealot terrorist. Pilate asks feebly and unwisely: "Then what shall I do with Jesus who is called Christ?" To this the Jews, sensing victory, cry out: "Let him be crucified" (Matt. 27:22). Pilate tries to silence this call for blood with the question, "Why, what evil has he done?" But the time for such a question is past. Pilate throws at them, "Your king, crucify your king?" To this the Jews yell at him, "We have no king but Caesar!" They also tell him that if he doesn't do as they say, they will report him to his superior, as a man who does not take care of that superior's best interest. With that the Jews have Pilate's hands hopelessly tied behind his back.

The Jews were just as incapable of digesting the concept of two kinds of kingship as Pilate was: their claim, "we have no king but Caesar," shows just how unable their flat theology rendered them. No king but Caesar? As though it were impossible to have both Caesar as *rex* and Christ as king, the one on the level of conserving grace and the other on that of redeeming grace.

Pilate has Jesus whipped — an "extra" that prisoners received in those days for being in court at all — and the soldiers are ready with suitable embroidery on the kingship theme. They have found some purple, the color of royalty; a wreath, reminiscent of the garland used at coronations, is now fashioned from thorns; a mock scepter, a piece of last year's cane growth, they try unsuccessfully to make this ridiculous king take in hand. The kiss of fealty, which they have seen men plant on the forehead of kings, is changed to spitting in his face to suit the occasion. And, finally, they caricature the "Hail, King" of the Roman coronation ceremony with "Hail, King of the Jews!"

Disgusted with himself, and even more with these Jews, Pilate orders a headboard prepared with the inscription, rendered in the three languages used in the area: "Jesus of Nazareth, King of the Jews." This angers the Jews, for it mocks their ancient ambition of going forward someday by going backward. Therefore, they ask Pilate to amend the inscription to read: "This man said, I am King of the Jews" (John 19:21). This is the last straw for the justly incensed Roman ruler, and he replies with finality: "What I have written I have written."

We see then that throughout his trial Jesus showed a profound unwillingness to speak of kingship without distinction. He taught very plainly that he has a rule-right, but that it does not compete with the rule-right of the *regnum*. He distinguished between an earthly kingship (the terrain of the *regnum*) and a spiritual kingship (that of the *sacerdotium*), the former responsible for God's conserving grace and the latter for his redeeming grace. All flat theologies must by their very nature run roughshod over Christ's sensitivity in this matter. Jesus' concept of kingship on two levels was too subtle for Pilate and too much for the Jews, even though they had had the benefit of long and persistent coaching by the Spirit of God. It also proves to be too much for all who continue to operate with a flat theology. To be able to deal with kingship on two levels requires one to first appropriate the concept of grace on two levels, which includes the concept of progressive grace. It is not a coincidence that every flat theology runs into deep trouble in the matter of rule-right; nor is it a coincidence that where the theology is flat it becomes impossible to keep the sword of the *regnum* out of the affairs of the *sacerdotium*.

Christian theology has a good deal of homework to do in the matter of progressive grace. Reformed theology has through a biblical sensitivity felt the need to distinguish between "the mediatorship of creation" and "the mediatorship of redemption," for Christ was the one *before* he was the other. This is a long stride in the direction of a theology of progressive grace. Reformed theology has similarly distinguished between Christ's "kingdom of power" and his "kingdom of grace" — another significant step in that direction. Reformed theology already has the concept of a kingship on the level of common grace plus a kingship on the level of redeeming grace in the fine intuition of the Heidelberg Catechism: it speaks of "our eternal king" as one who "governs us by his Word and Spirit and defends and preserves us in the salvation obtained for us" (Lord's Day XII). These are matters that have to do with Christ's kingship in the realm of redeeming grace; they leave to one side whatever implications, if any, Christ's kingship may have for the kingship that comes to expression in the *regnum*. However, Reformed theology has not been able to arrive at a consensus on the question of whether or not the juridical basis of conserving grace is located in the cross of Christ. Regarding this question, it is highly significant that when Pilate said he had rule-right that extended to life or death, Jesus did not say, "Yes, and it is from me that you have it"; he felt the need merely to say that Pilate's rule-right was "from above."[J]

[J] At this point we reflect on a controversy that raged during the Reformation between the Anabaptists and John Calvin. The former contended that the sword has no place in the affairs of redeeming grace and in their argument they pointed to the fact that Jesus had refused to settle a case that belonged in the affairs of the *regnum*, a disagreement as to inheritance. To this argument Calvin replied that "Jesus Christ is not a king in his person — but he is the guardian of all kingdoms, even as it is he that has founded and instituted them."[11] In this argument Calvin assumes that just because the Bible teaches that the Second Person of the trinity has something to do with rule-right per se, therefore Jesus of Nazareth has something to do with it, even with rule-right in such a place as medieval China. Surely not everything that can correctly be said of the Logos can also be truly said of Jesus of Nazareth — for example, that he was born of Mary.

"SONS OF GOD"

Since the advance upon pre-Christian sacralism came "by revelation" (to borrow an idiom from the writings of Paul), it was a foregone conclusion that it would be constantly in danger of being crowded off the stage again. As we shall see later, that did take place again and again. Nevertheless, there were some, notably Paul, on whom the idea of progressive grace did make a deep impression. His awareness of grace on two levels comes to expression in the "two-member" salutations with which he begins his epistles: "Grace be to you and peace from God the Father and from Jesus Christ our Lord" (there are some superficial variations, but the two-member feature is constant). In these salutations, "grace" (i.e., unmerited benevolence) and "peace" (i.e., the togethernesss of that which rightly belongs together) are invoked from "God the Father" in the Creator-creature relationship, and from "the Lord Jesus Christ" in the Redeemer-redeemed relationship. It is significant that a two-member salutation is used without exception by Paul, and that the only other New Testament writer to use a salutation (John in II John) also chooses that formulation. One wonders whether these writers of the New Testament had discussed the matter of progressive grace before they wrote, had first agreed on the theology contained in "God, who is the Savior of all men, especially of those who believe" (I Tim. 4:10) and the theology contained in the exhortation to "do good to all men, and especially to those who are of the household of faith" (Gal. 6:10). Both these expressions make very good sense in the context of progressive grace; in a flat theology they are quite indigestible.

The two-member salutation has frequently been tampered with, for reasons not usually stated. It has been quite commonly "improved" by attaching to it some phrase like "in the fellowship of the Holy Spirit," no doubt a well-intentioned (but nevertheless misguided) emendation in the interest of trinitarianism. This "improvement" (actually it is a mutilation) was born of a flat theology, and the fact that it could be done without so much as an arching of the eyebrows indicates how prevalent such flat theology is. The division of labor that shines through the two-member salutation is neither a novelty nor a solitary idea in Reformed theology. The Heidelberg Catechism, for example, divides the Apostles' Creed into segments, the first of which is said to deal "with God the Father and our creation" and the second "with God the Son and our redemption." This, we submit, is once again a groping in the direction of the third dimension, a more or less vague awareness of the progressive quality of God's grace. However, it counts against the Catechism's formulation that it slides imperceptibly from the former "our" to the latter "our." For the gist of the Catechism's theology is that these two "ours" are not coextensive, that God is the "Father" of *all* men on the level of preliminary grace, but on the level of redemptive grace is the "Father" of *believers* and of them only.

Although the "not of man" dimension of progressive grace was sure to come under attack from people who had not led their thoughts captive to the Word, there were some in all ages who sensed the thrust of the divinely triggered innovation whereby a composite society comes into being. Sad to say, even after the resurrection some had not absorbed the Master's revolutionary teaching very well; they continued to ask the old and now obsolete question: "Rabbi, are you at this time going to restore the *regnum* to Israel?" (cf. Acts 1:6). These continued to have great difficulty with the Redeemer's own job description: "My kingship is not of this world: if my kingship were of this world, my servants would fight, that I might not be handed over to the Jews; but my kingship is not from the world" (John 18:36).

* * * * *

With the New Testament innovation came a fully developed kerygma, a body of teachings with many ramifications, all neatly integrated as the stock in trade of the New Testament sermon. As was to be expected, New Testament preaching (taking the "sermons" recorded in the text of the New Testament to be illustrative) continued at first to be in saga form. The "sermon" preached by Stephen (Acts 7) is a good example of this: it recounts the vicissitudes of a *Volk*. But even this saga-sermon immediately moves into a more doctrinal exhortation, joined with a call to decision. This sermon moves from saga-recital to: "the Most High does not dwell in houses made with hands" (v. 48). It ends with an impassioned rebuke: "You stiff-necked people, uncircumcised in heart and ears, you always resist the Holy Spirit" (v. 51). In the matter of kerygma the New Testament strikes out in a new direction that takes us far beyond pre-Christian patterns and brings us to a new genre of human speech known as the sermon. As we shall see, this forward movement was not always allowed to go its way in later times; in the matter of sermon too there was an atavistic trend to return to things that had been superseded.

We also see things come full circle in the New Testament dispensation with respect to mission. It all started with John the Baptist and his "gathered" church of believers. Only converted people were accepted into the religious community which John had initiated; one could not be a member of the new fellowship if all he had to his credit was the happenstance of birth within a sacral society. The New Testament church, taking this as its point of departure, advanced the theory — and fleshed it out in practice — that no already existing incorporation either helped or hindered a prospective member of the body of Christ. No prior belonging was held to be either an asset or a liability. It was this innovation that caused the New Testament to turn its face toward humanity itself, in a mission that paid no attention to lines already drawn, to the creation of a church in which there was "neither Jew nor Gentile, bond nor free."

The mission of John the Baptist seems to have been quite exclusively *ad intra,* that is, directed toward those who were in the same cultural enclosure in which he found himself. As far as we know, John drew his followers from the Jewish nation only, although it is significant that he did seek to convert Herod, a man who was not of the already existing enclosure known as Jewry. Here we encounter a striking innovation. This concern for and attempt to bring about a change of heart in a non-Jew, this ambition to get him to adopt a new life-style, a thing John sought without any political or pre-religious motivation, shows us how far the Baptist had moved beyond the position held by Jonah in Old Testament times. But this missionary venture cost John his life.

With Jesus also we find at the first this same mission *ad intra.* Jesus said he was "sent only to the lost sheep of the house of Israel," a statement that gains significance when we note that it was in answer to the disciples' question about a non-Israelite woman, a Canaanite (Matt. 15:24). It was also at this stage in Jesus' ministry that he said to his disciples, "Go nowhere among the Gentiles, and enter no town of the Samaritans, but go rather to the lost sheep of the house of Israel" (Matt. 10:5-6). However, it is significant that before Jesus' ministry is over he is reaching out to the woman from beyond the borders of Tyre and Sidon: the barriers have been removed. Jesus answers her prayer by healing the child. Clearly, we witness in Jesus a forward movement in the matter of outreach. He grants the woman's request after he has kept her at arm's length for such a long time that his disciples have begun to feel conspicuous about it and ask Jesus to terminate the scene by telling her to get going. It is important that the turning point in Jesus' attitude toward this "outsider" came when, in reply to his statement that "it is not right to take the children's bread and throw it to the dogs," she replied, "Yes, Lord; yet even the dogs under the table eat the children's crumbs." Thereupon Jesus said, "For this saying you may go your way; the demon has left your daughter" (Mark 7:27-30). It was the woman's acknowledgment of a concept of "by-way-of" that made Jesus allow the anachronism to slip through, impelled him to do a thing for which the time was actually not yet quite ripe. It is also significant that the words spoken by Jesus at the well of Jacob, words which seemed utterly paternalistic — "You worship what you do not know; we worship what we know, for salvation is from the Jews" (John 4:22) — accompanied behavior which the disciples were as yet unable to accept, an hour-long missionary interview with a *Samaritan* woman. They prudently kept their mouths shut.

Such were the beginnings of mission. Soon Jesus was ready for his final word to the disciples: "Go therefore and make disciples of all nations, baptizing . . . teaching. . . ." (Matt. 28:19-20) or, as it is reported in Mark's Gospel, "Go into all the world and preach the gospel to the whole creation" (Mark 16:15 mg.). Now it was no longer an anachronism to do so: the salvation which was "of the Jews" had now been accomplished, even to the final flourish — the resurrection.[K]

The progressive sequences that we have traced in the mission policies of Christ are of course wholly indigestible to

---

[K]In the context of mission in the proper sense of the word, the distinction between *ad extra* and *ad intra* makes no sense. In the course of later history, the term "home mission" stood for the attempt to make believing folk out of people who were already part of what was known as "Christendom," and "foreign mission" stood for the attempt to make believers out of people who were not part of this "Christendom." The distinction between "home mission" and "foreign mission" becomes obsolete once the concept of "Christendom" (also known historically as "the visible church") has been dropped.

a theology that is blind to early and late. Unless the mission commands of Jesus are looked at stereoscopically, they are altogether incomprehensible and mutually exclusive — even contradictory. The New Testament church ushered in a full-orbed mission. Followers of Jesus went out in all directions, evangelizing all whom they met. Paul penetrated farther and farther on each missionary journey. We know that he contemplated a mission to Spain, and it is not at all unlikely that he went beyond Spain, perhaps even to the British Isles. (There is, at least, a rather venerable tradition that reports that Christianity was brought to these islands by "the *Sutor*," the "stitcher," and since Paul was a tent-maker by trade, it is suggested that the reference is to him.) In any event, as a result of the early church's missionary activities, pockets of Jesus-followers sprang up in an incredibly short time, to the farthest reaches of the empire and beyond. Some of the spokesmen for the early church seem to have gloated over the fact that the fortunes of the cause of Christ did not surge back and forth with the fortunes of the empire. They were happy that in some cases the cause of Christ had found a foothold outside the area under the sway of the Roman *regnum*.

The early church had its solemn transactions: principally baptism and the Lord's Supper, with the institution of footwashing not far behind. Baptism was primarily a badge of belonging; the Lord's Supper was a memorial. These solemn transactions took the place of the sacramental manipulations to which converts to the Christian faith had been accustomed in the sacral societies from which they had come. These Christian ceremonies were thus in danger, right from the start, of picking up sacramental overtones. As such, they had in them the potential for the crowding aside of authentic Christianity's means of grace, the preached Word. The danger inherent in sacrament-like performances soon became painfully real: that the Christian ceremonies would revert to pre-Christian connotations, that is, become again a sign of membership not dependent on decision. This reversion had already occurred in the Corinthian congregation of Paul's time. So great was the danger that the apostle sat down to do what he could to obstruct the atavism apparent in Corinth. (He introduced the subject with one of his "I would not have you ignorant" passages — a sure sign that something is weighing heavily on his mind.)

Paul felt that the Corinthian Christians had to be told that "our fathers were all under the cloud, and all passed through the sea, and all were baptized into Moses in the cloud and in the sea, and all ate the same supernatural food and all drank the same supernatural drink. . . . Nevertheless with most of them God was not pleased; for they were overthrown in the wilderness" (I Cor. 10:1-5). What is this if not a strong and emphatic warning that the Christian ceremony not be allowed to repeat the language of the pre-Christian sacrament? What is it if not a warning against allowing the ritual of the Lord's Supper to be the device whereby an already existing tribal togetherness becomes coextensive with the new togetherness? These words contain a stern warning that the decision dimension of the body of Christ not go into eclipse by means of the sacrament. Therefore, we have the interpolated admonition to run a test on oneself ("Let a man examine himself"), lest one make himself guilty of "not discerning the body of the Lord." The apostle is plainly worried that the totalism of the ethnic sacrament will rub off on the Lord's Supper. And he had good reason to be worried. The two were already amalgamating in Corinth, so that Paul had to caution: "You cannot partake of the table of the Lord and of the table of demons" (I Cor. 10:21).

As Paul contemplated the evil that was surfacing at Corinth, the evil of allowing the Lord's Supper to revert back to the pre-Christian sacrament of a unanimous society, he sounded a warning against "eating unworthily" as a result of failing to "discern the body." "Not discerning the body" has been taken to be a matter of seeing the "elements" but failing to see what they stand for, seeing bread and wine but failing to see them in their transubstantiated form. However, this interpretation of Paul's warning about "eating unworthily" and "not discerning the body" does not hit the mark. A much more plausible interpretation is that he who fails to "discern the body" fails to see the "body of Christ" which is *not* coextensive with any other body or any prevenient togetherness. One who fails to "discern the body" sees only an anteriorly existing mass, a mass held together by such considerations as cultural homogeneity, linguistic affinity, racial consanguinity, and political solidarity. But he does not have an eye for the new "body" that the act of faith creates, a new "body" that transcends the boundaries of all prior togethernesses: The evil Paul is combating when he speaks of "not discerning the body" is the evil of engaging in sacramental behavior as it is practiced in every sacral situation and, for that reason, failing to engage in it with an awareness of the new structuring of society that comes with authentic Christianity. That Paul's warning against that evil speaks only of not discerning the *body,* and says nothing about discerning the *blood,* adds greatly to the plausibility of the interpretation we have proposed.[L] The sin Paul has in mind, we may thus conclude, is the sin of taking part in sacrament as it occurs in the unanimous society and failing to partake of it as a ritual intended for use in the composite society. In this light it may be said that throughout subsequent history men have skirted too close for comfort to the sin of "not discerning the body."

Since the New Testament church consisted of members by decision, they engaged in private — that is, nonpublic — devotions (the sort of thing Plato wanted proscribed by law). Meetings were held off the street, in the private homes of believers like Prisca and Aquila, with "the church in their house" (Rom. 16:5). Later, when larger locations became necessary, meetings were held in the catacombs. The church went into these tunnels left by the chalk-mining operations partly because of the persecutions. However, such meeting places fit very well into the thinking of the early church and its concept of progressive grace; the conventicle was a natural to the early Christians. The new religion showed no desire or intention to replace the old sacralism with a new sacralism. It did not knock down the shrines on the city square and then pressure the city authorities to replace those with Christian icons or crucifixes. Early Christianity gave evidence that it thought of itself as something *other* than the religions which it was replacing, other in that it was geared to grace in two senses, and therefore to a composite society, rather than a monolithic one.

Early Christianity's behavior with reference to the *idolothyta* is a good illustration of its nonsacral quality. The entire

---

[L]It is interesting and significant that Calvin took the liberty of splicing out the language of the New Testament touching the matter of "eating unworthily" by adding *"et sanguinem"* ("and the blood"); Calvin wrote: *"non discernere corpus et sanguinem Domini est indigne accipere"* ("failing to discern the body and the blood of the Lord is to partake unworthily").[12] By so emending Paul's words, Calvin no doubt helped perpetuate the interpretation which we have called into question.

meat supply in the civilization in which Christianity was launched was *idolothyta* (literally, "idol-placed"): everything sold in the shambles had a mark of placement to the gods. This *idolothyta* reflected perfectly the sacralism of pre-Christian society. It is significant that no one in the church seems to have so much as suggested that the meat supply be marked instead with a symbol pointing to the religion of Jesus, the outline of a lamb, a cross, or a fish, for instance. The early Christians seem to have acted on the assumption that since an idol is a "nothing," the mark attesting to the placing before such a "nothing" was negligible. They ate "whatever is sold in the shambles, asking no questions." The only moral problem that remained was the problem of what to do in the presence of the "weaker brother" who still heard religious overtones in a butcher shop: to walk roughshod over the person's anachronistic sensitivities or in love to respect his conscience in the matter. It is clear, and significant, that early Christianity refrained from imposing, or seeking to impose, on society as a whole any of the articles of its faith. It did not take steps to create a new sacralism; it did not consider itself duty-bound to squelch the existing religiosities; least of all did it consider itself duty-bound to try to get the *regnum* to proceed to such squelching.

All this resulted from early Christianity's conviction that the state was meant to be secular — of this age, or *saecula*. It saw the state as an agency of preliminary grace, invented for the sole purpose of keeping society from chaos. There was no attempt to structure the institutions of redemptive grace after the lineaments of the institutions of preliminary grace, or vice versa. Early Christianity realized that one's membership in the state is a matter of course, not contingent on an exercise of choice, whereas membership in the church comes by way of a choice-making faith. Only decision prepared the way for its baptism. Naturally this meant that the early church saw human society as a composite thing made up of widely diverse elements, as diverse as believing and disbelieving are diverse. The early Christians were not given to anarchy — far from it. They did not think the *regnum* was of the devil, and they gave the state no trouble; at the same time, they did not think that it was an agency intended to serve the cause of redemptive grace, except in a preliminary way, by providing an orderly society. In all of this the early church continued in the modality of the proselyte members of the synagogue community it was replacing. Furthermore, it was destined to influence the future; for in abandoning the old sacralism that had been a feature of human society up to that point, it opened the way for a whole new order in human affairs. By ushering in the composite society it injected into the affairs of man a new principle and a new formula, the salutary implications of which can hardly be measured.[M]

On no issue did the new departure of the Christian vision evince itself more remarkably than in the matter of a definitive life-style. Through the concept of the composite society the early church was able to maintain high moral standards as evidence of the changed life. Through disciplinary preaching and action it sought to keep itself "unspotted from the world." The minimal requirement was "fruits worthy of repentance," that is, a way of life bespeaking inner change.[N] Every Chris-

[M] It is not too much to say that the concept of the composite society (a spin-off of progressive grace) has provided the formula for the pluralistic society that we in the United States have come to take for granted. A sacral society does not and cannot grant equal legal status to rival religions; the most tolerant thing it can do is check itself somewhat from handing out too many benefits to the "right" religion, thus imposing hardships upon the rest. Sacral society can be "tolerant," but the concept of freedom of conscience cannot exist in it. In contrast, the progressive grace concept makes a religious war unthinkable. Far from being the threat to civil quiet that sacralism makes it out to be, this concept nurtures civil quiet. The present war in Ireland results from the sacral heritage: both factions think in terms of a "right" religion enjoying the "benefits" of establishment. This shameful situation would have a better chance of righting itself if both sides were to renounce their sacralism. Even the running battle between Israel and its Arab neighbors is in large part a matter of two sacral societies locked in combat. Peace in the Near East would have a better chance if both sides could bring themselves to accept the nonconfessing, or secular, state.

[N] This requirement came to be looked upon in later times as perfectionism. However, this was a gravely unjust caricature. The primitive church did not think of the "saint" as unambiguously good nor did it look upon the "sinner" as unambiguously bad. It saw each Christian as a person in whom a new principle was in evidence; this was held to be that man's real self. But it saw that there were also remnants of the old nature against which there must be a fight, one that goes on as long as this life lasts. On the other hand, the primitive church saw the "sinner" as a person in whom evil is predominant, though it was evil tempered by vestiges of man's original righteousness. The early church considered every sinful act in the life of a Christian an inconsistency, just as it saw every good deed in the life of the "sinner" as an inconsistency. The "saint's" assets are in the new and his liabilities in the old, whereas the

tian was held to be a saint,º since the early church thought of society as a composite entity made up of saints and sinners. Along with this ran the conviction that martyrdom is to be expected. To be a follower of Jesus and not to experience hardship because of it was foreign to the early church's sensibility. It was axiomatic that "all who desire to live a godly life in Christ Jesus will be persecuted" (II Tim. 3:12). The presence or the absence of hostility from the side of the "world" became the touchstone for true discipleship. The early church urged its members to "consider him who endured from sinners such hostility against himself, so that you may not grow weary or fainthearted. In your struggle . . . you have not yet resisted to the point of shedding your blood. . . . For what son is there whom his father does not discipline? If you are left without discipline . . . then you are illegitimate children and not sons" (Heb. 12:3-8).

But the early Christians were also extremely effective and influential in society; it is doubtful that as small a percentage in any other society has made as great an impact. The reason for this is not hard to find. One might say that the human spirit thrives on controversy: all forward movement of the human spirit followed a confrontation of idea with idea. All societies that for one reason or another have not experienced cultural collision have become stagnant; only the composite society offers the ingredients out of which the forward thrust is made. This goes far toward explaining how and why authentic Christianity was throughout history the mighty forward-thrusting force that it was. On the other hand, the ages that have been called "dark" were times in which people operated with the notion of a "Christian civilization."

* * * * *

However, the early church was not to be spared the prob-

"sinner's" assets are in the old and his liabilities in the new (a new dating from the Fall of man). We shall explain later the origin and motivation of the slur "perfectionism."

ºIn later times the word "saint" came to stand for a sort of spiritual blueblood, one who had been beatified or canonized. The word never has this meaning in New Testament writings. It appears that this meaning was invented when the real meaning of the word "saint" had become an embarrassment, due to a development that we shall discuss presently.

lem that men have come to call "the problem of the second generation." As with every movement in the history of redemption, it was not easy to keep up the momentum gained in the initial thrust. Succeeding generations of men were "born in the church," and for these the Christian experience was bound to be less revolutionary than it had been for their fathers. As a result, the initial contrasts between "church" and "world" became less pronounced as time passed. Thus the conviction arose, especially among the more conscientious souls, that the church was losing its luster, was growing toward the world and becoming "worldly." Consequently, protest movements began to appear, "back-to" movements, whose ambition was to recapture the brightness of earlier times.

One of the earliest of these movements was Marcionism, named for Marcion, a wealthy shipowner in Asia Minor. This man led a protest movement during the middle of the second century A.D. Marcion's main complaint was that the church had become too much like that of the Old Testament. There can be no doubt that Marcion's criticism of the church was in large part justifiable. A great many of the converts to Christianity had been part of the Jewish community prior to their conversion. Their mentality was predisposed to have difficulty with the progressive grace structure of the new faith: they carried into the church a tendency toward a flat theology. Paul was Marcion's favorite writer, no doubt because Paul had done more than any other New Testament writer to set forth the preliminary quality of the Old Testament. Marcion proposed a return to Paul, so that his followers were sometimes called Paulicians. However, as much as Marcion was convinced that the New Testament is an improvement over the Old, he seems not to have hit on progressive grace as the concept whereby he could solve his theological difficulties. At any rate, he was not aware of the early and late quality of authentic Christianity. As a result, he had to select some of the biblical givens and reject others. This led him finally, as was to be expected, to reject even certain aspects of the teachings of his favorite apostle.

But it will always be to Marcion's credit that he was unwilling and unable to let the picture of Jesus Christ become clouded by the militaristic traits of Old Testament deity. What gave Marcion his trouble was that he did not realize that the Old Testament representation of God as the "God of battles" is still superimposed on the New Testament picture of a "God of grace"; for him the two were still one. The division of labor that had come to expression in the course of time through the revealing Spirit somehow failed to register with Marcion: for him *regnum* and *sacerdotium* were still undifferentiated. That is why he had insuperable trouble with a God who in the Old Testament stands "with outstretched arms as the enemies of Jehovah were being destroyed" but who in the New Testament stands "stretching out his hands in unselfish love." The problem with which Marcion wrestled was one that has troubled many serious souls ever since. It is the result of a flat theology. Marcion was no doubt on the wrong track, but not more so — perhaps even less so — than his contemporaries who could not even see the problem. Because they were beginning to think of *regnum* and *sacerdotium* joining hands, they were soon to try for a fusion of sword and cross. It will certainly not do to call Marcion a heretic with arguments drawn from a theology that precipitated such bloody scenes as the Crusades and the genocidal slaughtering of whole population groups like the Albigensians and Waldensians.

During these early times the church, which had hitherto been a rather loosely integrated structure, began to be highly institutionalized. What is particularly noteworthy is that some leading clerics began to assume the role of general supervisors. Especially important is the fact that the men whose "parishes" represented the larger civil units gravitated to the top in the church's affairs, a movement that presently led to the "papalization" of the bishop of Rome. This development is important because it shows that church and state were becoming more or less coextensive in people's thinking.

Whether it was this feature or some other sign that the church was becoming something other than it had been, there came into being still another protest group, named Montanists after one of their first leaders. Montanism sought to retain or recapture the erstwhile prophetic and experiential quality of primitive Christianity; it made much of what has later been called personal experience. Because Montanism was a protest against the ossification that had set in, it was natural that its adherents sometimes became extreme; they were often accused of being apocalyptic and visionary. This accusation was probably not unfounded, but the charge loses much of its point when made by people whose externalism had prompted the "heretical" protest in the first place.

The church was also troubled at this time by the protest movement known as Novatianism, named for a presbyter named Novatian. This group was deeply troubled by the developing laxity of conduct that had become a problem as the church became bigger and older. The Novatians wanted to have the rigorous entrance requirements that had been in effect in earlier times restored, with strict discipline to keep the church distinctive in the matter of conduct. For this reason they were spitefully called *katharoi* (Greek for "pure ones"). This movement also was very widespread and its adherents numerous. Personal holiness was its forte: Novatianism's prime emphasis was on a distinguishing style of life. The Novatians may have been guilty of a certain one-sidedness, but once again the accusation of "heresy" loses much of its edge when one remembers that those who used this accusation were themselves the cause of the protest, had by their laxity given it occasion.

All these movements set the stage for later protest movements: they gave the church a kind of precedent of the general content of "heresy" and an idea of how "heretics" were to be combated. In later times a dissident was automatically looked upon as a reincarnation of one or the other of these earlier dissidents. In fact, for a thousand years to come, when people heard the word "heretic," they already knew that they could expect one or more of the emphases of these early protest movements.

Primitive Christianity gave evidence very early that what had been gained under the pressures of the forward-moving Spirit of God could also be lost again — in whole or in part. But this must not blind us to the radical nature of the innovations that had occurred. It has been summed up in these words:

> Since Christ, then, there were henceforth on the earth two levels of sovereignty, a thing never before observed, either with the Jews or with pagans, namely, a temporal autonomous sovereignty, with its laws, its police, its power of physical constraint over those who commit social wrongs; and a spiritual autonomous sovereignty, directed toward the salvation of mankind, with its laws and discipline, but provided with spiritual means only. Both sovereignties derive from God, but each has its own mission. That of Caesar is divine in its origin, since all authority in this world is descended from God, but it is established in view of earthly purposes such as the punishment of criminals, the levying of taxes, and the good order of society. That of the Church is also divine, since it was established by

Christ, the Son of God, but it is purely religious and without material weapons. Being members of both societies at once, Christians are faced with a double range of duties. According to the Master's word, they have to try to "give to Caesar that which is Caesar's and to God what is God's."[13]

In these early times at least some of the church's leaders showed that they were able to think of an eventual combination of Christianity and the Roman state, of the carving out of some kind of "Christian sacralism,"[p] by making the Christian faith the "right" religion in the empire. One such leader was Origen, who as early as A.D. 250 asked suggestively:

> What would happen if the Romans were persuaded to adopt the principles of the Christians, to despise the duties paid to the recognized gods and to men, to worship the Most High. . . ? If they were to pray to the Word who of old said to the Hebrews when they were pursued by the Egyptians, 'The Lord will fight for you, you holding your peace' and if they were all to unite in prayer with one accord? They would then be able to put to flight far more enemies than those who were discomfited by the prayer of Moses.[14]

What Origen was suggesting, it must be noted, was that it would be good politics, beneficial to the *regnum,* if the ancestral deities were dismissed and the God of the Christians put in their place. We shall encounter this argument repeatedly in subsequent times — that the carving out of "Christian sacralism" pays off politically. Origen was saying that it would be good strategy from a political point of view if the sons of God were encouraged to rendezvous with the daughters of men, with a view to the probable offspring of such a coupling. We shall see in the next section of this book that this advice, uttered by a man of the *sacerdotium* in the hearing of the *regnum,* did not fall on deaf ears.

---

[p]We put this expression in quotation marks to indicate the anomalous result of placing this noun and this adjective together: if something is "Christian" it is not sacral, and if it is "sacral" it is not Christian.

Part Three

"THE BIRTH OF THE HYBRID"

So far in this study we have pointed out that human society has usually been sacral, held together by a common religion, but that authentic Christianity comes with a new and different structuring of human society in which the political community and the religious community do not coincide. This novel conception of the state as a creature of God's conserving grace and the church a creature of his redeeming grace was "not of man"; the world owes it to what theologians call special revelation. However, it should not surprise us when atavistic tendencies begin to appear, because the momentum gained by the drive of such special revelation is likely to slow down under the drag of the prior convictions of man in the raw. In this third section we shall seek to show how such a loss of momentum did indeed take place — and the breadth of its scale. It happened when an attempt was again made to carve out a unanimous society, this time in the signature of the Christian faith. This was the birth of the hybrid engendered by the union of the sons of God with the daughters of men.

Perhaps we should begin by saying that authentic Christianity's innovation of a composite rather than unanimous society did not cause it to be aloof from society as a whole. The early Christians remembered what Jesus had said about being the "salt of the earth," and they realized that this means two things: outright differentiation and forthright integration. They saw very clearly that salt is one thing and the commodity to be salted another; they saw just as clearly that if salt is to perform its flavoring and preserving function, it must be in close contact with that commodity.[A]

An eloquent contemporaneous testimony to the fact that the early Christians were not aloof from society but closely integrated with it is contained in what is known as *The Epistle to Diognetus,* written toward the end of the second century. After saying that "the soul dwells in the body but is not of the body and the Christians dwell in the world but are not of the world," this early tract goes on to say:

> Christians are not distinct from the rest of men in country or language or customs; neither do they dwell anywhere in special cities of their own, nor do they use a different language, nor practice a conspicuous way of life . . . but living as they do in Hellenic as well as in barbaric cities, as each man's lot is, following the customs of the country in dress and food and the rest of life, the manner of conduct which they display is wonderful and confessedly beyond belief. They inhabit their own fatherland, but as sojourners; they participate in everything as citizens, and endure everything as foreigners. Every foreign country is to them a fatherland and every fatherland a foreign country. . . . They reside on earth but their citizenship is in heaven.[1]

A question of some magnitude did arise in the minds of these early Christians whether a Christian could also be a ruler, not because ruling as such was held to be unworthy but because it was felt that the program of redemptive grace had first claim on the believer. Tertullian seems to have had considerable difficulty with this problem; but he also took pride in it that "we came on the scene but yesterday and already we fill all your institutions, your towns, your walled cities, your fortresses . . . senates, forums. . . ."[2]

The early church was extremely mission-minded. This was to be expected, for it conceived of human society as always made up of some who are in the enclosure and some who are still outside it, a view that regularly leads to mission. As a result, by the middle of the second century, it could be said that there was not a race of men upon earth among whom converts

---

[A] Aloofness from society is not unknown to history; in fact, it was far too common. But it is a matter of record that when it first appeared, and also subsequently, it came as a protest against the carving out of an allegedly Christian society, arose as a rebellion against the hybrid. It follows that the cause of such aloofness should be attributed to those who are its severest critics.

to the Christian faith could not be found. But these were also the days of persecution. We must keep in mind that these persecutions were not occasioned by any of the doctrinal items contained in the Christian creed, such as the deity of Christ or salvation by faith. Sacral societies like the ones all around the early church are not bound together by doctrine but by cult, by sacramental act or gesture. For that reason they are not sensitive to deviation in doctrine but are extremely sensitive to aberration in cultic details. The persecutions resulted from the fact that the Christian faith was undermining the homogeneity of the sacral society, was eroding the unanimity at the level of men's highest loyalty. That it was this consideration rather than some item of doctrine that prompted the persecutions is apparent from the sentences pronounced on early Christians. The following sentence is typical: "Whereas Nartzalus, Speratus, . . . have confessed that they live in accordance with the religious rites of the Christians, and when an opportunity was given them of returning to the usage of the Romans, have persevered in their obstinacy, it is our pleasure that they should suffer by the sword."[3] The early Christians were sentenced for the kind of conduct Plato wanted proscribed, as set forth in his *Laws*. What was needed to escape the martyr's fate was not a repudiation of belief held by the Christians but cessation of religious dissonance and resumption of the "usage of the Romans."

The persecutions were inspired by the sacralist fear that the sacrament-bound society would come apart. This fear came to clear expression in the measures taken by the pagan emperor Decius, who, alarmed at the erosion of the ancestral faith and at the spread of Christianity, ordered all householders to perform the pagan sacramental acts, upon completion of which they were to sign the following notarized statement: "I, N. N., have always sacrificed to the gods and now in your presence I, in keeping with the directive, have sacrificed, have caused a libation to be poured out, have tasted of the sacrificial victim."[4] House-to-house checks spotted all who constituted a threat to Roman sacralism, and those who were found guilty of noncompliance were subject to dire punishment.

Since it was this fear that gave rise to the persecutions, it is not surprising to find early churchmen toying with the idea of a new consensus at the shrines, a new sacralism whereby all Rome's citizens would be bound together once more in a common faith, that is, in a common sacramental act. The very thought is a denial of the essential contours of the authentic Christian faith. To make the religion of Jesus the religion of a realm is to divest discipleship of decision, and that is to negate discipleship itself. Christianity generalized is Christianity surrendered. By making the religion of Jesus the religion of a whole language group, men strip it of one of its definitive dimensions and reduce it to a mere culture-religion.

However, the plan to do just that was raised from both sides — from *regnum* and *sacerdotium*. As early as A.D. 175, a churchman named Meliton of Sardis was whispering into the ear of the rulers that "only when Christianity is protected and promoted . . . does the empire continue in size and splendor."[B] A little later, Origen was making the suggestion that if the entire Roman empire were to unite in the adoration of the true God, then the Lord would fight for her, she holding still; then she would slay more enemies than Moses did in his day.[C] Such advice, if followed, would bring back the monolithic society of the pre-Christian world and would also provide the formula whereby the church could liquidate its competition by hands other than its own, thus keeping its own garment unsoiled by the blood of its victims ("she holding still"). It must not escape us that neither Meliton nor Origen mentions a benefit to the church: they argue that it would be good politics, that the suggested course of action would benefit the empire. We must note the significance of this idea of *political* advantage, for it frequently comes to the surface when things begin to drift toward "Christian sacralism."

The movement toward "Christian sacralism" began in A.D. 313 with the promulgation of the Edict of Toleration (also known as the Edict of Milan because it was first published in that city). This edict declared the Christian religion to be *religio licita* (a permitted cult), a status it had not had

---

[B]According to Eusebius (IV, 26:7), Meliton tried to make the emperor take the bait by saying that Rome and the Christian religion had both been born in the days of the first emperor, Augustus — a fabrication if there ever was one!

[C]Reference is to Exodus 14:14, where we read: "The Lord will fight for you, and you have only to be still." This latter clause was used all through medieval times to supply the biblical warrant for the practice of having heretics liquidated on the church's orders but by the sword of the *regnum*, with the church merely "looking on."

before. The immediate effect was the cessation of persecution, for the edict made the old charge of sacrilege-treason no longer possible. This change of climate allowed the Christians to come out of hiding, and it became apparent that the followers of Jesus were far more numerous than anyone had surmised. Through the Edict of Toleration the God of the Christians received space in the yellow pages. It could have been foreseen, however, that it would not sit right with the Christians to let him become one of many; their God was a God that ends all gods. The Christians continued to urge people to renounce the ancestral faith and its gods, embrace the one and only, and come to baptism.

As a result of either this intransigence on the part of the Christians or their unexpected numerical strength, soon after the Edict of Toleration a second edict was enacted that made Christianity the one and only legitimate faith. Christianity became the "right" religion, and all the rest were by implication "wrong." This sudden change of fortune for the Christian cause was largely the work of the emperor Constantine. For the part he had played in that mighty change he has been known ever since as Constantine the Great by all who think the Constantinian change was a benefaction for the cause of Christ. We must take a close look at that change to see whether such a high appraisal of it is warranted.

There is no evidence that Constantine had the faintest conception of progressive grace or the remotest understanding of authentic Christianity's unique structuring of human society. All that happened was that the roles were reversed: the Christian faith now occupied the place from which the ancestral faith had been expelled. Whereas Christianity had been persecuted hitherto, it now found itself in position to do some persecuting of its own — which it began at once to do. And the reasons were the same; they are reasons inherent in sacralism.

Constantine considered himself the supreme authority in matters pertaining to the new faith, exactly as he had previously with reference to the old faith. He made it his business "to demonstrate with unequivocal verdict . . . just how the divine being should be worshipped and what kind of cult is pleasing to him."[5] He claimed for himself the prerogative of determining whether a given person's name was to appear on the church's membership list; only he had keys for opening and closing. When the emperor saw that the Arian controversy was likely to pose a threat to the "Christian sacralism" he was assembling, he wrote to Athanasius, who wanted Arius expelled: "Now that you are acquainted with my will, grant unimpeded entry into the Church to all who wish it. If I hear that you have stood in the way of any of them when they claim to be members of the Church, or have debarred them entry, I will immediately send someone who will depose you at my command and remove you from the country."[6]

Constantine was just as intolerant after his "conversion" as he had been before: now gatherings in the signature of the old religion were forbidden, often in the very words of the earlier proscriptions against Christian gatherings. The mere placing of a votive offering at an ancient shrine was forbidden by law. Unbaptized persons were now required by imperial law to attend indoctrination classes, with a view to baptism. Those who refused to go to the font after such indoctrination were subject to severe penalty. Any person who after such forced baptism relapsed[D] into the old ways was subject to *exterminatio*.[E]

Constantine began at once to bestow all kinds of favors on the new religion. Elegant church structures, forerunners of the medieval cathedrals, were built at public expense, frequently on the ruins of an earlier shrine to some pagan deity. Sunday, the first day of the week, which had been known to the early church as the "Lord's Day," was now proclaimed a legal holiday with the pagan name "day of the sun." This return to the pre-Christian name for the Christian day of rest was no doubt due to the emperor's continued reverence for the sun as a deity. For many years after Constantine's "conversion," coins struck in his mint continued to carry emblems honoring *Sol Invictus*, the unconquered sun. Since it was the sun that had been instrumental in leading Constantine to his "conversion" (by causing the "vision" on which he doted), he

---

[D]Here in history begins that severity toward relapsed persons that was to be practiced for a thousand years to come. This severity should not surprise us: it is the inevitable concomitant of sacralism. If *regnum* and *sacerdotium* are understood to be coextensive, then a person who makes bold to withdraw from the latter cannot be tolerated in the former. Sacralism cannot endure the "heretic," and one who relapses thereby declares himself a "heretic," that is, a person who makes choice.

[E]The word *exterminatio* as applied to "heretic" may have at the first carried its etymological meaning ("putting outside the borders"), but it soon came to have its present, derived, sense ("liquidation").

thought that *Sol Invictus* should continue to be honored. Did not the Christians themselves meet for prayer on the day of the sun and in their prayers turn toward the east, the place of its rising? And was not God referred to in their Holy Book as the "sun of righteousness"?

Constantine began at once to subsidize the Christian church with lavish money payments, and functionaries of the church were paid out of the public treasury. This led to an unholy scramble for appointment, often by persons who had neither theoretical nor experiential knowledge of the new faith. This scramble was accelerated by a decree that freed all clerics of public burdens, such as the paying of taxes.

It seems that the emperor — always a liberal spender — was especially liberal toward the churches in Africa. This was probably because it had become apparent from the start that the Constantinian venture was going to encounter resistance in Africa. There had already been for some time differences between the churches in North Africa and those across the Mediterranean, but no antagonisms anything like those destined to develop very soon. Members of the two intermarried freely and entered into all other social ties. But when the emperor began to meddle in the church's affairs, the disagreement between the two groups picked up a new dimension. As the French scholar Martroye has pointed out, "the hostility resulted from the rigors ordered against the Donatists, when the interest of public quiet led the emperors to renew the old Roman doctrine of religion subordinated to the civil ruler."[7] The Donatists were accustomed to having Rome run things on the political level, and they no doubt realized with alarm that because of the Constantinian change the church would henceforth also have to take orders from Rome. This no doubt contributed to the Donatists' attempt to obstruct the change. Perhaps Constantine's unusual lavishness with the African churches was his attempt to disarm the Donatists in this fear. At any rate, he instructed Caecilian, the bishop of Carthage, as follows:

> "Whereas I have decided that . . . provision should be made for expenses to stated numbers of the servants of the lawful and most holy Catholic Church, I have written to Ursus, the accountant of Africa, instructing him to cause to be paid to your reverence 3,000 *folles*. You will therefore, upon receipt

of the aforesaid sum, order the money to be distributed to all the previously mentioned persons in accordance with the list which has been sent to you by Hosius.^F If you discover that it is inadequate in order to fulfill my wishes in this matter towards all of them, you must without hesitation demand whatever you discover is needed from Heraclides, the intendant of our domains. For I have ordered him personally to cause to be paid without delay any sums which your reverence may demand of him."

At this point the emperor added, no doubt with the Donatists in mind:

"And since I have heard that certain persons of turbulent character wish to distract the people from the most holy Catholic Church by some base pretence, you must know that I have given such orders personally to Anullinus the proconsul and also to Patricius, deputy of the prefects, that among all their other business they will devote especial attention to this matter, and will not submit to seeing anything of this kind happen. Accordingly, if you should observe any such persons persisting in their insane designs, approach the above-mentioned officials without any hesitation, and refer the matter to them, so that they may deal with them as I ordered them personally. May the divinity of the great God preserve you for many years."[8]

It becomes apparent from these orders that the idea of an iron or bamboo curtain is not an invention of the twentieth century. Here the emperor is constructing an iron curtain around the church, making it impossible for anyone to leave it. The political motivation behind all this is painfully apparent; it fairly glowers at us at every point in the record. Another example is the letter Constantine sent at this time to Anullinus, proconsul of Africa:

Whereas from many considerations it appears that the annulment of the worship in which the highest reverence of the most

---

^FReference is to Bishop Hosius of Cordova in Spain, whom Constantine had selected to be his advisor in church affairs. That Constantine sent Caecilian a list of names drawn up by Hosius is interesting, to say the least. One is led to ask whether Caecilian did not know who his subordinates were or had no inventory of the clerics under his supervision. It is probable that Constantine had Hosius draw up the list so that no persons inclined toward Donatism would be included, for Hosius was anti-Donatist. We learn from this procedure that politics have a way of getting into the church when the church gets into politics.

holy power is maintained has brought the greatest dangers upon the commonwealth; and the lawful revival and protection of this same worship has caused the greatest good fortune to the Roman name, and exceptional prosperity to all the affairs of men, the divine beneficence affording this, it has been decided that those men who in due holiness and the observance of this law offer their personal services to the ministry of the divine worship shall receive the due reward of their labors. Accordingly I desire that those who within the province entrusted to you provide personal service to this holy worship in the Catholic Church, over which Caecilian presides, who are commonly called 'clerics,' shall be kept immune from all public burdens of any kind whatever, so that they may not be diverted by any sacrilegious error or slip from the service which is owed to the Divinity, but may rather without disturbance serve their own law, since their conduct of the greatest worship toward the Divinity will in my opinion bring immeasurable benefit to the commonwealth. Farewell, our dearest and most beloved Anullinus.[9]

It is quite clear that Constantine promoted the new faith mainly for its "immeasurable benefit to the commonwealth." He has left no evidence that he placed any high value on Christianity's doctrine of sin and grace, divine forgiveness, pardon and renewal, or love and mercy. It speaks for itself that Constantine, like Plato before him, would see in the private cult of religion a frightful threat to the sacral ideal. Thus, before the Constantinian change had come full circle, the death sentence had been prescribed for either holding or attending a conventicle.[G]

One of the most far-reaching enactments intended to support the new sacralism was the legal identification of heresy with sedition, or crime against the state. Deviation on the plane of the *sacerdotium* became deviation on the plane of the *regnum*. We have seen how this was operative at Jesus' trial, and we have argued that failure to distinguish between these two is the inevitable outcome of a flat theology. Even though the confusion of heresy with sedition follows naturally from

---

[G]For a thousand years to come this sacralism-inspired suppression of the conventicle, the nonpublic gathering for religious purposes, was in force throughout all of Europe. The conventicle is the gathering of "heretics," that is, "choosers"; sacral society cannot permit any choosing.

sacral presuppositions, the fashioners of "Christian sacralism" saw to it that the identification of the two kinds of infraction was hardened into imperial law. This identification stood firm for the whole span of time known as the Middle Ages, and became a leading issue in the Reformation. We read in the Codes of Justinian that "heresy is to be construed to be an offence against the State . . . ; everything that is of evil and practiced on the level of religion is to be counted as crime."[10]

With the coming of "Christian sacralism" the old dream of going forward by going backward was realized; in Constantine's change the spirits of the Maccabees and the ghosts of the Zealots rode again. The kingdom of Christ, which the Savior in his hour of trial had declared to be "not of this world," was now as much a kingdom of the world as any that had ever existed. The sword that Jesus had told Peter to put away was again drawn from its sheath — by men who wanted to be known as vicars of this Peter. And these self-styled vicars began at once to instruct the *regnum* to hack and to hew with it in the very domain from which Jesus had banished it. The kingdom of Christ now pitted army against army, sword power against sword power, and from this point on warfare was under the water of baptism, a very "Christian" enterprise. By the year 416 the army was declared closed to all but Christians. Calling down fire from heaven to destroy those who stood in the way (behavior which Jesus had rebuked in unmistakable terms) was now under the benediction of that same Christ.

Not only did the church now pronounce its blessing on wars fought for political aggrandizement, as a tool for "causing the empire to wax greater and greater," but it also began to give its support to acts of violence perpetrated in the name of religion. For example, Christians burned a Jewish synagogue to the ground in a place called Callinicum. They had been saying in the ears of the emperor that he was to strip the heathen temples of their ornaments; they had recommended that the heathen idols be melted for the minting of coins. As they put it: "Since the ruining of the heathen temples was begun the divine power has caused your power to wax greater and greater." So why not burn down Jewish synagogues? Jews were surely not that much better than the devotees of the ancestral deities. When the emperor Theodosius heard of the atrocity, he ordered the Christians to rebuild the synagogue. Thereupon, a leading spokesman of the fallen church, none

"THE BIRTH OF THE HYBRID"

other than Bishop Ambrose, addressed the emperor: "I am of a piece with these bishops; I say that it is I that burnt that synagogue, that it is I that gave the orders to set it on fire — in order that there be no place left where Christ is denied." He told the emperor that anyone who gave orders for the Christians to rebuild the synagogue was denying the faith: "Must then a house be built for those who deny Christ, built with the church's moneys! Are you going to let Jews triumph over Christ's church? Are you giving a trophy of victory over Christ's people? Rejoicing, O emperor, to infidels? Festival to a synagogue? Humiliation to the church of Christ? God says to you 'I gave you the victory over your enemies and do you now give my enemies the victory over my people!' . . . Whose business is it to avenge the synagogue anyway? Christ's would you say? The Christ whom they have killed and whom they deny . . . ?"[11]

The reader will have noticed that by this time the point which the Almighty had agonized to get across to his people in the days of Saul and Uzziah had been completely lost again. The division of labor that had been worked out had been rendered obsolete, the *regnum* and *sacerdotium* entertwined once more, woven together as closely as they had been before the revealing Spirit had begun to wrestle with men. Society had once more become as sacral as it had been in the days of Nebuchadnezzar. In a word, the sons of God and the daughters of men had given birth to an illegitimate hybrid, an ungainly and ugly creature but, as is often the case with hybrids, a rugged one. It promised to be on the scene for a long time to come.

* * * * *

The nature of the change that took place in the soul of Constantine — his "conversion," as it has been called — has been variously assessed. Those who held that the coming of "Christian sacralism" was a boon were likely to paint it in glowing colors. Eusebius wrote hundreds of pages in praise of the man and the movement. Abraham Kuyper, a leading Reformed theologian of our time, seems to have been almost as enthusiastic about the Constantinian change as was Eusebius. He wrote:

> When the first contest eventuated in this that the emperor bowed to Jesus, then . . . the kingship of Christ began to be triumphant in society. . . . The kingship of Christ from this time

on stood as a direction-giving power above the imperial power, which, in order to strengthen its influence, tried for an ever-increasingly close integration with the kingship of Jesus. . . . When in the fourth century persecution ceased and the imperial power evinced a readiness to accommodate itself to Jesus, the basic victory became apparent. . . . This principial victory continued on during the entire course of the long period known as the Middle Ages.[12]

In thus assessing the Constantinian change, Kuyper was just echoing the evaluation reflected in the prayer with which the Synod of Dordt (1618-19) was opened. This synod had been convened by and was conducted under the sovereignty of the *regnum,* who held and refused to divulge — although asked — the credentials of the delegates from abroad. It was called to settle a question pertaining exclusively to the *sacerdotium* (that of nascent Arminianism), and the sentence pronounced upon those whom the Synod found to be in error was civil — *exterminatio* (in its literal sense). In the opening prayer, lavish praise was heaped upon the *regnum* "for walking in the footsteps of your illustrious predecessors, Constantine, Theodosius. . . . "

On the other hand, many Protestants of our time, especially those who live in the New World, would have a decidedly less lofty appraisal of Constantine and his innovation. Although they might not speak of him as "the murderous egoist who possessed the great merit of having conceived of Christianity as a world power and of acting accordingly,"[13] they will find it increasingly hard to disagree with the late Karl Barth's assessment. He contends that when the church let her life be underwritten by the world, so that she became a power in the world next to other powers, then the church became a *Volkskirche* in open betrayal of her holiness, her message, and her witness, and she walked straight into a monstrous fiction and illusion.

We can be sure that Constantine's conversion had the marks of a troubled politician rather than those of a troubled soul. The usual conversion theme of sin and grace, of pardon and renewal, is strangely absent in this "conversion." In defense of the emperor, it should be remembered that those churchmen who sold him the idea of carving out "Christian sacralism" had not stressed the usual theme but had dangled before his eyes the great benefits the step would have on Constantine's career, with special emphasis on his military career, and on the affairs of the *regnum* in general. Since the churchmen had used political bait in seeking to gain the emperor to their side, it is not surprising that the man's conversion was politically tinted and tainted. It must also be borne in mind that the subject of this "conversion" was an emperor at war: Christianity appealed to him because he had become convinced that it would help him in the business of winning wars. His opponent, Maxentius, was "adept in magical arts" of the pagan religion and the dark powers behind it; he carried representations of these powers on his implements of war, and it was with these that he hoped to win. It is in this context of military rivalry that the conversion of Constantine must be seen. The "vision of Constantine," as it has come to be called, the cross in the sky and the accompanying legend *in hoc signo vinces* ("conquer in this sign"), served to offset the "vision" of his opponent. Constantine saw that in the cross he had located strong medicine, stronger than that of Maxentius. The military man's interests predominate in the whole affair.

This goes far to explain why Constantine seems not to have lifted a finger to work the newly espoused faith into the lives and affairs of the civilian; it was at the war front that the conversion made a difference. He forged the bits of iron his superstitious mother had sent him, allegedly the rusted nails of the cross of Christ, into a bit for his favorite war horse and into rosettes for the bridle. The *labarum* (the representation, found in Christian art ever since, of a long-stemmed letter "p" with an "x" worked into the stem) was a monogram Constantine affixed to his field tent and to the shields of his soldiers. The prayer that he made his pagan soldiers recite after him (the Christians among them had Sunday leave in order to attend the worship services of the now favored religion) was a military man's prayer: "Thee alone we know to be God; thee we confess to be king; upon Thee do we call for aid; from Thee we gain our victories; through Thee we have prevailed over our enemies. Thee we thank for past benefits and from Thee we hope to have future ones. Thee we beseech, begging Thee long to preserve for us our Emperor Constantine and his God-loving sons, safe and victorious."[14]

In view of the circumstances that surrounded the birth of Christendom (as the hybrid has been called), that its architect was an emperor at war, it comes as no surprise that the hybrid became an instrument of war. The religion of the cross was martialized; the cross now had a blade welded to it. Ever since the days of Constantine, when the church first reached the point where it could get political advantages from wars, it has supported all kinds of wars in the name of the Prince of Peace. In the words of a recent writer: "The meek and peaceful Jesus had become a God of battle; and the cross, the holy sign of Christian redemption, had become a banner of bloody strife. . . . The God of the Christians had changed into a God of war and conquest. . . . The sign of the cross to which Jesus had been led because he refused to sanction or lead a patriotic war, and on which he had died for the salvation of men, was now an imperial military emblem, one bringing good fortune and victory."[15]

The genesis of the *labarum* tells the story of the debauchery of the Christian faith in the Constantinian change. The "sign" that Constantine saw was probably caused by a sundog, a halo of rainbow colors on either side of the sun due to the presence of ice crystals in the air; the resulting bending of the sun's rays is often accompanied by a vertical shaft of light above and below the sun. We know that Constantine was something of a sun-worshipper at the time (and for some time after, considering that coins struck by him after his conversion continued to have representations of *Sol Invictus*), and this made him sensitive to anything in which the sun played a part. It appears that in its original form the *labarum* looked like a cross with a circle above the horizontal bar — thus bringing Jesus and the sun-god together. This was later altered into the emblem we see on church art and furniture today.

In the Constantinian change we witness a massive atavism, a gross return to a position that had supposedly been superseded. In it we witness a return to the structuring of society before the Spirit of God had begun to wrestle with the spirit of man. That for which King Saul had been rejected by God was reintroduced, with considerable acclaim, by a king whose name has come to be written "Constantine the Great."

What had happened is that the church as *Corpus Christi* (the body of Christ) had given way to *Corpus Christianum* (the body of the christened).[H] The novel vision of authentic

---

[H]The terms *Corpus Christi* and *Corpus Christianum*, which we will be using from this point on, run parallel with the terms "the invisible church" and "the visible church" respectively. *Corpus Christi* is the church as seen in the composite society, whereas *Corpus Christianum* is the church as seen in the unanimous society known as "Christendom."

Christianity and its novel structuring of human society had disappeared; in its place had reappeared the structuring to which the world was accustomed and to which it is doomed to return except for the Christian world-view. As a Dutch scholar has put it recently: "The *Corpus Christianum* structurization fits neatly into the oneness of religion, of culture, of state, which is a distinguishing feature of virtually all non-Christian religions. In the light of this situation we are obliged to see the thing called *Corpus Christianum* as a syncretic mixing of the gospel and an antiquated pagan way of seeing things."[16] He might also have put it this way: with the coming of *Corpus Christianum* we witness the birth of an ungainly hybrid.

* * * *

One of the most discouraging features of the Constantinian change is the fact that some of the best minds of the church imposed on themselves the difficult task of putting together a theology that would support the new order. Augustine of Hippo made it his life's task to devise a map of the church that would fit on top of the map of the empire, that would make *Corpus Christi* into *Corpus Christianum*. For this service he was canonized as Saint Augustine. Because of the high esteem in which he is held to this day by both Catholics and Protestants, we must take a new and closer look at his policies and achievements in the Constantinian change.

The task to which Augustine set himself was far from easy. The New Testament was still in men's hands, with its blueprints of a church that ignores all existing boundaries as it draws its own. A way had to be found around this difficulty if the dream of an empire-church were to come true. Augustine sought to escape the dilemma in which he found himself by the device of a church in two senses *(ecclesiola in ecclesia)*, a little church folded away in the tissues of a big church — *Corpus Christi* tucked away in *Corpus Christianum*. Augustine thought that by means of this device he would be able to preserve the believers' church of the New Testament as he constructed the empire-wide church. However, there was a further difficulty. If the "little church" were held to be discernible, serious-minded people would so concentrate on it as to make them lose all interest in that massive thing now also called church. So Augustine — with gratitude we may be sure —

seized upon the very biblical idea of predestination, the idea of election in eternity. By this means he was able to make *Corpus Christi* an entity that was by definition indiscernible to the human eye, and it was this invisibility that kept it — as an idea — from cancelling out the large and very visible church of the masses. However, at this point Augustine encountered yet another hurdle: the New Testament pictures the church of Christ as quite discernible, altogether visible to the human eye by a distinguishing life-style. The New Testament says of individual Christians: "by their fruits shall ye know them," and by conduct "such as becometh saints." How then can such Christians become indiscernible when joined together in the church?

Augustine was inventive; with all his self-imposed hurdles, he had to be. He found a way around this obstacle too. He made the exemplary life indicative not of discipleship, as the New Testament has it, but of heresy! He began to refer to the probity of those who were resisting the innovation of *Corpus Christianum* as "quasi." Where John the Baptist had applied the water of baptism whenever he saw "fruits worthy of repentance," Augustine now began to apply words of reproach. He invented the explanation that the patently superior conduct of the Donatist "heretic" was a matter of *quasi laudabilis conversatio* (make-believe praiseworthy deportment) — an expression the world was destined to hear for more than a millennium to come.[1]

Having permitted himself these aberrations from authentic Christian thinking, it was natural that Augustine would have his troubles. The system of truth inherent in authentic Christianity is too well-integrated to prevent the wresting that was taking place from causing distortion all along the line. Augustine's "solution" to the problem he had raised for himself only made trouble break out at other points. There was the matter of prediction. People believed firmly in the idea of predictive prophecy; this would lead them to expect that the mighty changes that were taking place would have been touched upon predictively. But the New Testament contains no prediction that could be said to find its fulfillment in the Constan-

---

[1] It was this issue that gave the Germanic languages their principal term for the "heretic." Because the "heretics" claimed to have undergone a cleansing, the Greek word *cathar* (meaning "cleansed") was used. From it High German derives its word *Ketzer*, and Low German *ketter*.

"THE BIRTH OF THE HYBRID"

tinian change. It does not speak of an age of persecution followed by an age of no persecution; it knows of no welding of cross and crown, no uniting of *regnum* and *sacerdotium*, which had been separated with so much travail in Old Testament times. If Augustine were not now an apologete (that is, one who takes a position and then seeks to construct an argument in support of it), he would have given up. At the very least, the New Testament's uncooperativeness should have made him check himself and the steps already taken. However, before long he and his followers were identifying the change that had put an end to cross-bearing with the millennium as pictured in the Apocalypse.[J] They began to say that the commands contained in the "Great Commission" of Matthew 28:19 had been carried out now that all the nations were under the water of baptism.

One of the hurdles in Augustine's path was that the changes he was advocating required the use of coercion. This was a particularly rough stretch in his rocky road. The New Testament insists so consistently that people must choose freely to accept or reject, to belong or not to belong, that any sacralist — such as Augustine was now becoming — would have to be inventive indeed to justify the use of force in the things of faith. It was during Augustine's running battle with the Donatists that his theology of coercion took shape. Although the controversy with the Donatists had many ramifications, the heart of the disagreement was the question of how to delineate the church of Christ. During this controversy Augustine described the church as *Corpus Christianum*, and the Donatists continued to think of it as *Corpus Christi*. Augustine was quite aware that this was the central issue. He wrote: "The point at issue between us and the Donatists is the question where this body is located, that is, where the church is to be found."[17] The Donatists continued to see the church as a small body of the saved surrounded by the unregenerate. They said that with the Constantinian change "the tares have verily increased

---

[J]It is no mere coincidence that the idea of the Second Coming was submerged with the coming of "Christian sacralism." Except for an occasional sporadic revival (usually in the context of other "heretical" ideas, as in the case of Joachim of Fiore), it was quiescent all through the ensuing millennium and more. Its revival had to wait until "Christian sacralism" had been rejected. It lives today in those areas, and only in those areas, that have rejected *Corpus Christianum*.

but the wheat has decreased"; they held that because of those innovations "the field of the Lord continues in Africa alone,"[18] since in their eyes a church that embraced a total citizenry was no longer the church of Christ. When the Donatists talked of going their own way in protest against the idea of a church that included everyone (for which Augustine was fighting), he wrote: "I hear that you are in the habit of quoting that which is recorded in the Gospel, that when the seventy followers went back from the Lord they were left to themselves in this wicked and impious desertion and that the Lord even asked the twelve who remained whether they didn't want to go too . . . but what you forget is that at that time the Church was only just beginning to burst forth from the newly-planted seed and that the saying had not then been fulfilled as yet: 'All kings shall fall down before Him, all nations shall serve Him.' It is in proportion to the enlarged fulfillment of this prophecy that the Church now wields greater power, so that she may now not only invite but also compel men to embrace that which is good."[19]

To further support the bizarre idea that coercion was now right and proper, Augustine also referred to the parable of the wedding feast (Luke 14), saying to the Donatists: "Christ shows this plainly enough in the parable of the wedding feast. After he had summoned the invited ones . . . and the servants had said that it had been done as ordered and that there was still room the Master said 'Go out into the highways and hedges and compel them to come in so that my house may be full.' Observe that with reference to those who came in during the former period it was 'bring them in' — by which the incipient situation in the Church was signified, during which she was but growing toward the position of being able to coerce. Since it is right by reason of the increased strength and might to coerce men to the feast of eternal salvation therefore it was said later . . . compel them."[20] Augustine came back to this passage and this questionable hermeneutics time and again. For example, in his *De Correctione Donatistarum* he wrote: "Wherefore, if the power which the Church received by divine appointment in its due season, through the religious character and the faith of kings, be the instrument by which those who are found in the highways and hedges — that is, in heresies and schisms — are compelled to come in, then let them not find fault for being so compelled. . . . "[21] In a sermon on Luke 14:16,

Augustine returns to this theme: "Whom thou shalt find wait not till they choose to come, compel them to come in. I have prepared a great supper, a great house, I cannot suffer any place to be left vacant in it. The Gentiles came from the streets and lanes: let the heretics come from the hedges, here they shall find peace. For those who make hedges, their object is to make divisions. Let them be drawn away from the hedges, let them be plucked up from among the thorns. They have stuck fast in the hedges, they are unwilling to be compelled. Let us come in, they say, of our own good will. This is not the Lord's order. 'Compel them,' saith he, 'to come in.' "[22] Such exegetical stunting could be called clever if the matter had not been so serious. No responsible exegete would hang such a heavy load on so frail a peg, the mere sequence in a parable of the verbs "bring" and "compel." This is not adequate support for the idea of two episodes in the life of Christ's church. Nor would Augustine have hung so much on this flimsy peg had he been able to find a sturdier one.[K]

The reader must be sure to observe that Augustine here posits a spurious early and late, one not derived from Scripture but from his own flat theology. Augustine had failed to perceive the concept of early and late over which the revealing Spirit had toiled so hard. Then, having incorporated this spurious early and late into his thinking, he saw it in the most unexpected places. For example, with reference to the things recorded in Daniel 3, he wrote: "There was given under Nebuchadnezzar a figure both of the times which the Church had under the apostles and of the times she has now. In the age of the apostles and martyrs was fulfilled that which was prefigured when the aforesaid king compelled pious and just men to bow to his image and he cast into the flames all who refused. Now however is being fulfilled that which was prefigured shortly after in the same king, when having been converted to the true God he made a decree throughout his empire that whosoever should speak against the God of Shadrach, Me-

[K] The Donatists were apparently not greatly impressed by Augustine's pious attempt to open the way for a persecuting church. They continually repeated in their sermons that nothing essential had changed now that the Roman empire had accepted Christianity. The only change, said they, was that whereas in pre-Constantinian times the devil had used force, he now worked through allies inside the camp. For the true Christian the results were the same. Their leader, Petilian, saw no difference between persecution in pagan times and persecution in Donatist times.[23]

shach, and Abednego would suffer the penalty which his crime deserved. The earlier time of the king represents the former age of emperors who did not believe in Christ, at whose hands the Christians suffered because of the wicked; but the later time of this king represents the age of the successors to the imperial throne, now believing in Christ, at whose hands the wicked suffer because of the Christians."[24] This is, of course, an attempt, born of desperation, to find support for a spurious concept of early and late. Moreover, by what hermeneutical principle does that which happened in the days of Nebuchadnezzar become predictive prophecy?

A complaint was raised by some (Augustine surmised that their spokesman was a certain Vincentius) who were having difficulty accepting the idea of compulsion in the things of the faith that there was "no example found in the writings of the Evangelists and Apostles of any petition presented in behalf of the Church to kings of the earth against her enemies" — precisely what Augustine and his large following were doing. In his "Letter to Vincentius," Augustine replied: "Who denies this? None such is to be found. But at that time the prophecy, 'Be wise now, therefore, O ye kings; be instructed, ye judges of the earth: serve the Lord with fear,' was not yet fulfilled." Little did Augustine realize, it seems, that it is risky to change a command into a prediction, as he does here. His failure to absorb the authentic concept of early and late was once more leading him to a spurious one. In yet another desperate attempt to find biblical warrant for the idea of coercing to the faith, Augustine quoted the experiences of Paul, saying: "You have also read how Paul . . . was compelled by the great violence with which Christ coerced him to know and embrace the truth; for the light of men's eyes is more precious than money or gold. . . . This light, suddenly taken away . . . he did not get back until he had become a member of the Holy Church. You think coercion should not be used to deliver a man from the error of his ways yet you see . . . that this very thing is done by God."[25] It does not seem to have occurred to Augustine that he was thereby giving mere men the right to play at being God!

Augustine found out very soon that the New Testament is so uncooperative that one must take recourse to the Old Testament if he is to sustain "Christian sacralism." This he did, and it gave him some relief; for the Old Testament (especially in its earlier deposits) can be quoted handily in support of it. It was easy for Augustine to slide back from Constantine to David and from the church-state now known as Christendom to the church-state that was Israel. That backward slide is easy in the context of a flat theology. Thus it comes as no surprise that the Old Testament seen in the context of a flat theology has always been the happy hunting grounds of all who strive to justify that hybrid known as *Corpus Christianum*. It remained that all through the ensuing millennium or more.

Although the "proof-texts" assembled in support of the hybrid were far from adequate, the apologetes for the new order got their way because they represented the popular position; they said the things people wanted to hear. Before long people were looking upon the fusion of *regnum* and *sacerdotium* as unquestionably correct. All sorts of far-fetched arguments were advanced in support of the hybrid. One of the church's teachers spoke of the civil rulers as the left side of the body of Christ, the clergy being the right side. Another spoke of two hierarchies together forming Christendom, one secular and the other ecclesiastical. Still another drew a parallel between the two natures that come together in Christ and the fusion of *regnum* and *sacerdotium*.

A monstrous doctrine of "two swords" was worked out, a fiction whereby all the weaponry of the *regnum* was made available to the church. In fact, the fallen church's theoreticians began to teach that the sword of the magistrate was given to Peter and that it was therefore only by the sufferance of the pope, allegedly Peter's heir, that the magistrate had it to use. This construction, of course, implied that the civil rulers had better use the sword as the church liked to see it used — or else. The text on which this doctrine of the "two swords" was based was Luke 22:38, where it is reported that when the disciples said "Look, Lord, here are two swords," Jesus said that this was "enough." A variant of the "two swords" notion was the idea of "two arms." It became an unquestioned doctrine of the church that both the "arm" of the magistrate and the "arm" of the clergy were limbs of the body of Christ, with the understanding that they functioned just as the two arms of a human body cooperate to serve a single head, from which each takes orders. Naturally the "other arm" (as the secular arm came to be called) became a very handy appendage when there were "heretics" to force into line. In fact, the constraining of some "heretics" became the main chore of the "other arm." As Pope Pelagius put it in the year 553, "Unto the coercing of heretics and schismatics the Church also has the secular arm, if men cannot be brought to sanity by reasonings."

To maintain some kind of self-respect, the fallen church, as it consigned men to death by the "other arm," said something about stopping "short of death and mutilation of members." However, this was just so much window-dressing, a crass artificiality. Besides, it was an abuse of the figure of speech: swords are not intended to nudge people; their purpose is to function on the level of "life and limb." Moreover, this caution about "stopping short" was never meant to be taken seriously by anybody. The church — as well as everyone else — would have looked up in incredulous amazement had an executioner done any such thing as "stopping short of death and the mutilation of members." Tongues, hands, heads, to mention only a few members, were cut off in spite of the provision — and by the thousands. The only thing the pious phrase about "stopping short of death and mutilation of members" showed was that, in spite of its fallenness, the church still had a haunting memory of what it once was, still recalled the high estate from which it had fallen. Perhaps the provision contained its tacit confession of what the church of Christ was meant to be but no longer was.

The Constantinian change put an end to membership by decision: from that time on people were said to be Christians without any foregoing struggle of soul, which is impossible. They had never pondered an alternative, nor did they know there was one. They were Christians willy-nilly — a contradiction in terms. What was left of faith went flabby, for faith can be faith only when it stands in lively tension with its opposite. Grace lost its conditional quality, and salvation became something that is done to people. The call to conversion grew silent, and the urge to accept was heard no more. Evil as this elimination of decision was, it was compounded by the fact that the fallen church began to look upon the call to decision as evident proof of heresy. The word "heresy" derives from the Greek verb *hairein*, "to make a choice," and that is precisely what the church did not want anyone to do. Choice-making leads to a composite society, thus putting an end to a unanimous society. It was the "heretic's" theology of choice that made him objectionable: not so much *what* he chose but *that* he chose made him intolerable.

It was in the course of this campaign against decision that the church's theology went sacramental. Sacrament as a concept is dependent on the idea of automatic grace. (In theological terms this is called working *ex opere operato*: in common-sense language it is called working magically.) Once again it was Augustine who led the way in this sacramentalization of the faith. In his rounds with the Donatists he had argued that just as the malefactor on the cross was saved even though "the necessity in the case kept him from baptism," just so the baptized child is saved even though "the necessity in the case keeps it from faith" — that is, the "necessity" of its nonage.[26] The formula of automatic grace saved the day for the new theology. It provided the foolproof recipe for the concoction of *Corpus Christianum*.

With the loss of the concept of decision, mission in the only tolerable sense of the word was precluded. Those who engage in mission place alternatives before people; what kind of mission can there be where there are no alternatives? Now that the whole empire was assumed to be Christian, a further missionary challenge was no longer there. The fallen church taught that the Great Commission had been intended for the twelve apostles and their immediate successors during the span of the church's "immaturity," when the "invite them" days had not yet been replaced by "compel them" times. This thinking concerning the Great Commission was in vogue all through medieval times up to Reformation and beyond. During the millennium that followed the birth of the hybrid, the church, being coextensive with the empire, increased in size as the empire increased and in no other way. This kind of church expansion, which is not to be confused with mission, lasted almost to modern times. We have a good example of it in the conquest of Mexico, where a conquistador representing the *regnum* planted a flag, and a padre representing the *sacerdotium* placed a cross next to it.

In the days of *Corpus Christianum* a country was divided into parishes: each parish had its cleric — called by a dual call, from church and state — and every person residing in such a parish was by definition that cleric's parishioner. A parish ordinarily followed the lines that defined the already existing political unit. The relative importance of the political unit determined the relative importance of the coinciding parish, now called a see. In this way the bishop of Rome was eventually at the top and thus became the pope, because his parish was the political capital. No person was allowed to preach or even discuss the things of religion in any such parish except the person who had been sent by the dual call. This restriction likewise was destined to be followed for well over a thousand years, up to the Reformation and beyond. The effect of this parish arrangement was that a person would think twice before going on a preaching mission of his own. Any area to which he might go was already some cleric's parish, so that the would-be missionary was an intruder by definition. Paul's passage about persons who "make their way into households . . . who will listen to anybody, and can never arrive at a knowledge of the truth" (II Tim. 3:6) was construed to refer to such "intruders." In this way the church was able to exercise complete thought control and erect barricades against any "revisionism." The church persuaded itself that it was right to apply this passage to the roving evangelist, the "unsent" preacher, for these people seemed to be forever studying Scripture, always learning, and yet "never able to arrive" at what the church saw as truth.

As a result of the Constantinian change, the kerygma of the early church was stifled: preaching a body of truth which the hearer could either accept or reject became a thing of the past because such preaching served very poorly the fallen church's passion for the unanimous society. Because preaching the Word led inevitably to the composite society, it was eliminated; in its place came sacrament. Thus, in place of salvation by way of believing response to the preached Word came salvation by way of passive submission to sacrament, which was dispensed by official dispensers and by them alone — and to everyone indiscriminately.

It was at this point in history that the concept of sacrament became dominant in the Christian tradition. Sacrament correctly understood is a manipulation of "elements" whereby a togetherness already in existence is said to take on a religious dimension: thus a prior togetherness becomes a togetherness on the religious level. It was at this time that the togetherness of the empire became a religious togetherness through sacrament. Sacrament, thus defined, an inevitable feature of all pre-Christian societies, now became the central feature in the resulting Christendom. In the face of such sacramentalization of the faith, preaching became obsolete and kerygma went off the air. It is very important to observe that in this exchange of pulpit for altar the Donatist rival church dragged its feet: there a serious attempt was put forth to keep and preserve the institution of preaching. Professor Frend points out that "the sermon and reading from Scripture played a considerable part in what is known of the Donatist services."[27] In its sermons the Donatist rival church instructed its adherents that nothing essential had changed now that the Roman Empire had accepted Christianity; the only difference between the pre- and the post-Constantinian epoch was that in the one the devil used force, but in the other he had allies in the Christian camp itself and could rely on fraud. For the true Christian the result was the same.[28]

It is common knowledge that the word "sacrament" is not found in the New Testament — neither the word nor the concept.[L] The word as well as the concept was grafted on the Christian heritage; they are not native to it. The church did indeed have, from its inception, certain sacred "handlings" or ordinances, notably baptism and the memorial meal; but it did not call them sacraments or think of them as sacraments. It was with the Constantinian change that these sacred ordinances were transformed into sacraments, that is, into manipulations of "elements" whereby the already existing togetherness of the empire — the largest thinkable at the time — was said to take on the religious dimension. We use the term "transformed" because the authentic ordinances were not only of no use to the fashioners of the new order but a definite handicap: both baptism and the memorial meal lead straight to compositism, which was exactly what the new fashioners wished to avoid. Therefore, these ordinances had to be radically revised and reversed.

The memorial meal was transformed into the mass. Outstanding in the alterations performed on the Lord's Supper was the elimination of decision, a removal of any sense of "take it or leave it." If all are to be involved, it becomes un-

[L] The word *sacramentum* does occur in the Vulgate, where it stands for the Greek *mysterion*. But *mysterion* never connotes a manipulation of "elements." Instead it stands for that transaction whereby special revelation was given. With the pre-empting of the word *mysterion*, the very concept of Word revelation was robbed of its base.

wise to insist on decision; for the call to choice-making leaves open the possibility of nonparticipation, and with that the dream of homogeneity takes wings. The accent had to be moved from the recipient to the dispenser. In the wake of this shift of accent, the "take, eat" of the authentic Lord's Supper was conveniently dropped and in its place came the salvation-conveying wafer to be set on the tongue of the recipient (better called the "object"), who was in the most passive posture imaginable — kneeling, with opened mouth. In time the other "element," the wine, was no longer dispensed to the object, no doubt because it proved quite unmanageable to convey a sip of wine into a purposely passive mouth. Another item in the transformation of memorial meal into sacrament was the substitution of altar for table. *Sacramentum* was a word of pagan vintage that conjured up in men's minds an altar on which a sacrifice was made, so that sacrament at a table was virtually a contradiction in terms. Small wonder that the table was eliminated and an altar introduced in its place.

The deepest cut in the surgery performed on the memorial meal, the most far-reaching of all the adjustments made, was in the concept of grace. If compositism was to be overcome and the homogeneous society achieved, then grace had to be made automatic, not dependent on any such thing as the attitude of the object. It had to be made to work as a matter "of course." The fallen church worked out in language that cannot be improved upon for clarity this theology that salvation comes to men exactly as a lawn is watered when the gardener turns open a valve. The idea of automatic grace is of the essence of the theology of salvation by way of sacrament, and the heart of the concept of sacrament is the elimination of the conditional quality of the gospel. The sacramental theology that was devised stands or falls with this representation of salvation imparted in a way comparable to the injection of serum into the patient by a nurse equipped with a hypodermic needle.

The other of the two authentic ordinances of the New Testament church, the rite of baptism, was similarly taken in hand and distorted to make it fit the new order. The authentic rite was by its nature a compositism-precipitating thing: it was closely tied to decision. This feature of baptism was an embarrassment to the fashioners of the new order, so they excised it. For this reason baptism at once was virtually reduced to *infant* baptism. The nonage of the object was a valuable concept in that it tuned out the concept of decision. Baptism became christening, which is best defined as Christian baptism divested of the feature that distinguished it from circumcision. Christening is Christian baptism forced back into the cast-off clothes of circumcision — baptism changed into sacrament. Christening is a new circumcision. Like circumcision, it intends to mark with a Christian mark a togetherness that follows already existing boundaries. Christening must thus be looked on as a part of the Constantinian heritage.ᴹ

It is an old cliché in ecclesiastical literature that "baptism has come in the place of circumcision"; but, strangely enough, no plausible reason is ordinarily given for the changeover. From somewhere — certainly not from Scripture — the notion has found acceptance that circumcision was discarded and baptism put in its place because circumcision was "bloody" and was for that reason made obsolete by the shedding of Christ's blood. However, the reply to this notion is that the New Testament is not that squeamish about blood. Surely the idea of blood was allowed to remain in the other ordinance, the memorial meal. So why should it be lifted out of the baptism ordinance? The plain fact is that there is no plausible reason for the substitution of Christendom's christening for circumcision: the two speak precisely the same language. Both point to inclusion in the religious community because of a foregoing inclusion in the tribal-national community. Christening is Christian baptism after it has been stripped of the signification objectionable to "Christian sacralism" and given a different meaning, one that sustains that sacralism.

With the coming of christening, baptism became inescapable — intentionally so — for two reasons: first, because it was done during the first few hours of a human being's life; second, because the coercing power of the *regnum* was invoked. The *regnum* and the *sacerdotium* joined hands to make sure no one was skipped; indeed, the *regnum* made the baptism of

---

ᴹWhether a given baptism is authentic baptism or a case of the sacramentalized distortion known as christening can be determined by the way it is viewed by the society in the midst of which it takes place. If the society applauds, it is probably a case of christening; if the society looks askance, it is probably authentic baptism. G. R. Beasley-Murray relates that during baptismal services in India each baptism was accompanied by a hiss of disapproval from onlooking villagers and former associates of the person being baptized.[29] From this reaction it is apparent that the baptisms in question were authentic and not cases of christening.

every infant born in its domains mandatory. The *regnum* and *sacerdotium* trained their heaviest artillery on all who participated in a rebaptism, a practice that arose at once among persons and groups who could not make their peace with "Christian sacralism." Those who participated in what was called a "rebaptism" declared thereby that christening was humbug; to let that go unpunished would be to allow a crack to form in the monolithic concept of the unanimous society. Thus, it is not at all surprising that capital punishment was soon prescribed for any person who performed or submitted to a rebaptism. In all of this the church's theoreticians, notably Augustine, not only did not resist but cooperated fully.

Though it seems almost unbelievable, Augustine was driven by the force of "logic" to look upon christening as a "better baptism," better for the same reason that every feature of the Constantinian change seemed better to him. The distortion of "repent ye" to "do penance" was an improvement in Augustine's eyes: he argued that "repentance was not perfectly treated of until the Novatians opposed." (The Novatians had insisted that repentance must reflect itself in an improved way of life if it is to be considered real, a matter in which they surely had the New Testament on their side.) Augustine argued similarly that the concept of baptism had become "better" as a result of the rounds with the Donatists, which means that in his view christening was baptism bettered. Further, Augustine urged that the idea of the "oneness in Christ" had undergone a change for the better with the launching of *Corpus Christianum*.[30] Of course, all of Augustine's arguments that things had become "better" were but corollaries of his spurious concept of early and late, to which his flat theology had forced him. Augustine's logical mind would let him stop at nothing once he had chosen a direction. *Corpus Christianum*, said he, was a "better" delineation of Christ's church than the one that had obtained hitherto. He pronounced a horrible anathema on anyone who balked at the "better" delineation of the church, upon all "who declare that the church is something instead of that communion which embraces all nations." Illustrative of the attack on all ecclesiastical dissidents were the draconian measures being taken to force them into line, such as confiscation of property, laws making it impossible to inherit or bequeath, regulations interfering with buying from or selling to "heretics," expulsion from the land of birth, etc. — all of them civil punishments. Confronted with such evil legislation, Augustine not only did nothing to obstruct such laws but haughtily asked persons caught by them whether they thought he was obliged to obstruct them:

> Was it my duty to obstruct these measures, in order, forsooth, that you might not lose what you call your own, and might without fear rob Christ of what is His: that you might frame your testaments according to Roman law, and might by calumnious accusations break the Testament made, with the sanction of the Divine law to the fathers, in which it was written: "In thy seed shall all the nations of the earth be blessed": that you might have freedom in your transactions in the way of buying and selling, and might be emboldened to divide and claim as your own that which Christ bought by giving Himself as its price: that any gift made over by one of you to another might remain unchallenged, and that the gift which the God of gods has bestowed upon His children ... might become invalid: that you might not be sent into exile[N] from the land of your natural birth, and that you might labour to banish Christ from the kingdom bought with His blood, which extends from sea to sea, and from the river to the ends of the earth? Nay verily; let the kings of the earth serve Christ by making laws for Him and for His cause.[31]

It was surely no innocent or inconsequential thing to serve as midwife at the birth of a hybrid such as this![O]

[N]Out of the Constantinian change came the practice, almost standard through the following millennium or more, of banishing "heretics." This punishment follows very naturally from "Christian sacralism;" for if church and state are one, then expulsion from the former entails expulsion from the latter, by *exterminatio* in the etymological sense if the victim was lucky, by *exterminatio* in the derived sense if he was not.

[O]In the venerable old church history by Neander we read: "It was by Augustine, then, that a theory was proposed and founded, which tempered though it was in its practical application by his own pious, philanthropic spirit, nevertheless contained the germ of that whole system of spiritual despotism, of intolerance and persecution, which ended in the tribunals of the inquisition."[32] Indeed, the idea of an "iron curtain," with all the inhuman horror that goes with it, can be traced back to Augustine's system. After all, the Donatists asked simply for the right to secede, a request that Augustine denied them; they were not permitted to go their own way. The whole arsenal of the empire was employed to keep them from going. In defense of this policy, Augustine again took recourse to the Old Testament, saying: "Did not Israel ... seek to exterminate the two tribes and a half which had their possession beyond the Jordan when it seemed they were separating themselves from the unity of the nation?"[33] The Russian tanks in Budapest could thus be justified with quotations from Augustine.

Now that the church was empire-wide, there was at once a need for a great many parish priests, a need that far exceeded the available supply. Consequently, many persons were ordained who were poorly qualified intellectually and even more poorly qualified spiritually. It was inevitable that some began to look upon the priesthood as an easy way of life, and it became equally inevitable that the more serious-minded would stumble over the situation of manifestly worldly men trafficking in holy things. It became a prominent issue in the controversy that began to rage between the empire-church and the Donatists, who insisted that an utterly unspiritual cleric was incompetent to handle the means of grace. This was an argument that was to be heard over and over.

But to this telling argument Augustine also managed to find an answer. We may read it in his letter to a certain "Lady Felicia," a high-minded woman of noble birth who was apparently being drawn to the Donatist camp because of the much higher moral standards maintained there. She had showed considerable alarm at the libertine character of many in the emerging empire-church. Augustine advised her to "be not too much troubled by these offences," seeing that "there are some who hold the honourable office of shepherds in order that they may provide for the flock of Christ; others occupy that position that they may enjoy the temporal honours and secular advantages connected with the office." Then, in an attempt to justify the anomaly of the unchallenged presence of patently false shepherds, he argued that "concerning the bad shepherds [Christ] admonishes the sheep with these words: 'The Scribes and Pharisees sit in Moses' seat; all, therefore, whatsoever they bid you that observe and do; but do not ye after their works; for they say, and do not.' . . . there are both good and bad in the Catholic Church, which, unlike the Donatist sect, is extended and spread abroad, not in Africa only, but through all nations. . . . But those who are separated from the Church, as long as they are opposed to it cannot be good; although an apparently praiseworthy conversation seems to prove some of them to be good, their separation from the Church itself renders them bad. . . ."[34 P] Little did Augustine realize, it seems,

[P] Here we encounter an argument that was to be bandied back and forth for a thousand years to come, namely, that the apparent moral rectitude of the "heretics" was not enough to offset their "sin" of seeking to obstruct "Christian sacralism." In time the argument became common that to speak of "the Scribes and Pharisees" as pastors *in* the church of Christ is odd indeed; for Jesus spoke of them as very certainly *outside* his church, said of them that they were on the way to perdition.

In this letter Augustine reverted to his precious idea of "compelling" — no doubt as a warning to Lady Felicia not to try anything funny. In regard to the flock he argues for her benefit: "The good are represented by the name of sheep, but the bad are called *goats:* they feed, nevertheless, side by side in the same pastures. . . . Those presumptuous servants, who have lightly ventured to separate before the time which the Lord has reserved in His own hand, have, instead of separating others, only separated themselves from Catholic unity; for how could those have a clean flock who have by schism become unclean?"[35] Here Augustine touches on a notion that prevailed all through the middle ages, that all attempts at separation before the Judgment Day are premature. The parable of the field sown with diverse seeds was supposed to teach this. In vain did the "heretics" point out that Jesus had said this of the *world* and not of the *church*, showing that this parable provides for the composite society, not for a composite church. In this the "heretics" surely had the New Testament on their side, for Jesus had said that the field on which the compositism occurred was the "world."

* * * * *

We have already seen how, with the coming of the hybrid, baptism became required by the *regnum* — essentially baptism by force. In the millennium that followed people were often coerced into "having themselves regenerated by the water of baptism." Sometimes whole tribes were made to pass through a shallow stream, and amid the splashing a cleric would pronounce the words of baptism. It is said that Charlemagne gave orders that every Saxon who chose to remain unbaptized was to be put to death. It is also reported that at least one cleric kept his sanity in the midst of so much absurdity and said: "The unfortunate Saxons have lost the sacrament of baptism

---

that the moral excellence was a ruse of Satan, bait which he used to catch more fish. The text about Satan as "an angel of light" came in very handy in this argument and was hence commonly used, up to Reformation times. and beyond.

because in their hearts they have never had the foundation of faith; it should be known that . . . belief is a matter of the free will, not a matter of compulsion. How can a man force someone to believe what he does not believe? You may indeed force him into being baptized but not into believing."[36]

The reader will probably see forced baptism as a piece of devilish mockery — and it is. But it must not be forgotten that if church and state are considered one, then forced baptism is altogether reasonable. The state can tolerate no citizen who refuses to be considered a member of the state, nor can the church tolerate such a one if it considers itself coextensive with the state. In "Christendom," good standing in the state requires good standing in the church and vice versa. Forced baptism is therefore completely reasonable in a sacral situation, as reasonable as universal military service or common taxes; forced baptism is implied in the very idea of "Christian sacralism." Moreover, it must be kept in mind that christening is in itself a kind of forced baptism, one that opens the way for forced baptism in the life of adults. In the framework of *Corpus Christianum* it makes good sense to say, as a famous doctor of jurisprudence did say in medieval times:

> "When a man misbelieves in matters of the faith, he is to be returned to the true faith by instruction; if he refuses to believe but wishes instead to hold to his wicked error, then he is to be brought to justice as a heretic and burned. But in that case secular justice must come to the aid of the Holy Church; for when a man is condemned as a heretic by the examination of the Holy Church, then the Holy Church must hand him over to lay justice and this lay justice must then burn him, seeing that the spiritual justice ought never to put anyone to death."[37]

Such was the jurisprudence that results from a flat theology; it comports very well with the practice of forced baptism.

This jurisprudence admits of no distinction between infractions on the level of the *regnum* and those on the level of the *sacerdotium*. For this reason it does not know the difference between *excommunicatio* and *exterminatio*. Such blindness to a necessary distinction is apparent even in the thinking of so great a mind as Thomas Aquinas, who taught that: "In regard to heretics there is a sin for which they deserve not only to be separated from the Church by excommunication but also from the world of men by death."[38] When confronted with Jesus' teaching that the "tares" should be allowed to stand, Aquinas got around the difficulty by saying that this command of Christ loses its pertinence when there is no chance of mistaking the identity of the plant in question.

Medieval theologians, again following Augustine, expanded Christ's *compelle intrare* ("compel them to enter") to include *compelle remanere* ("compel them to stay"). The Fourth Lateran Council taught that "they who have once been converted to the faith are not to be permitted to turn back from it." Augustine, it will be remembered, had used this argument against the Donatists when their talk of going it by themselves had reached his ears. It was an official teaching that when heretics returned from error, their penitence was to be accepted, "but not to the point of escaping the death penalty thereby." Here we again meet that rigor practiced against apostates throughout the heyday of *Corpus Christianum*.

We see then how the hybrid distorted the religion of the New Testament. Each distortion led to further distortions, until what was left bore slight resemblance to the faith depicted in the New Testament. The Christian faith had been thrust into the format of things as they are in the world apart from special revelation. The New Testament became an embarrassment to the hybrid. This fact contributed to the eventual eclipse of sacred Scripture. One detects not only an almost complete neglect of Scripture but also a positive hostility toward it. The fallen church was well aware that *Corpus Christianum* would never be secure as an idea if people had access to the sacred writings; so it went out of its way to keep these writings out of the hands of people, especially lay people, of whom the church felt it could never be sure. Because Scripture was likely to give *Corpus Christianum* trouble when it was available in the vernacular, translations into the common tongue were particularly offensive. All through medieval times it was frightfully dangerous to have a copy: for example, the Synod of Toulouse (1229) forbade translations into the vernacular and spelled out punishment for anyone who possessed a copy. The Synod of Terracona (1234) repeated these thunderings, serving notice that all copies were to be turned in to the local bishop within eight days. Innocent III decreed that since the Scripture is so "difficult" that even learned men are unable to make out its meaning, the common man was not to get near it. For his biblical support he used the passage from

Exodus 19: "Every beast that touches the holy mountain shall be thrust through with a dart."

Such concern over the circulation of copies of Holy Scripture in the vernacular is, of course, adequate proof that such translations were by no means uncommon. Orthodox "heresy" owed its existence to a knowledge of Scripture, and that made possession of a copy a matter of maximum importance. The number of translations done for this purpose was large. Ludwig Keller, who as a lifetime librarian was in a position to know, informs us that "the Gospels had been published twenty-five times before 1518, the Psalter thirteen times, and portions of the Gospels times without number."[39] It is not always demonstrable that these translations were done by "heretics"; but since the official church declared open season on these translations and their owners, it is very questionable that *it* would be providing them. Because the fallen church worked very hard to keep Scripture out of the hands of lay folk, it was of course extremely dangerous to possess a copy. The length to which the medieval "heretic" went in order to escape the hand of the church by storing it in the human memory, a depository to which the church had no access, is almost unbelievable. One after the other, inquisitors reported that "heretics" knew the New Testament by heart in the vernacular, that they would hear no other preaching for they alleged that all that the clerics preached without proving it from the Old and New Testament was nothing but falsehood.

Of all the distortions that came with *Corpus Christianum* and the unanimous society, none was more evident than the loss of a definitive life-style. This was an inevitable consequence of the Constantinian change. For, as Professor Frend has put it: "Once the premiss of the Church as a body of the Elect has been dropped, then most of the puritanical beliefs with which this concept was associated automatically become obsolete."[40] When the church is said to embrace a total society, it must of necessity lower the bars in the matter of conduct. Thus it did lower them in the days of the birth of the original hybrid and all through subsequent times during which the hybrid walked the earth. The church no longer spoke of "fruits bespeaking repentance": it became wholly latitudinarian, so that a person could live a life of hopeless profligacy and remain a good "Christian" nonetheless, allegedly a far better "Christian" than was the "heretic" who in keeping with

New Testament requirements worked for the new life. Soon there was no discipline left, neither concerning life nor doctrine; the only sin recognized as censurable was the "sin" of seeing society as a composite entity and acting accordingly. At this juncture — and at it alone — did the church make use of its "keys of the kingdom."

With the coming of the Constantinian change, persecution for the faith had come to an end; henceforth one could be a "Christian" without experiencing hardship for it. It had become good politics to belong, bad politics not to belong. With this a facet of the original vision was blurred. The early church had taught that "all who would live godly shall suffer persecution"; but this was no longer the case. Serious-minded people began to miss something in the Christian experience, a heroism that had been on the earth when professed allegiance to Christ could take a man to the lions. A kind of nostalgia developed for a faith that could stir people's blood — a yearning for martyrdom, even a volunteering for it. In the days of the Donatists this bizarre phenomenon already appeared in the *Circumcelliones,* who of their own volition joined those who were going to their death for religious convictions. Neither was such enthusiasm for martyrdom unknown in later times.

This issue of whether persecution is a necessary part of the authentic Christian faith was one that divided the Donatists from the Catholics. The church that exists in the format of *Corpus Christianum* is regularly the *subject* of persecution (that is, the performer of the act), and the church that sees itself as *Corpus Christi* is regularly the *object* of persecution (that is, the receiver of the act). The presence or the absence of persecution therefore became the test of the genuineness of faith. Since the New Testament presupposes that one will experience hardship for his commitment to Christ, the absence of such hardship was for Augustine a major problem, for whose solution he was driven to carve out a spurious early and late. An equally great problem for Augustine was that the rival church of his times, the Donatists, did experience persecution for their faith. As he struggled with this problem he made use of the argument — one that became a standard — that it is not the suffering as such that makes the martyr but the cause for which he suffers. The Donatist cause, Augustine quickly added, was "unworthy"; thus their martyrdom was not really martyrdom. This issue of whether hardship for one's faith is its acid test was rife all through medieval times. As Oscar Cullmann has pointed out, "The Gospel knows nothing of that confusion of the Kingdom of God with the State which is characteristic of the theocratic idea of Judaism"; and, as he says, the church is not to assume that persecution by the state is necessary, yet "it must always reckon with the fact that it *can* be persecuted by the state."[41] It certainly is correct to say that if the relationship of church and state is such that persecution for the faith is by definition unthinkable, as was the case in medieval times, something has gone decidedly wrong.

Another outstanding evil that swept in with the Constantinian change was the alteration of authentic Christianity's concept of God. God was emperorized, martialized, and regalized; he was changed back into the Old Testament lineaments of God, when as yet the coercing *regnum* and the soliciting *sacerdotium* were sketched on one canvas, before conserving grace and redeeming grace had each received its own structuring. God as he reveals himself in the Creator-creature relationship in the Old Testament is not differentiable from God as he reveals himself there in the Redeemer-redeemed relationship. Thus, as one reads the Old Testament and compares it with the New, one cannot avoid the impression that the God set forth in the latter is not just a carbon copy of the God set forth in the former. The God of the Old Testament seems much more stern, more a God of justice and vengeance, than the God of mercy, grace, and compassion whom we meet on the pages of the New Testament and whom we see exemplified in the person of Jesus Christ. The problem posed here has troubled people from very early times; it has especially troubled all those who hold a high view of the Word of God. It is almost insuperable in the framework of flat theology, but it becomes much more manageable in the context of the doctrine of progressive grace.[q] For the divergent God-concepts that emerge in a comparison of the two Testaments run parallel with the differentiation of king and priest, of *regnum* and *sacerdotium*. The God of the Old Testament is the God of *regnum* and *sacerdotium* as yet undifferentiated; therefore, the

---

[q]In a flat theology, serious-minded people have seen no other way out of the difficulty than by the device of accepting and rejecting. This was the "solution" proposed by Marcion. In a three-dimensional theology, one in which early and late are seen as being of the essence of things, an escape from such accepting and rejecting is provided.

sword (that symbol of conserving grace) is still allowed to invade the terrain of redeeming grace. It is the division of labor concerning which the revealing Spirit was so anxious in the days of King Saul that caused the sword function to disappear from the terrain of redeeming grace.

With the birth of the hybrid this division of labor was stopped and reversed; the domain of the king flowed together again with the domain of the priest. It was this reuniting of what had been separated that caused the God of Christianity to become once more primarily sovereign and imperial rather than a father, a ruler rather than a friend. This unwarranted emphasis (because it is atavistic) on God as ruler remains to this day a feature of all flat theologies. In this connection it is significant that Paul refers to God only once (II Cor. 6:18) as *Pantokratōr* (the All-ruler), the designation by which he is regularly known in the Old Testament and for which Constantine had a fixation. Even in this lone instance in Paul's writings it is in a quotation from the Old Testament, which he is able to use only after he has injected the idea of God's fatherhood into it. However, Constantine rarely referred to God as "father" (in fact, only twice in his known writings); even when he does call God "father," he envisions him as a stern possessor of authority rather than as a loving protector and companion of his children. The following is a typical sample of Constantine's idea of God: "So will you win the grace and the favour of the Lord and Father of all, God the Founder and Father of all, Whom many of the previous Roman emperors, led astray by frantic error, strove to deny, but whom an avenging fate consumed. . . ."[42] Constantine's God was nothing so much as a super emperor.

It speaks for itself that anything done to one's concept of God will have repercussions in one's concept of Christ. Along with the martialization of God came a similar martialization of Christ: the "suffering servant of Jehovah" was emperorized, contrary to the prophecy that he would not "cry out in the streets" (as a victorious king) but would come "meek and lowly." The one riding a lowly and utterly unwarlike mount, the foal of an ass, was placed on a prancing steed, the mount of a victorious emperor. The Savior, the friend of sinners who had fled from the scene when others had thoughts of taking him by force and making him a king — this Savior was neatly transformed into a being whose central interest was to rule and judge. It will be recalled that such was the Christ of Martin Luther's childhood. Here again we meet a spurious concept of early and late. The New Testament does picture Christ's change of mount from a humble donkey to a prancing steed. However, it associates the humble mount with Christ's first coming and the proud mount with his second coming. In Constantinianism this change of mount was short-circuited so that it allegedly took place in the fourth century. Because of this premature shift from donkey to horse, medieval man had one more reason to stop praying "Yea, Lord Jesus, come and come soon!"

With the theology of the imperialized Christ came an inordinate emphasis on salvation as pardon and a slighting of salvation as renewal. This imbalance is inherent in the imperialization of Christ because emperors can pardon and, if they are in the mood for it, do pardon; but emperors cannot renew. When we recall that Christianity from its inception was definitively a religion of renewal (think of John the Baptist and his emphasis on "fruits worthy of repentance") quite as much as a religion of pardon, we see that with the birth of the hybrid, theology began to put all its weight on one of its two feet, began to stress pardon and to slight renewal. One can scarcely overstate the amount of evil inherent in this imbalance. One of the features of this imbalance is the failure of the Christian faith to be the agency of betterment and renewal that its founder wanted it to be, on the individual as well as the social level. If men are merely pardoned, the world is not changed: merely justified people are no better neighbors for that. Seen in this light, Luther's idea of "justified and sinner at one and the same time" is rank error — as some of his contemporaries were quick to point out. For, if an allegedly justified man is the same sinner he was before the transaction, then his alleged justification is a fiction and a farce. He who has been justified has also been made just and hence is no longer the unjust creature he was before.[R] From this imbalance has come,

---

[R]The imbalance of which we have been speaking comes to clear and startling expression in the fact that the word "justification" has in virtually all traditional theology an exclusively forensic dimension. In the New Testament the word has both a forensic and a moral aspect, speaking at once of the Christian's relationship to God and his law and of his relationship to his fellow man. Justification is an ambiguous word — intentionally ambiguous: it contains both pardon and renewal. A justified person is one who has been both acquitted *and* made just.

by way of reaction, the current one-sided emphasis on social amelioration known as "the social gospel," a correction — albeit an over-correction — of the imbalance. Likewise, from it have come a flock of so-called holiness churches, churches in which the forensic aspect of salvation is crowded aside by a one-sided emphasis on the moral aspect. These too are history's way of balancing its ledger. At present, cries go up that the church is "irrelevant"; a church that talks only (or even predominantly) of pardon *is* irrelevant, although it must be added that a church that speaks only of renewal will probably in the end turn out to be just as irrelevant.

* * * * *

It would be quite unrealistic to suppose that a change as momentous as the Constantinian change could take place unopposed. As long as there were still people who had known the church as it was prior to its fall, there was bound to be opposition. One of these was Hilary of Poitiers, who saw what was happening and tried to get others to see it. However, the church not only turned a deaf ear to such voices but began to suppress them. But as long as people continued to have access to the New Testament there was bound to be resistance to the antics of the hybrid. As we have already intimated, such opposition to "Christian sacralism" manifested itself at once; and it never died down in the centuries that followed. It may be said that the heart of medieval "heresy" in western Europe throughout the middle ages was a persistent protest against *Corpus Christianum* and all the implications of the Constantinian change.

The church sought to silence criticism from within, usually by means of the arm of the *regnum*. This explains why most of the opposition to the Constantinian change came from the outside, from persons and groups that had been pushed out. This was true, for example, of the "heretics" known as the Waldensians. Peter Waldo had no intention of going outside the church: he was forced to go on his own because the church forbade him to preach, since his preaching included a great deal of rebuke aimed at the church's fallenness. We who take for granted great freedom of speech must remember how wholly different was the climate in which medieval dissenters had to operate. If we do not, we will be likely to draw the wrong conclusions from the relative paucity of written relics left by the prevailing church's rival.[s] As with an iceberg, only a small part of the total mass of life and activities of the medieval "heretics" is visible. For example, we know that a whole century before the Reformation there were underground churches in the southern Low Countries — rightly or wrongly called "Hussite churches" — congregations that had their own catechism classes, their own ministers, membership lists, in fact, all that goes with life as a church. They even maintained some kind of "classical" connection with other units of their kind, for we find them practicing pulpit exchanges. These rival churches have not, as far as is known, left a word in writing. The only record left of them is contained in what we would today call the police record, in which their liquidation is reported.[43] Thus, when groups prefer to be silent for reasons of survival, we must not draw the wrong conclusions. When ministers in the rival church withheld their names, even from their own followers, a practice that grew out of the experiences by which names that were known could be extracted by torture, we must be careful not to misinterpret the silent record. There is a cryptic quality to just about everything that has come down to us from these rival church circles. For example, we find the rival church referring to itself as "the little flock of Christians referred to falsely and with false names as p.o.v.o.b."[44] The initials undoubtedly stand for "Picards or Waldensians or Beghards," all of them names so incriminating that it was deemed prudent neither to own them nor write them out in full. They were all well-known terms of opprobrium ascribed to rival church people who wanted to be known simply as "the little flock of Christians."

Not only were rival church members extremely reticent about themselves and their affairs, so that they left a sketchy literary record; they also denied things about themselves and their affairs which we know to have been true. Long before the Reformation, the so-called Bohemian Brethren (a manifestation of the rival church in what is now Czechoslovakia) and the Waldensians (a rival church in the Piedmont) had many connections with each other, even to the extent of accepting a common ordination to the ministry and borrowing whole

---

[s]Henceforth we shall refer to the underground protest movements as the "rival church" or, interchangeably, "free churches." They were indeed free in the modern sense of the word, that is, not integrated with *regnum* — neither helped nor hindered by it.

pages from each other's catechism book. Nevertheless, they denied before the *regnum,* which was putting the clamps on them, that there had been any contact between them. A student of medieval "heresy" said over a century ago: "The general fact of an oft-repeated exchange of doctrinal utterance . . . is demonstrably the case in spite of repeated denial of any fellowship with each other or of acquaintance with each other's teaching."[45] The undeniable fact is that the rival church was extremely widespread throughout all of Europe in medieval times, and any representation showing that they had no progeny in post-Reformation times is surely erroneous.

A second thing to remember as we study the history of the rival church is the extreme hazard to "heretics" for meeting in conference. Conferences are held in order to arrive at consensus; they serve to bring right and left together, to keep various emphases from leading to fragmentation. Such conferences were denied the "heretics." As a result, we have no such thing as a Westminster Confession in the signature of the rival church. Such approximations of "symbols of unity" as we do have are relatively recent, drawn up after the medieval system of thought-control had begun to erode. For the most part, we will have to be satisfied with sporadic glimpses of the rival church's nature and essential thought system. Since it was impossible for medieval "heresy" to work out an articulate and orderly system of doctrine and practice, we are forced to approximate it ourselves, using such building materials as are available.

It should also be kept in mind that the medieval rival church was led by its very theological assumptions to appear more or less occult. It was not out to create a "believing society," a *Corpus Christianum;* its ambition was to bring into being a company of true believers, a *Corpus Christi,* within society as such. It sought to make converts on a person-to-person basis, at best by some sort of cell-group method; this implied that is was not interested in broadside propaganda. Nonpublic assembly had been the method in primeval Christianity, and it was one of the things unsympathetic observers were unable to understand and scolded the Christians for. We read in the *Octavius,* with reference to the Christians of those early times: "Why do they make such efforts to hide and conceal whatever it is that they worship? Honorable acts always welcome publicity, only crimes delight in secrecy. Why have they no altars, no temples, no well-known images? Why do they never speak in public, never meet freely, unless it be that the hidden object of their worship is either criminal or disgraceful?"[46] This nonpublic policy came to an end in the church with the birth of the hybrid, and it continued in the rival church alone. This esoteric quality of early Christianity had given rise to all sorts of unsavory reports concerning the Christians (they occur already in the *Octavius*), and these were transferred to the rival church in post-Constantinian times. They became regular clichés and were repeated, often verbatim, right up through Reformation times and beyond.

We must remember as we seek to discover the true lineaments of medieval "heresy" that in written historiography we are confronted with caricatures, besmirching pictures drawn by the enemies of the people they purport to describe. Some of these caricatures are so patently absurd — even though offered by the church's official spokesmen — that they deserve only laughter: for example, that the "heretics" rode to their conventicles on broomsticks supplied by the devil. One who seeks a reliable picture of Martin Luther from the Catholic writers of the day will come up with a caricature; so it is with the hostile church's picture of the medieval rival church. With these precautions in mind, however, it should not be impossible to derive from the available sources a view of medieval "heresy" that is at least tentatively correct. The resulting picture leaves little doubt that the heart of medieval "heresy" was a sustained opposition to the Constantinian change.

* * * * *

We propose now to examine this "heresy" in the light of some of the names invented by the angered church as terms of opprobrium to discredit its rival and their cause. The "heretics" of the free church had not coined these smear names for themselves, and the established church took it very ill that they refused the names. We find a faithful son of the church, David of Augsburg, complaining: "These hypocrites give themselves diverse names and don't call themselves what they in reality are, that is, heretics, but call themselves *the True Christians* or *the Friends of God* or *God's Poor Ones* and that kind of names."[47] We should not distinguish sharply between the different names, for it was common practice all through medieval times to use whichever name had the greatest smear value at the moment, and they were often mere clichés.

The name *Cathar* may have been the most effective in the church's smear campaign, for it harked back to the days when it was used to label a sect that had a concept of ultimate dualism at the center of its theology: this sect had taught that good and evil are equally ultimate. The Manicheans (from whose errors Augustine had to fight himself free) had been such *Cathars;* they had taught that the Old Testament is the work of the Evil Principle and the New Testament the work of the Good Principle. Because the post-Constantinian "heretics" were committed to progressive grace and were thus aware of the preliminary quality of the Old Testament, the church in its endeavor to eliminate its rival grasped the possibility of accusing it of the dualism of the older heretics, of "pitting the Father against the Son," as it was sometimes put.

What are we to make of the charge of dualism? It is certainly true that the rival church had a stereoscopic view of the gracious dealings of God: they spoke of "the old law" and "the new law," terms they had quite certainly derived from the book of Hebrews (for they were always well-versed in the New Testament writings). But the charge of dualism does not demand serious consideration. One of the best-informed scholars in the field of medieval "heresy," Herbert Grundmann, has concluded that when heresy makes its appearance in the West in the first half of the eleventh century, there are, as far as can be determined, no dualistic doctrines present anywhere at all. This authority points out that the charge of dualism is copied over virtually verbatim from the writings of St. Augustine. He also points out that what people in those days said about the "heretics" of their times is commonly introduced with such expressions as "they say that" or "it is rumored." These devices indicate that the reporter was dependent on others for his assertions. In this connection we must recall the oddities of the medieval mind: it is proverbial that when a medieval person became curious about the number of molars in the lower jaw of a horse, he would page through Aristotle or some other authority to find out, rather than looking for himself. There is a world of truth in this representation of the medieval mind. It would have been characteristic for a person of those times to turn to Augustine or some other authority to learn what a heretic was, rather than conduct firsthand examination of the living example before him.

In any event, we may by and large dismiss the charge of dualism as a feature of the medieval "heretics," although it is a little too sweeping to say that there was not a trace of dualism anywhere. There certainly were dualistic traits in some eruptions of medieval heresy, for example, in Albigensianism; the same is true of the Bogomils in the Balkan areas. But it is very significant that there were reports of "sharp dissension" between the "heretics" and these sects. The orthodox "heretics" seem to have been aware of the dualism, which they put far from themselves.[T]

There was another feature of the free church people of this time that tended to popularize the charge of Catharism; it had to do with life-style. *Cathar* derives from the Greek verb *katharidzein* ("to cleanse or purify"). As we have noted, the medieval "heretic" continued to see salvation as a matter of renewal, continued to think in the idiom of John the Baptist's concept of *metanoia* and "fruits bespeaking conversion." For the "heretics" the essence of Christianity was located not in the church as the dispenser of salvation but in a religious way of life. If there is one feature of this "heresy" that stands out it is the heretics' virtuous life-style. One could fill a book with testimony to this fact. We read of a young woman picked up for heresy because she resisted the advances of the local priest. A group of "heretics" who were being put to the flames testified as follows (and no one contradicted what they said): "We undergo this because we are not of this world; you however love the world, have peace with the world because you are of the world. . . . We and our fathers, the generation of the apostles, continue in the grace of Christ and will continue in it unto the end of the age. In distinguishing between you and us Christ has said 'by their fruits shall ye know them' — our fruits are the

---

[T] We have spent some time on the charge of dualism as it was used against the rival church people in pre-Reformation times because the charge was revived in Reformation times as people sought to besmirch the so-called left wing of the Reformation, in which the earlier free church tradition resurfaced. To this day the charge of "basic dualism" is still heard as theologians, especially in Europe, discuss the "left wing." Ordinarily those who make the charge are themselves caught up in monism born of a flat theology, which tends to run common grace and special grace together, and fails to differentiate between the Creator-creature relationship and the Redeemer-redeemed relationship.

tracks made by Christ" (*vestigia Christi*).⁴⁸ The reader will have noted that these "heretics" claimed great antiquity for themselves: they said they were "the generation of the apostles." They also contended that they were what was left of the real church and that the big difference between their own free church and the other body was apparent in the diverse lifestyles. We hear it said of them: "They defend their heresy with the words of Christ and the apostles, saying that the entire church is found with them, this because they alone continue in the footsteps of Christ and in the apostolic way of life."⁴⁹ The tensions that came to expression between the church which enjoyed establishment status and the free church in medieval times were inevitable: one who believes that the church is *Corpus Christianum* must make room in it for all, the impious as well as the pious; one who believes that the church is *Corpus Christi* is in position to make acceptable conduct the *sine qua non* of membership. Therefore, it was also inevitable that lifestyle would become the touchstone of orthodoxy to the adherents of the rival church and proof of heresy to the adherents of the established church. Of this situation the literature of the times speaks often.ᵁ

In view of these tensions between the established church and its underground rival, it comes as no surprise that in the latter the Epistle of James was always a favorite. In an old catechism used by the Waldensians, the question was put: "How many kinds of faith are there?" The answer was: "Two, dead and alive!" In one of the Waldensian tracts we read:

> Saint James has shown and said quite plain
> That no man is saved by faith alain;
> If faith is mingled not with deed
> Then vain it is and surely dead.
> Saint Paul confirms this language brave
> That what one hears can not him save;
> If with man's faith works join not hand
> Then goes he not to gloryland.⁵⁰

There is hardly a reference to the rival church which does not contain a reference to the above average moral rectitude found there. For example, the inquisitor Sacconi said of them:

> "They preach much from the Gospels and say among other

ᵁFor examples of some of this literature, see the Appendix.

things that a man should do no evil, nor lie, nor swear. When they preach from the Gospels and Epistles they corrupt them with their explanations, as masters of error who know not to sit at the feet of truth, teaching and expounding the Scriptures being wholly forbidden to layfolk. They say that their church is the true church and that the Roman church is not a true Church but is the Church of malignants.[v] They reprobate Church wealth and ecclesiastical 'regalia' or the high feudal privileges of bishops and abbots. They seek to abolish all ecclesiastical privilege and they maintain no one should be compelled to the faith. . . . They condemn the Church's sacraments and say that a priest who lives in mortal sin cannot make the body of Christ,[w] that transubstantiation takes place not in the hands of the priest . . . but in the mind of him who received it worthily."[51]

Reference to the moral rectitude of the "heretic," the trait that earned them the designation *Cathar,* is indeed plentiful. Another of the inquisitors has left us the following testimony:

Because men see daily that these people excel in outward holiness whereas most of the priests of the Church follow after vices, notably those of the flesh, they think they can be better shrived by them than by the Church's priests. . . .[x] Heretics are known for their manners and their words. In their manners they are composed and moderate; they do not dress showily, wearing neither luxurious garments nor vile ones. They practice no merchant's trade, so as to avoid falsifications, oaths, frauds. They live as laborers or artisans and for teachers they have cobblers. They multiply no riches but are content with necessities. Moreover, they are chaste . . . temperate in eating and drinking. They do not go to taverns or to dances or to other vanities. They avoid the oath. They are forever working or learning or teaching — which implies that they pray but

---

[v]The church's translation of "I hate the company of evildoers," found in Psalm 26:5, contained a word meaning *"assembly"* or *"congregation"* and also the word *"malignant."* The "heretics" were quick to see in this verse an adumbration of the fallen church, whose assemblies they could not join either.

[w]This "make the body" must not be taken to imply that the "heretics" believed in transubstantiation; they did not. The explanation of this language is that these are the words of a Catholic.

[x]These words about "shriving" (absolution) must not be taken to imply that the "heretics" believed in shriving. Again, we must remember that these are the words of a Catholic, for whom the salvation experience consisted of being shrived.

> little. They go to Church feignedly . . . so as to catch the preacher in his words. They are known for their precise and moderate speech. They avoid all scurrility and back-biting as well as loose speech and lies and swearing. . . . They compare the Roman Church with their own; the doctors of the Church, say they, are pompous in dress and manners . . . are incontinent, whereas among us, say they, each man has his own wife with whom he lives chastely. . . . The Church's leaders, say they, are rich and avaricious, love pleasures . . . fight and lead others to war . . . eating the bread of idleness, whereas ours work with their hands. . . . It is because we hold to the true faith in Christ and teach his true doctrine that the Scribes and Pharisees persecute us without cause and unto the death — just as they did with Christ. . . . The clergy, now as then, lay burdens on men which they do not touch with their own little finger. They compel men to obey the traditions of men rather than the commandments of God. They lay upon the sinner grievous penances whereas we, following Christ's example, tell the sinner to go and sin no more. . . .[52]

Such then was the reputation that evoked the hateful term *Cathar*. We turn now to an examination of the epithet "heretic." We have been placing this word in quotation marks because these people were not heretics in the usual sense of the word, that is, off the beam theologically. The people of the rival church were orthodox:[y] their Christology was the Christology of the New Testament; their doctrine of sin and grace was evangelical; their God was the God of the creeds. Lea, in his well-known work on the Inquisition, correctly refers to these "heretics" as "sectaries holding fast to all the essentials of Christianity." Even spokesmen for the prevailing church witnessed to the orthodoxy of these people. William of Newburgh, for example, said of "heretics" that had fallen into the church's hands in his area: "When questioned one by one of

[y]The testimony to the orthodoxy of the rival church is voluminous as well as virtually unanimous. One inquisitor after the other testified to the orthodoxy of his victims. One of them lists as one of the three things that make these "heretics" dangerous the fact that "they exhibit such a fine show of piety, living justly before all men and believing all the articles of the Creed. . . . Their sole evil is that they revile the Roman Church."[53] In the New Testament there are two areas in which serious deviation leads to discipline: *doctrine* and *life*. It is plain from the above quotation that the "heretics" did not deviate in either of these two areas: their belief was orthodox and their life morally right. Their only "sin" was that they "reviled the Roman Church" or, to put it in the terms of this study, they rejected "Christian sacralism."

the articles of the faith they answered correctly as to the substance of the Physician on high; but, perversely concerning the medication whereby He deigns to heal human infirmity, namely the Holy Sacraments. They solemnly renounce baptism, the eucharist, the sacrament of marriage, and dare wickedly to derogate from Catholic unity which is supported by these props."[54] Clearly, these "heretics" did not err in doctrine; their "wickedness" consisted in that they had broken with the sacral idea of salvation by sacrament, the props which supported *Corpus Christianum* (which William calls the "Catholic unity"). In other words, their "sin" was that they believed society is composite and thus had made a choice — were heretics.

According to the account of a sixteenth-century clerk of courts, a man who was thus in a position to know, it was customary for these "heretics" as they recited the Apostles' Creed as a suitable summary of their faith, to stumble over the word "catholic" in the article about the church.[55] The word means "as to the entirety," and hence it is not surprising that the "heretic" had difficulty with it: a church "as to the entirety" was precisely what he did *not* believe in. The church "as to the entirety" is *Corpus Christianum,* and we know how these "heretics" felt about that concept. Moreover, the word "catholic" raised bad memories for those who could not in good conscience go along with the Constantinian change. In A.D. 380 the emperor Theodosius had decreed: "We desire that all people whom the benign influence of our clemency rules shall turn to that religion which tradition declares to have been delivered to the Romans by the blessed Peter. . . . We order those who follow this doctrine to accept the title of *Catholic Christians;* the rest we judge to be madmen and raving, worthy of incurring the disgrace of heretical teaching. Nor are their assemblies to receive the name of churches. They are to be punished, not only by divine retribution but also by our measures, which we have decided on in accord with the divine inspiration."[56] In the light of this ancient legislation, enacted in order to make the life of the dissenter impossible, it is certainly no wonder that the "heretics" choked on the word "catholic" in the creed. For the rest they were orthodox. Even in this matter they were orthodox, more orthodox by far than was the prevailing church, which considered itself coextensive with "all those whom the benign influence of the emperor's clemency rules."

"THE BIRTH OF THE HYBRID"

A measure of the orthodoxy of these "heretics" may be seen in the lengths to which the established church went to keep the New Testament out of their hands. The New Testament made the "heretics" too strong. To realize that this is where the shoe pinched, one needs only read the papal thunderings against the Bible in the hands of its rival. For example, a directive issued by Pope Innocent III in 1199 said:

> Our brother, the bishop of Metz, informs us that in his diocese and in your city a great many lay-folk, both men and women ... have French translations of the Gospels and the Epistles of Paul, the Psalms . . . and other books, which they read together and from which they preach in their clandestine conventicles, vilifying those who do not attend, and resisting to their faces the priests who would instruct them, arguing that they find in their books much better instruction. Now it is undoubtedly true that the desire to know the Scriptures and to exhort men to follow these is not reprehensible . . . but what is to be condemned is the holding of secret assemblies . . . the arrogating to themselves the right to preach, the jeering at the ignorance of the priests. For, the Scriptures are of such profundity that not merely the simple and unlettered folk but even the learned ones cannot attain to a knowledge thereof — so that it is enjoined in the Law of God that every beast that touches the holy mountain is to be thrust through with a dart . . . since in the Church it is the doctors who are charged with the preaching, therefore no man may usurp this office.[57]

If there was intolerable unorthodoxy on the scene, it can be found, it seems, with the man who wrote the above directive — with him rather than with the people he was castigating. It is impossible to believe that people thus eager for the Word of God were heretical in the current sense of the word; it is easy to believe that they were orthodox in the sense of being true to the Word.

Nor was the New Testament an idle letter with these "heretics": it was that on which they lived. Many a leader of the rival church and many common members of it had learned whole books of the New Testament by heart. This is clear from the testimony of their greatest enemies. For instance, Etienne de Bourbon, a Dominican monk who spent his long life hunting down heretics, had this to say about them:

> They know the Apostles Creed fluently in the vulgar tongue; they learn by heart the Gospels and the New Testament, in

the vernacular, and they repeat these aloud to each other. . . .
I have seen a young cow-herd who had lived in the home of a
heretic for one year but had attended so diligently to all that
he heard that he had committed to memory during that one
year forty Sunday Gospels, not counting the feast days. . . . I
have met up with some lay-persons who were so steeped in their
doctrine that they could recite great portions of the Evangelists,
such as Matthew and Luke, especially all that is said in them
of Christ's teachings and sayings, so that they could repeat
them without a halt and with scarcely a word wrong here or
there.[58]

The "heretics" were also called "schismatics" (derived from a Greek verb meaning "to split"). The "heretics" were undoubtedly schismatics if by that we mean persons who believe that authentic Christianity leads to the composite society. The empire-church accused them of "rending the robe of Christ"; but whether or not they were guilty of such rending depends on how that "robe" is to be construed. If "robe" is understood to be coextensive with the empire, then these "heretics" were indeed rending it. But if it is thus understood, it also follows that Christ himself was guilty of such "rending": for he said that he had not come to send peace (meaning in Bible language "togetherness") on the earth but the sword (meaning in Bible language an instrument for cleaving). He had conceived of his assignment as a matter of rending all earthly togetherness (in extreme cases even the togetherness of family). Therefore, if there was unorthodoxy on the medieval scene, it was the unorthodoxy that had given birth to a culture-wide church. It was the all-embracing church that was the heretic, not the "heretic" who opposed it.

Closely related to this term of opprobrium was the derogatory word "sectarian." The rival church was called a "sect."[z] These words find their root in the Latin verb *sequor* (meaning "to follow"). Again it must be said that the "heretics" were indeed followers; but the question immediately arises whether

[z]Although "sect" and "sectarian" are still heard in American speech, they are anachronisms in the New World. These words have meaning only as correlatives of a "right" religion; where there is no religion enjoying establishment status, it makes no sense to speak of a *sect*. The use of the word "sectarian" in America is somewhat frightening because it implies some sort of ultimate loyalty, perhaps called "the American way" or some such thing. It may be said that to speak of something as "sectarian" on the American scene is to violate the spirit of the First Amendment.

it is possible to be a Christian in the authentic sense of the word and *not* to be a follower. The medieval "heretic" admitted to his tormentors that he was a "sectary" — adding in the same breath "I follow Jesus Christ."

Moreover, the "heretics" attended conventicles. Although the English language does not seem to have an equivalent, the Germanic languages very early developed a term of opprobrium that brought out this aspect of the "heretic's" evil ways — *Winckler*. The word *Winckel* means first of all a nook or corner; *Winckler* came to stand for the "heretic" who went to religious gatherings in nooks and corners. Soon the word picked up the idea of something illegal or unauthorized (as in *Winkelehe*, a common law marriage). Once again it must be granted that the "heretics" were indeed *Winckler*. But the question then becomes: who was unorthodox, the "heretic" or the inclusive church? The New Testament knows no other gatherings in the name of Christ but such as are espoused by the believing element. It was an emperor — with the fallen church looking on approvingly — who had declared the conventicle illicit, just as the pagan emperor Decius had called the nonpublic gathering of his day illicit. It will be recalled that in the days of Theodosius the word "catholic" had been linked to the word *"church"* by legal enactment, and he had said that all other meetings were "not to be called churches." He said he was doing this "in accord with the divine inspiration"; but we have every reason to dispute this lofty claim. The revealing Spirit is not that self-contradictory.

From the days in which the hybrid first saw the light, the conventicle had been under such heavy fire that anyone who attended only the conventicle was not likely to survive. Out of this situation grew a practice that came to be known as Nicodemitism. The name is derived from the Nicodemus of the New Testament, who, although at heart a disciple of Jesus, sought to keep the fact hidden for the sake of survival. Nicodemus was two-faced so that he would not be thrown out of the synagogue. Those who practiced Nicodemitism nourished their souls in the conventicle of the rival church but attended the meetings of the established church occasionally, just often enough to make the inquisitor look the other way.[A]

[A] The fact that the "heretics" continued to attend the rites and rituals of the established church has made some investigators conclude that

If this practice seems cowardly to us, we should seek to visualize the necessities of the times, in which any other course of conduct almost certainly meant death at the stake. Moreover, in the eyes of the "heretic" the activities of the prevailing church were a meaningless sham, activities at which one could be physically present without appreciable damage to his soul.

However, the "heretics" seem not to have been altogether at ease about the duplicity inherent in Nicodemite policies. They sought for biblical arguments to quiet the voice of conscience. They found one, for example, in the deportment of Naaman the Syrian, a man who was healed of leprosy. Although he had become a devotee of Israel's God, he asked to be allowed nonetheless to do valet service in the house of Rimmon, even bow along with the king as he worshiped at Rimmon's shrine, and yet be "pardoned of the Lord in this thing." The Nicodemites, like everyone else in those precritical days, found support for their double-minded practice in some rather out of the way — and questionable — places. One of these "proof-texts" found in the search for permission for the Nicodemite policy was the prayer uttered by Elisha just as Elijah was about to leave him: "Let, I pray, a double portion of thy spirit be upon me." This was read by the Nicodemites as a prayer asking that "thy spirit be double in me," meaning: "Give me what it takes to play our game of duplicity successfully." This questionable exegesis may have found some support in the translations that were in the hands of the "heretics," the exact texts of which are not in all cases known to us; but the interpretation seems like a shaky rationalization of a practice they already felt guilty about. In any event, centuries later, on the eve of the Reformation, a man high in the church's power structure complained that in his area (the southern Low Countries) "one-third of the populace, if not more, attend the conventicles."59

Still another term of opprobrium with which the ruling church sought to defame its rival was the term *Schleicher*. This German word means "one who crawls in" and connotes sur-

---

the "heretics" were and remained "good Catholics." This explanation of the "heretics" is quite common in the writings of some scholars, especially those of the past. It is surely subject to re-evaluation; for people who under their breath refer to the empire-church as a "den of robbers" and call its building "piles of rocks" are far from being "good Catholics." They are simply prudent.

reptitious entry. A variant of this smear word was *Leufer*, meaning "walker," or one who goes on foot from place to place. The terms were applied to the roving missionaries, who were accused of crawling into a parish and there preaching with the intention of gaining converts to their gospel and new members for the free church. The prevailing church, employing the kind of hermeneutics characteristic of it, leaned on II Timothy 3:6 in its assault on the *Schleicher*. In this passage we read of persons who "creep into houses, and lead captive silly women laden with sins, led away by divers lusts, ever learning, and never able to come to the knowledge of the truth" (KJV). This passage was regularly used by the empire-church in its running battle with the "heretical" missionary, who did indeed "creep into houses" (known as parishes) and did indeed "lead captive" some of their inmates.

These *Leufer* often travelled hither and yon disguised as peddlers; when it seemed possible without too much risk, the "peddler" would shift the subject from his wares to "the pearl of greatest price," the gospel of salvation and its Christ. Customarily the *Leufer* went out in pairs, thus emulating the disciples of Christ, and they were apparently very common. It seems safe to say that it was unlikely that one would live out his life in a medieval town anywhere in Europe without having personal knowledge of *Leufer*, so prevalent were they. Judging by the countermeasures taken by the enraged church, the effectiveness of these missionary endeavors carried on by the rival church must have been phenomenal. The church became frantic about the *Schleicher*. In an effort to neutralize the effect of the migrant missionaries and their clandestine preaching, it persuaded the *regnum* to extract an oath from every male of accountable age binding him to report the whereabouts and activities of all *Schleicher*.[B]

The church even went so far as to organize a special order of priests whose prime assignment was beating down the *Schleicher*. It had sent one of its most ardent and capable heresy hunters, Bishop Diego of Osmo, and a few of his asso-

---

[B] It seems that the aversion to oath-taking, a continuing feature of "heresy," was inspired by this policy. The oath was a means for the detection of the "heretic"; small wonder that the "heretics" looked upon it as an invention of the devil. The argument concerning the correctness of oath-taking was a prominent issue in medieval times; it resurfaced in Reformation days.

ciates to try to convert back to the Catholic fold a pocket of "heretics." Diego and his helpers worked hard at the job for a year or more — without success. The spiritual leaders of the "heretics" were so well-versed in Scripture (the only authority they recognized) that they proved to be more than a match for those who had come to convert them. As a matter of fact, Scripture indeed was on the side of the "heretics," which the church knew very well as seen from the fact that it tried its utmost to keep Scripture out of the hands of the "heretics." So discouraged were Diego and his helpers that they begged to be released and given another assignment. At this point the church hit on the idea of fighting fire with fire, of beating the "heretics" at their own *Schleicher* game: it put a new kind of priest on the road, a new order known as the Dominicans (named for Dominicus, one of Diego's associates). These were to engage in itinerant preaching as did the "heretics" (for which reason they were popularly called *Predikheeren,* "preaching sirs"), travel without the pomp and show of power characteristic of the other orders, dress like the *Schleicher* (in undyed homespun and simple sandals), and emulate the latter in every other way. The only difference between the *Schleicher* and their newly created imitators was that the former were hostile to the church and the latter friendly. No doubt the presence of the new order made the work of the *Schleicher* more difficult and dangerous. But the creation of the Dominican Order failed in its purpose: it was unable not only to stamp out "heresy" but also to prevent its spread and growth.[c]

Still another term of derogation invented by the medieval church in its battle against the free church was "Sacramentarian." This designation is likely to be misunderstood, for it did not indicate a person who puts heavy emphasis on sacrament; quite the opposite, it indicated a person who opposed the heavy

[c]In several areas the Dominicans were roughly received, even stoned in a few instances. This less than friendly reception has never been satisfactorily explained. Catholic writers are inclined to say that the news of the creation of the new order had not as yet reached those areas and that the "faithful" populace thought the itinerant preachers were *Schleicher,* whom they had been taught to oppose. The fact that one such stoning took place in Paris, to which the news of the creation of the new order must have already come, argues against this interpretation. It is more likely that the people, often massively on the side of the "heretics," resented the church's move against them and for that reason tried to drive the Dominicans away.

emphasis on sacrament that prevailed in the established church. A sacramentarian was an antisacramentalist. As was natural, the rival church would have nothing to do with sacrament, because sacrament is a device wherewith an already existing togetherness is said to become a religious togetherness. For this reason the "heretics" always scoffed at the very idea of salvation by sacrament; they were against all the church's sacraments.

Along with their rejection of baptism as sacrament, they were also against the "sacrament" of marriage, which gave their enemies the welcome chance to say that they were against marriage as such, that they had their "wives in common," a charge that was untrue. They also opposed the "sacrament" of penance, as well as the mass. The "heretics" were said to "deny that the substance of bread and wine blest by the priest at the altar is actually changed into the body and blood of Christ" (*Corpus* I, 19), and that is to deny the heart of the sacramental system. Of a group of such "heretics," burned at Cologne in the year 1163, we read that they were people "who consider all men who are not of their sect to be heretics and unbelievers; they spurn the sacraments of the true Church and say that only they have the true faith and that all others are worldly men who are under condemnation; they say that the body and blood of the Lord is nothing, ridiculing the mass and calling it awful names, for which reason they do not partake of it" (I, 41).

It was of course terribly dangerous to feel that way about the official church's most prized possession. And since every parish priest had a foolproof way of knowing the deportment of each of his parishioners in regard to sacrament, a member of the free church was not likely to go undetected. Several techniques were devised to detour that difficulty. Perhaps the most common escape route was Nicodemitism, the practice of partaking feignedly. Sometimes the "heretics" would accept the salvation-bestowing wafer only to hold it in their mouths until they were outdoors, where they would spit it out again. One man confessed that he had tried to do this but swallowed it nonetheless "because it slipped down too quickly." There are cases reported of "heretics" who put the morsel of bread in a handkerchief and later slipped into the emptied church to hang it on the altar, with a note attached saying that they were returning it because they had no interest in it.

There was another reason why members of the rival church became sacramentarians: they saw in the sacramental traffic carried on in the official church a case of outright idolatry, a matter of behaving before a creatural object in a way in which one is permitted to conduct himself before only the Creator. This conviction likewise precipitated a problem for the "heretic." It was customary for a platter known as the *ciborium* to be carried through the streets during a procession; the platter carried bread that allegedly had been transubstantiated. All adults were expected to "gaze adoringly" and to kneel before the "host" as it went by. To find a way around this difficulty was not easy, for one would have to deviate from standard procedure, in the presence of his neighbors. We read of one "heretic" who solved this cruel problem by absenting himself each time the "host" went by, ostensibly to heed the call of nature. However, he did it a few times too often. Another sacramentarian, whose name was Van der Eeke, solved the problem by kneeling as ordered, but with the outer husk of a walnut held in each eye socket. This man was punished by *exterminatio* for his behavior; his sentence read: "Fifty years expulsion from Flanders because he as the sacrament was going down the street made bold in derision thereof to put two nut husks in his eyes and one in his mouth as he knelt before the holy Sacrament, which are matters of evil example, not to be tolerated without punishment" (II, 279).

The "heretics" were also called "Anabaptists," a word meaning rebaptizers. The word is loaded, for it implies that the first lustration was genuine baptism — which was precisely the point at issue. No "Anabaptist" ever acknowledged that he was involved in a *second* baptism. In their more hostile moments, enemies of the rival church also called them "Katabaptists," a word meaning "averse to baptism." This term was also extremely unfair, for no one in the rival church was averse to baptism; they were against christening, that is, against baptism as a sacrament. Their rebaptism was a part of their Sacramentarianism, part of their assault upon *Corpus Christianum*. We know that already in the days when *Corpus Christianum* was being invented there were those who thought so little of christening that they rebaptized those whom they accepted into their own rival church fellowship. Medieval theologians were well aware that rejection of christening was nothing new; as early as 1050 the church spoke of men who "are introducing ancient heresies into modern times, alleging that the body of the Lord is not so much the body as a figure and a shadow of it. . . . they turn the baptism of infants upside down" (I, 9). In 1184 Lucius III warned against heretics "who concerning baptism . . . are not afraid to think and teach otherwise than the Holy Church preaches and practices" (I, 54). Somewhat earlier the church was aware of people who taught that "the mystery of baptism and the sacrament of the body and blood of the Lord are nothing" (I, 2). At about this same time the church warned against people "who say that the substance of bread and wine which is blest by the priest on the altar is not actually changed into the body and blood of Christ nor that the sacrament of baptism is effective unto the salvation of infants" (I, 19). In a similar vein the church spoke of its opponents in the rival church as "those who under the mask of religion condemn the sacrament, the baptism of infants . . . we condemn such as heretics and expel them from the church and order them to be coerced by the civil power; all who come to their defence shall be taken in hand" (I, 29).

Sometimes the offended church looked upon the "heretics'" rejection of christening as their central "heresy," the cornerstone of their whole edifice. In their book *Heresies of the High Middle Ages,* Wakefield and Evans quote some of these opinions: "The first item of the heretics is that they deny that little ones below the age of understanding can be saved by the baptism of Christ, that somebody else's faith is able to help those who are unable to exercise their own, seeing that according to them not somebody else's faith but one's own saves in baptism, the Lord having said 'whoso believeth and is baptized shall be saved but whosoever believeth not shall be condemned'" (p. 120).[60] More often, however, the rejection of christening is mentioned as simply one of the features of the "heresy" that was prevalent in the rival church. The usual description of the "heretic" had something in it concerning the rejection of christening. For example, we read in regard to the "heretics" that "they hold the baptism of children not yet at the age of understanding to be worthless, no matter who the sponsors" (p. 102). Further, "they also say that the sacrament of baptism of infants has no efficacy for salvation" (p. 105). And many other examples: "they give no credence to our baptism" (p. 130); "they render void the priesthood of the Church and condemn its sacraments, save baptism alone and this they approve only for adults. . . . They do not believe in infant baptism because of the text of the Gospel 'he that believeth and is baptized shall be saved'" (p. 131). At another time some "heretics" being questioned were told: "You put together a captious and slanderous attack upon infant baptism by following without much insight, the verbal formulas[D] and noting in them a defect of misrepresentation where none exists" (p. 154). "Asked about baptism of children and whether they were saved by baptism, they answered that they would not discuss this but that they would answer questions on the Gospels and the Epistles" (p. 190). The "heretics" were also said to hold "that infants are saved without baptism" (p. 346), and "that children baptized by the priests of the Roman Church do not attain salvation" (p. 372). Finally, "heretics accuse the Church as follows: 'They baptize little children who do not believe and who have no knowledge of good and evil'" (p. 605). No one in medieval times looked upon this aversion to christening as in any way a new departure from the faith. Bernard of Clairvaux said of the 11th century: "I do not recall having heard anything new or strange in all their meetings, numerous as they are, but things that have been worn thin by use and have been long agitated by the heretics of olden times, things that have been well-threshed by our theologians" (p. 138). When some "heretics" were apprehended at Liege in 1147, it was said that they were caught up in "newly discovered snares of ancient enemies" (of the faith). Occasionally it was said that they were "like unto the Donatists in Africa" — as indeed they were.

There is every reason to believe that it was not infant baptism as such that was repudiated by the medieval "heretics" but infant baptism that had been transformed into christening: they were against it in the context of *Corpus Christianum* but not necessarily in the context of *Corpus Christi*. They were opposed to christening because it was one of the supporting pillars of "Christian sacralism." It was said of some free church people of medieval times: "They confess the Catholic faith by mouth, but not with the heart; in their secret meetings . . . they say that they alone as disciples of Christ have the right to baptize. Whence they baptize the children of their own believers. . . . Out of this practice the sect of the Rebaptizers

---

[D]The reference to "verbal formulas" is to those passages in the New Testament (such as Mark 16:16) in which baptism is said to follow upon faith. The "heretics" tested all theological issues by the New Testament. By saying that they would only reply to issues broached in it, they avoided getting entangled in the church's metaphysics.

arose from them" (p. 234). We know that at the time of the birth of the hybrid there were already people who were called "Anabaptists." To "baptize a second time," of course, follows naturally from the rejection of christening: one who repudiates christening must resort to the baptism of those who have made a decision to believe, which is known as "rebaptizing" to those in sympathy with the hybrid. There is reason to believe that such "second baptisms" have been practiced ever since. Early in the thirteenth century there was a category of "heretics" known as the "Rebaptizers" who were said to have appeared simultaneously with the "Leonists" — an alternative name for Waldensians. Since we do not know just when the system of thought known as Waldensianism arose (it was almost certainly prior to the life of Peter Waldo), we do not know just how far back in history these "Anabaptists" go.

The "heretics'" rejection of sacrament led them to minimize "office." Faithful sons of the church said of the "heretics" of their day: "Many of them are well-versed in Scripture, which they possess in Teutonic translation; others repeat baptism; others do not believe in the body of the Lord [i.e., transubstantiation]; others say that the body of the Lord can be constituted by any man or woman, ordained or otherwise, in any dish or goblet and at any place;[E] others hold that extreme unction is unnecessary; others minimize the pontificate and the priesthood." Because the "heretics" held to a greatly reduced view of "office," they saw nothing incongruous in lay administration of the "ordinances." Many a "heretic" was put to death "for having administered the sacrament without priestly vestments," that is, for officiating although of "lay" status. This too was a common part of the Sacramentarian heritage.

Along with their other "heresies," these orthodox "heretics" continued to insist that the church was a fallen creature because it was the subject rather than the object of persecution. Moneta of Cremona said of them: "The heretics say that the Church should suffer persecution in this world, not practice it on others; but the Roman Church persecutes others the while itself remaining free from persecution."[61] Prominent likewise

[E]This "constituted by" must not be taken to mean that the "heretics" believed in transubstantiation. We have here the words of a Catholic of the times, in whose eyes the memorial meal (which the "heretics" did observe) was a matter of "constituting the body of the Lord"; he knew no other name for it.

in the vision of the underground church was the complaint that the official church gave its blessing to warfare. In criticizing this posture, the prevailing church said that the "heretics" "seek to prove that the Roman Church is not the Church because it blesses the *carrocio*[F] prepared for unjust battle, that is, for battles against brothers and neighbors, and so urges men to fight unjustly."[62]

* * * * *

Such then was the rival church of medieval times and such was the "heresy" of those times. It is apparent that it consisted of a broad and sustained attack on the Constantinian innovation, a sweeping aversion to all that went with the exchange of *Corpus Christi* for *Corpus Christianum,* a massive protest against "Christian sacralism." It was, in a word, a broad disapproval of the hybrid that had resulted when the sons of God and the daughters of men had been together.

Adolf von Harnack, perhaps the greatest authority of all time on the history of doctrine, was quite aware of the existence of the "heretics" throughout the centuries between the age of Constantine and the Reformation, as well as of the rival church ideas that tied them together. In an article dealing with a specific eruption of the "heresy" of which we have been speaking, he said: "During these twelve centuries attempts were never lacking to rupture the bonds of the State-Church/Priests-Church and to reinstitute the apostolic congregational structurization."[63] In our terminology, this adds up to the assertion that throughout the twelve centuries during which the hybrid roamed the earth there was a continued effort to stop it in its tracks and to return to things as they had been before the Constantinian change. It is safe to say that, far from being successful in its attempt to suppress its rival, the prevailing church was losing the fight. There was more of this "heresy" around on the eve of the Reformation than there had

---

[F]The *carrocio* was a cart on which an altar was placed, plus the standards of the *regnum,* and it served as a sort of sacramental symbol for the soldiers as they went to battle. Constantine would have loved the *carrocio*. The question being asked on every hand in our times — whether a Christian can participate in warfare — was not heard until the pedigree of the hybrid was called into question, that is, not until *Corpus Christianum* had been repudiated.

ever been before.ᴳ What Coulton has said about Waldensianism is true of "heresy" in general: "In spite of slaughter in detail and slaughter in mass, generation after generation, there were more . . . in Luther's time than in Pilichdorf's."⁶⁴

The controlling idea in all of this "heresy" was that the church of medieval times was a fallen creature, and that it had become necessary to reinstitute the church of the New Testament. The usual representation was that the fall of the church had occurred in the days of Constantine. For example, in a rather lengthy tract entitled *The Net of Faith*,⁶⁵ written a century before Luther, Peter Chelcicky of Poland said:

> By the use of force no man is brought to faith in Christ, as unlikely as that a man should acquire a knowledge of the Czech language by studying German. . . . By means of the secular power Antichrist has pulled all power to himself under cover of the Christian faith. Since we believe that it was by meekness and humility unto the cross that Christ has delivered us from the power of Satan therefore we cannot allow that the perfecting of our faith comes by worldly power as though force were a greater benefit than is faith. . . . When Emperor Constantine in his heathen mode of existence was taken up into the church by Pope Sylvestre and the latter was fitted by the former with external rule—then the destruction of the church was inevitable.

Dabszynski, a Polish scholar who was attached to the University of Craçow in the middle of the 15th century, wrote: "Sylvestre, the first pope, took his power from the dragon named Constantine and his venom was diffused over the whole church. Led by Satan Sylvestre deceived the emperor and got possession of Rome by fraud."

In the chronicles of the rival church known as the Hutterite Brethren we read: "When Sylvestre received Constantine . . . then the emperor provided all who called themselves Christians in his whole realm with great peace; at that time the pestilence that walks in darkness and the destruction that wastes at noonday crowded in mightily, the cross was lifted and welded to the sword — all by the cunning of the devil."⁶⁶ Pro-

---

ᴳA Waldensian who was asked in about 1500 how many Waldensian pastors there were in his area replied "some four hundred." We are told that in the 14th century the Waldensians held a secret synod in which there were some five hundred delegates. What became of this legacy of dissent when the Reformation occurred is a question usually left unanswered if not unfaced.

fessor Frend has accurately observed that "in the last resort the difference between the Donatists and Catholics turned on the relation between church and society."[67] At the end of his study of the Donatist rival church, he sums up that controversy in these words:

> Donatism and Catholicism represented opposite tendencies in early Christian thought. The Churches were in fact two societies, differing fundamentally in outlook on both religious and social questions. . . . Was the Church 'within the Roman Empire', sustaining and sustained by the Christian emperors, or was the Empire the representative of the outer 'world' whence the Christian must separate himself in order to progress in faith? Were social evils and injustices to be fought in the name of Christ, or were they to be tolerated for the sake of unity? To all these questions the Donatists and Catholics gave different answers. The issues were not those of 'truth' versus 'heresy', but of two opposed attitudes toward society, attitudes that have persisted throughout the history of the Christian Church down to the present day.[68]

As we have shown in the foregoing, the issue between the two schools of thought (identified as *Corpus Christianum* versus *Corpus Christi*) had many facets; many specific issues were involved in the major issue of the legitimacy of the hybrid. Whether the issue was christening, the existence of sacrament, the conduct of mission, the need for a definitive life-style, salvation as pardon plus renewal, even the issue of engaging in an "unjust war," etc. each was always one aspect of the larger issue of the rightness or wrongness of the hybrid known as Christendom — the issue of grace in two senses.

There was yet another facet in this controversy over the delineation of the church, one to which Professor Frend refers in passing in the above quotation. It is the issue of economics, which we must leave largely undiscussed in the present study. Already in the Donatist rebellion against nascent "Christian sacralism" the complaint was heard that the economic justice inherent in the gospel and demanded by the gospel was being blurred, that the proponents of the new order were closing their eyes to the things the New Testament had to say in the area of "mine and thine." This complaint, coupled with a call for an economics that reflect a Christian sensitivity, was heard

"THE BIRTH OF THE HYBRID"

all through the ensuing millennium.[H] It came to be referred to — by the enemies of the rival church — as an agitation for "community of goods." This aspect of the conflict between the two ideologies surfaced again in Reformation times (to which we shall turn in the next chapter of this study). All the earliest leaders of the Reformation gave evidence of having heard and taken to heart the medieval rival church's clamor for an economics informed by the New Testament. Luther, for example, said early in his career that in a society influenced by the Christian vision there would be no begging. A spokesman for the old order, the Catholic polemicist Jerome Emser, took Luther to task for this unmercifully. He asked whether Luther was unaware that many people, of whom he gave examples, "earned heaven by begging as well as by giving to beggars." He warned his contemporaries that if the ideas of Luther on this score were to gain adherence, many good works would be *"gestopft"* (terminated). Luther and other Reformers also assailed the usury that was rife in the economics of the day, a system derived in its entirety from pagan sources. However, for various reasons — among them the scare of the emerging Peasant War — Luther and the others reversed their earlier convictions in the matter of economics. However, the economic sensitivities continued in the rival church, which resurfaced as a result of the Reformers' swing to the right. For this, these rival church members called down upon themselves the ancient and threadbare argument about "community of goods," a charge that stands unretracted in the thirty-sixth article of the Belgic Confession.

In the next — and final — chapter, we turn to the fact that "also afterward," when the sons of God established further intimacies with the daughters of men, hybrids continued to be born.

[H]In the year 1535, the emperor Charles V received a memorandum from the Council of the Archbishop of Cologne, telling him to suppress the Anabaptists because "they seek to introduce community of goods, etc., even as has been the nature of the Anabaptists throughout the ages, even as the old histories on imperial law over a thousand years testify."[69]

Part Four

"AND ALSO AFTERWARD"

Episode One

Early in 1525 a child was born to Conrad Grebel, a young scholar whose father was in the Great Council of Zürich. He did not baptize his baby because he had become convinced that christening finds no support in the New Testament. When the news of Grebel's break with christening reached the ears of the *regnum* of Zürich, it caused great consternation. They stood squarely in the tradition of "Christian sacralism," and for that reason they saw in the activities of Grebel a dire threat to the social order. This "Christian sacralism" had been fashioned by Constantine for political reasons, and it had been of great political usefulness ever since. The *regnum* was always deeply concerned with the concept of *Corpus Christianum* and thus the Zürich fathers wanted the rite of christening kept intact. They decided to move and to move fast.

However, there was the protocol established by ancient law and historical precedent requiring the *regnum* and the *sacerdotium* to work together if and when it was necessary to move against heretics. The *sacerdotium* had to try the accused first and declare him to be in heresy before the *regnum* could proceed against him with its sword of steel. To satisfy this established way of proceeding, the city council arranged for a confrontation. The date was set for January 17, 1525. The intention of the confrontation, which actually had all the features of a trial,[A] was that the finger would be pointed at those who — with Grebel as their spokesman — were rocking the boat. At the meeting Zwingli, who was not prepared to incur the displeasure of the council, argued in favor of the traditional position regarding christening. He must have realized that by so doing he was turning on his former colleagues and collaborators in the ongoing reformation. He must have also realized that in so doing he was going against his own former self.

The confrontation was held as planned, and it ended as planned. After an intense, often stormy, debate it was decided that Zwingli and those who had sided with him had won the argument. This implied that Grebel and his faction were now legally "in heresy" and thus in line for restraining and punitive action from the side of the *regnum*. As in the old sacralist tradition, a person officially in error theologically was by that token guilty of sedition, so that the Grebel party could now expect civil action against themselves. The *regnum* lost no time in acting on the decision. On the same night, the city council met in a second meeting to implement action against the dissenters. An edict was promulgated ordering all parents who had unbaptized infants to present them for baptism within eight days, or face expulsion from the city. Grebel and Felix Manz (another clergyman who sided with Grebel) were ordered not to speak derogatorily of christening again; certain others who were not citizens of Zürich (and hence not under the council's jurisdiction) were told to quit the city at once. Thereupon, these and many others who shared their convictions retreated to the home of Manz's mother in nearby Zollikon,[B]

[A]This was customary: a century earlier, John Hus thought he was going to a discussion but soon found out that it was a trial instead. The same was true of Luther at Worms. In medieval times truth was not something arrived at by a meeting of minds; it was a matter of *papa dixit* (the pope has spoken). Truth, like many other things, was decreed.

[B]Felix Manz was the son of an unwed mother: his father was a priest, the canon of Grossmünster in Zürich. There were many such illegitimate children, conceived of a priest and one of his parishioners. Erasmus, the great humanist, as well as Henri Bullinger (Zwingli's successor) and Leo Jud (also active in the reform in Switzerland) were in their number. Such persons had an above average chance to get an education. The fact that more than one of them figured in the Reformation may have been due to their personal knowledge of how great the need for reform was.

where an all-night meeting was held for Bible study, prayer, and mutual encouragement.

From this point on the reform movement in Switzerland was two-pronged: it had become bifurcated, with Zwingli and his followers who had knuckled under to the *regnum* in one camp, and those who with Grebel and his associates had chosen not to knuckle under in the other. On May 28, 1525, Zwingli wrote to Vadian (Joachim Watt) that the struggle with the Catholics was "but child's play" compared with the conflict that was developing between the two camps within the Reformation.

A new hybrid had been born — to fulfill the phrase in the Genesis story, "also afterward." True to the nature of the beast, it had no sooner struggled to its feet than it began an all-out program of liquidation of all those who resisted hybrids. All the fury of persecution was revived against the same old nemesis, a way of thinking and of conduct that would make society composite. This new wave of persecution served to make the "heretics" even more sure that they were on the side of the angels; they were bearing the cross of Christ after him, experiencing hardship because of their commitment to him, which in the tradition of the rival church since the days of the original hybrid had been considered the condition of true discipleship.

Zwingli and his party had gone magisterial: they were now working in a reform movement propelled by the *regnum*.[c] They operated with a flat theology, where the distinction between preliminary (conserving) grace and subsequent (redeeming) grace was sure to be stifled. On the other hand, Grebel and those who stood with him were now leading a nonmagisterial reform, one in which the concept of progressive grace could flourish. Once more there was a "right" religion carried on by the *regnum* and a "wrong" one nourished in a free church. For this free church the ancient smear word "Anabaptist" was given a new usefulness; for, although the word calls attention to but a single facet of the issue (and is to that

[c]One of the first to study the rise of the rival church in Reformation times, the Catholic scholar C. A. Cornelius, had this to say of Zwingli's turn to the right: "As correct as this was in the eyes of the State and as much as these developments gave to Zwingli's program greater respectability, so poorly evangelical was it and so certainly did it have to lead to cleavage and conflict within the party."[1]

extent not wholly appropriate), it stuck, and it has been in use to this day to denote the "left wing of the Reformation," as it has been called.

The question must be asked — and also answered — how the bifurcation (which, as we shall see, was by no means confined to the land of the Alps) was brought about. How is it to be explained that so early in the Reformation — considerably less than ten years after the posting of Luther's theses — a deep rift had opened in the movement, one that ran across the whole face of Europe and was not bridged for centuries to come? The usual explanation of the bifurcation is that it all began with the events of 1517, and that the Anabaptists represent the "left wing of the Reformation" because they went further and more headlong than the mainline Reformers.

The terminology "left wing" will not do as a description of the rival church of the Reformation. "Left wing" is a term borrowed from the parliamentary scene, and it stands for a faction that wishes to go faster and further than does the "center," and much faster and further than the "right." But Grebel and his faction were not "left wing"; in some respects they were "right wing" instead. For example, in the matter of justification by faith, the concept that may be called the center of gravity in the body of typically Reformation thought, Grebel and his party stood well to the "right" of Luther. The Epistle of James, the book of the Bible with which Luther was embarrassed because it made too much of the need of a definitive life-style, was actually a favorite with the people who rallied to Grebel's side. In this specific matter the so-called left wing was right wing. The trouble with the label "left wing of the Reformation" is that behind it lies the assumption that the bifurcation was the result of quantitative difference, when the difference was actually qualitative. The Reformation in its final form was continuous with the *Corpus Christianum* tradition, whereas Anabaptism was continuous with the *Corpus Christi* tradition. In other words, the Reformation ultimately embraced the hybrid, whereas Anabaptism was always hostile to it. The difference of opinion that led to the bifurcation takes us back far beyond 1517. Throughout post-Constantinian times the rival church had had the policy of trying to live the New Testament life within the context of the existing empire-church; it saw no chance of eliminating the empire-wide church, and thus tried for a way of life that would get by in its presence, patronizing the church as *Corpus Christianum* just enough to keep it from pouncing. With the changing pattern of European political life, the possibility came into view of eliminating the competition between the two churches by making Christendom over to fit the evangelical doctrines. This was to go after much larger game than the medieval rival church had aimed at. However, as those of the rival church came to see things, it was the repetition of an ancient evil, the evil of "Christian sacralism." It was at this point that the rift occurred.ᴅ

Because the Reformation in its final version was magisterial, those who stand in the tradition of magisterial reform show the Reformation as beginning in 1517, when for the first time the possibility of state support loomed up. This explains why history books written by historians in this tradition begin the story at the point when reform carried by the *regnum* of the particular country begins: in Germany with the "Protestant" princes, in France with the coming of the Condes, in England with Henry VIII, in Holland with the *Compromis* of 1566 (the year in which for the first time coalition between nobles and consistories became a possibility). However, by so doing these historians throw a pall of silence over all that preceded 1517; they omit the very important first chapter of the story they are telling. Not all historians following that tradition are as blind to the first chapter as the Dutch historian whose voluminous account of the Reformation in Holland (a work that for generations was one of the standard works) devoted one page to all that went before 1566; but many of them fall into the error of neglecting that early history. Those who ignore all that went before the magisterial reform will end up with a misunderstanding not only of the magisterial reform but of the Reformation as a whole.

The Reformation did not begin on the night of October 31, 1517. Luther's brave deed of that night no doubt encour-

---

ᴅIt is significant that at precisely this time a new word appeared in European parlance, the word *Neuevangelischen* ("new evangelicals").[2] This term (first used of the Zwinglians) implies that there were now two kinds of evangelicals on the scene, the old kind and the new. The older ones (who invented the term "new evangelicals") were those of the old rival church, and the new ones were the magisterial reformers and their following. Both were distinguishable from the Catholics; and each was distinguishable from the other in their diverse evaluation of the hybrid.

aged and inspired all who already had reformation in their banner; but Luther *found* followers before he *made* any, followers who later — when they saw where Luther was going — peeled off again. C. A. Cornelius contends that "to Luther came others who, before his activity, had already distanced themselves from the doctrines of the official church, men who were encouraged by his activity to give expression to their ideas and to organize them into systems."³ However, these did not stay on, and the reason for their leaving was that they were too averse to the hybrid to go along with magisterialization. Luther himself testified about their departure in language that cannot be mistaken: "In our times the doctrine of the Gospel, re-established and cleaned up, drew to it and gained many who in earlier times had been held down by the tyranny of the Antichrist, the pope;ᴱ however, there went forth from us at once Anabaptists, Sacramentarians, and other rabble-folk . . . for they were not of us even though for a time they walked with us . . . for they have not had in mind the pure doctrine nor did they seek it."⁴ ᶠ

ᴱThe reference can only be to the rival church of pre-Reformation times, known by all sorts of names, among them "Pickards" and "Waldensians." Luther does not identify them because he wrote this after the bifurcation had occurred, and it would be poor politics to acknowledge that his movement had at the first attracted "heretics."

ᶠ"The pure doctrine" was Luther's formulation of *sola fide* ("by faith alone"). He meant thereby that man cannot earn his salvation, neither in whole nor in part: as such it is surely in keeping with the teachings of Scripture. However, there was in Luther's conception of the salvation experience a disproportionate emphasis on salvation as pardon at the expense of salvation as renewal. It was at this point that the heirs of the old rival church arched their eyebrows. They thought Luther meant by *sola fide* something like "faith standing alone" or "faith unaccompanied," and that they could not accept. The old rival church had invested too much in the attempt to recover the life-style of authentic Christianity to accept a theology in which almost nothing was said about a distinctive way of life. The old rival folk were especially fond of the book of James, and it startled them to hear Luther call James a "right strawy epistle" which he "didn't want" in his Bible; he even said — not in jest — that he was some day going to "heat the kitchen stove with that Jakie." One of the older pastors of the old rival church, Lucas of Prague, took Luther to task for his neglect of "fruits worthy of repentance" and wrote to him: "Nohow and never will you be able to ascribe justification to faith alone, for you have the Scripture against you. . . . Leave, I pray of you, some standing room for good works; in this matter you go against Christ and cling fast to error."⁵ When it became evident that Luther was not going to heed this admonition, "there went forth . . . Anabaptists, Sacramentarians, and other rabble folk . . . . "

"AND ALSO AFTERWARD"

It is an intolerable oversimplification to begin the story of the Reformation with the posting of the theses because that has implications that simply cannot be accepted. For one thing, we have then the inexplicable situation of a school of thought (known as Anabaptism) that is like the Melchizedek of the book of Hebrews — "without father, without mother." All the other schools of the Reformation scene have the founder's name attached to them, for example, Lutheranism, Zwinglianism, Calvinism. Cornelius faces the question concerning this anonymity by pointing out that all the early leaders of Anabaptism were unanimous in the idea that the church should consist of true Christians and of them only, and that it was necessary to follow the example of the apostolic church, to separate from the world and assemble a righteous and holy people. He adds that the identity of those who first entertained this idea is not known. This is very strange if one assumes that the Reformation began in 1517. Anabaptism was not a tempest in a teacup.[G] The whole Reformation was influenced by it, perhaps more than by any other tendency of the times. There was hardly a court in Europe that did not have matters pertaining to this eruption of "heresy" on its docket. And yet, as Cornelius has pointed out, the movement had no apparent head. This is unthinkable — on the assumption that it all began with the events of 1517. It is as though a movement like communism could erupt spontaneously from the North Sea to the Mediterranean without any names attached to it, no mention of Marx or Lenin. The strange silence about who was at the head of Anabaptism becomes completely understandable once we recognize that it was a resurgence, a revitalization of ideas of long standing, ideas that were never absent from the medieval scene and can be traced back all the way to the days of the birth of the original hybrid.

Moreover, the common mistake of beginning at the year 1517 has impossible psychological implications: it requires that we assume a volatility which the human spirit simply does not have, a jumping back and forth that is psychologically unthinkable. If we begin the Reformation in 1517, we have to posit the following gyrations in the souls of masses of people: first

---

[G]As early as the year 1528, a mere three years after the meeting at Zürich, there were in Swabia alone four hundred special police whose task was to nab Anabaptists. When it became apparent that this was not stemming the tide, the number was raised to one thousand.

a weaning away from the ancestral faith as a result of the *sola fide* agitation emanating from Wittenberg; then an emphatic and massive assault upon that very *sola fide* — simultaneously, in all parts of Europe, and all within the space of seven short years, at a time when communication was far from what it is now. Human beings are simply not that whimsical and volatile, certainly not within the populations of Germanic peoples, and surely not in large masses and simultaneously over all of Europe!

The bifurcation that took place points to antibodies in the bloodstream of many who looked up hopefully at the news from Wittenberg, antibodies that were the legacy of long-continued resistance to the medieval order, a long-standing heritage of rival church "heresy." How else shall we explain that from the beginning those who abandoned the magisterial reformers to form their own free church demonstrated a pronounced sacramentarianism, a prosaic and antisacramental view of the Lord's Supper? It has been suggested that they picked this up from Zwingli because he is the only Reformer who took a position on the sacrament anything like that of the leaders of the new rival church. But Zwingli was the archenemy of the Anabaptists, and thus it is not likely that they borrowed their common-sense view of the ordinances from him. Moreover, Zwingli himself confessed that he had got the idea that formed the heart of his view of the Lord's Supper from a Dutchman, one who certainly did not get his concept from any Reformation figure. The source was as available to the rival church as it had been to the man who brought it to Zwingli. It is a heritage of pre-Reformation dissent as it ran in the medieval rival church for centuries. Although it is perhaps true that Zwingli derived the linguistic formula — "this is my body" = "this signifies my body" — from the Dutchman who had come to confer with him, it is virtually certain that he derived his theology concerning the matter from the rival church of earlier times. We know at least that when Henri Bullinger disclosed to Zwingli his own common-sense view of the Lord's Supper in 1523, which he said he had concocted from Augustine "and the Waldensian writings," Zwingli immediately gave his enthusiastic support to it.[6] This makes it certain that he had been bombarded previously by a theology that came from the writings of the earlier "heretics." Zwingli did contend that he "knew the Waldensian ideas only from hearsay," but this may well have been just another diplomatic gesture inspired by the well-known tendency to avoid all possible evidence of association with earlier "heresy."[H] For all we know, Zwingli had read widely in the literature of the old rival church, specifically as found in Waldensian tracts. But it is significant that at the time Bullinger first disclosed to Zwingli his prosaic view of the sacrament, Zwingli added at once that it should not be divulged to anybody "because the time is not ripe for it as yet." When he did consider the time "ripe" for the revelation of the views that later became associated with his name, he did not acknowledge the debt he owed to the earlier "heretics" (neither directly nor via his friend Bullinger); it was subsequently quite lost in the record. This is understandable if we keep in mind what the acknowledgment of such relatedness could have entailed; when we recall that protest groups in pre-Reformation days flatly denied having anything to do with related groups, even though they were demonstrably indebted to them, we cannot expect Reformation leaders to confess continuity with older groups.

However, one contemporary, Guido de Brès (author of the Belgic Confession of the Reformed churches), indicated that the "heretics" of his day did confess orally to being one in spirit with the older "heretics." He wrote: "Many of your people say that if you want to find the truth you must hunt it on the lists of heretics who were rejected."[7] No doubt the "heretics" of Reformation times were less hesitant to *say* that they stood in the tradition of ancient "heresy" than *write* it, for the written word is always more incriminating than the spoken word. However, some written things issuing from the rival church do occasionally show indirectly that their saga did not begin in 1517. One such voice, in criticism of Luther's slight emphasis on the changed life, said, "Leave us a little room for our works; the papists teach correctly in this matter but you are a poisonous snake." He added: "The older priests have not been able to lead us astray but the present ones are doing it; their books are the books of heretics."[8] Who were

[H]We cannot stress too strongly that it was poor policy to acknowledge any indebtedness to or affinity with Waldensianism. Jean Crespin, a contemporary Protestant and author of *Book of Martyrs*, wrote: "For a long time the world had held the Waldensians in such horror that every manner of absurd opprobrium had been laid to their charge and it seemed impossible that the earth should sustain them."[9]

these "older priests" who had tried, without success, to lead astray the "us" of the old rival church? The reference can only be to the priests of the empire-church of pre-Reformation times. And who were the "present ones" who were also trying to lead these people astray and were having some success? The reference can only be to the magisterial reformers. When we recall that members of the rival church had called Melanchthon's famous *opus* "a heretical book" (largely because of its slight emphasis on a distinctive life-style), the outlines of the situation become clear. The above pastor, who still had memories of life in the older rival church and who had been able to shield his flock from the Catholics seeking to prey on them, finds himself now confronted with a new kind of predator — the magisterial reformer. But acknowledgments of a connecting link between the older rival church and the one that was coming to expression as a result of the bifurcation are rare, as is to be expected.

If modern historians are wont to begin at 1517, this was not the case with contemporaneous minds. They point to the ideological continuity between the new free church and the former one. One of these was Bartholomäus von Usingen, former teacher of Martin Luther, who wrote in 1529:[10] "In these times those who are called Anabaptists or Catabaptists because of their repeated baptism came forth out of Picardism."[1] It was commonly said of the Anabaptists that they derived their strength and nourishment from all sorts of ancient heretics and, adorning them with a beautiful front (a left-handed compliment of the "heretics'" high morals), they peddled them anew on the world. Neither did it escape Luther's eye that those who were breaking step with him had antecedents in the old rival church of medieval times. Smarting under their scoldings for the latitudinarianism in the matter of conduct, he wrote:

> This is a comfort against the *Schwärmgeister* and all those who are so offended at the church's weakness. For from the beginning the heretics have cherished this notion that the church must be holy and without sin. When they saw that some in it were slaves to sin they forthwith denied that this was the Church;

---

[1]"Picardism" was one of the terms of opprobrium hurled at the rival church in medieval times. The etymology of the word is uncertain: some say it derives from Picardy, a province in France that was notorious for its "heresy"; others consider it a variant of "Beghard," another old smear word.

and so they made a sect of those whom they claimed to be the true Church. Out of this came the Donatists and the Cathars and many others as well as in our times the Anabaptists, etc. who all cried out with the same passion that the true Church is not the Church (because they saw that sinners and godless people are mixed in with it) and they separated themselves from it.

Luther also said that "it is the greatest wisdom not to be offended when evil people go into the Church and come out of it.... The greatest comfort is that we know that they do not do the Church any harm but that we have to put up with it that wheat and tares are mixed together." He contended that by this drive for "their all too great holiness they bring about that they are no Church at all but a naked sect of the devil."[11]

Another contemporary who saw clearly the continuity between the new free church and the old one was Urbanus Rhegius, a Lutheran pastor. Referring to the Anabaptist leader Bernard Knipperdollink, he wrote in a book to which Luther wrote the preface:

"Aha, here Bernard resorts to a genuinely Donatist trick. They too condemned and abandoned Christendom on account of some evil and false Christians. . . . Nevertheless there have always been some true and devout Christians in the mass and we hope they are present also with us. Moreover, the fact that wicked rascals are present with us . . . is none of our business; we haven't instructed them to drink and gourmandize, to be immoral or covetous. . . . We don't want to rend the net because there are some bad fish in it. as the super-saintly Anabaptist Bernard is doing. He gives himself away at this point and shows that he has the same Anabaptist devil in him which blinded also the Donatists in Africa. They likewise opened their eyes wide and saw with a hypocritical face that many wicked people were wearing the name Christian, people who were in reality genuine heathen; and they proceeded to go off by themselves, apart from Christendom, and made off that they wanted to raise up a truly reformed Church, one in which there was nothing but saints. And they were so pure in their own eyes that they declared the baptism performed in Christendom by evil priests to be no baptism and they baptized anew. By this method they thought to raise up genuine holiness. They scolded Augustine for staying on in the assembly of the wicked, to which he replied that there were indeed evil people in his fellowship . . . and that external fellowship of good and evil does no harm to the former's salvation, seeing that they don't approve of their evil and godless mode of existing. We are not to cause a separation; he who separates from the Church becomes a heretic[J] and a schismatic. Let Bernard consider himself told off, for he is a neo-Donatist who takes offense at the evil lives of others and he has . . . gone about to raise up a holy and unspotted Church . . . he and his company cut loose from Christendom. . . . I would forsooth prefer to be a coarse publican in the Christian Church, or a patent sinner, rather than be the holiest Pharisee of all in Bishop Bernard's *spelunk*."[12]

So clear was it to this contemporaneous theologian that Anabaptism was not some new thing but a resurgence of an old issue that he entitled this polemic against them *Refutation of the New Valentinian and Donatist Confession.* . . . So similar were the two rival churches, the two rebellions against the hybrid, that sometimes in the course of his argument Rhegius calls the Anabaptists "Donatists" — omitting the "neo": "God raises up the magistracy against heretics, faction-fashioners and schismatics in the Christian Church, in order that Hagar may be flogged by Sarah. . . . The Donatists murder men's souls, make them go to eternal death and then they complain when men punish them with temporal death. Therefore, the Christian magistrate must make it his first concern to keep the Christian religion pure with sound teaching . . . all who know history will know what was done by such men as Constantine, Marianus, Theodosius, Justinian, Charlemagne and others." The present tense of the verbs in the above sentence shows that Rhegius was thinking of contemporaneous "Donatists," more commonly called "Anabaptists." Calvin was likewise aware that history was repeating itself in the rival church that was annoying him. He wrote of the Anabaptists: "Such were of old the Cathars and the Donatists, who were similarly infatuated; such in the present day are some of the Anabaptists. . . ."[13] Luther also saw the similarity: "Saint Augustine was greatly bothered in previous times by the same kind of customers and seducers."[14]

The law enforcement agencies saw clearly the repetition of history in the resurgence in their day of the ancient rival church ideas and emphases; they invoked the Codes of Theodosius, which they called "a placard or Edict calling for

---

[J] It will not escape the reader's attention that in Rhegius' mind heresy is not a matter of doctrine but one of making a choice between alternatives.

"AND ALSO AFTERWARD"

the death of the heretics, namely such as in those days practiced rebaptism, as your sect does now."[15] It was under the terms of these ancient legal enactments that the first Anabaptists of the 16th century were punished. This is understandable, because these legal enactments were originally devised to eliminate those who were obstructing the formation of *Corpus Christianum*. Since, as Roland Bainton has pointed out, "the Anabaptists sought to replace *Corpus Christianum* as a socio-political unity with a voluntary nonpolitical reality called *Corpus Christi*,"[16] these ancient codes were entirely pertinent in the fight against the Anabaptists.

There was no aspect of the ancient quarrel that had erupted in connection with the original hybrid that did not recur in connection with the one "also afterward." There was, for example, the unwelcome readiness of the Anabaptists for martyrdom, the undeniable light-heartedness with which they shouldered the cross. This had been a trait of the Donatists — in its lunatic fringe almost a volunteering for martyrdom. And it had recurred frequently in the millennium that followed. It was seen in a renewed form among the Anabaptists — a sort of volunteering for martyrdom. Luther saw the similarity and said: "St. Augustine had a lot of trouble with the Donatists long ago; they also . . . begged for martyrdom, asked the executioner to slay them in order that they might qualify as martyrs; and when no one laid a hand on them they had a way of jumping off bridges or falling from houses, so that they broke their necks — as they recited the passage 'Whose loveth his life more than. . . .' "[17] In an *Advice* drawn up in 1536, we read concerning this readiness for bearing the cross:

> That these people are possessed by the devil and blinded, is apparent from the way they go willingly to death, to the fire, to the water. That is the way the devil commonly works. In the Gospel we read of a lad whom he threw into fire and water often (Mth. 17:15) . . . as also he drove Judas to the noose. It is plain that he drives people in the same way still . . . just as he drove the Donatists who even let themselves fall into the water or caused themselves to be burned. The devil even tried to make Jesus such a martyr when he suggested to him that he throw himself down from the temple tower.[18]

One wonders whether the writers of this *Advice* thought that the disciples of Jesus who were found "rejoicing that they were counted worthy to suffer dishonor for the name" (Acts

5:41) were perhaps also impelled by the devil. The readiness for martyrdom was always a mighty asset for the cause of the rival church — and its opponents knew it. That is why steps were often taken to make speech impossible to the martyr, by such devices as the tying of a piece of wood crosswise in the victim's mouth. But, as seen from the shabby argument resorted to in the above *Advice,* the opponents of the "heretics" were at a loss for a decent case against them.

Another similarity that did not escape contemporary observers was on the point of life-style. To this also there is a chorus of testimony. Luther, for example, wrote in an attack on the Anabaptists: "When they observe us and the offences with which Satan perverts our congregations then they deny that we are a Church and they find it impossible to extricate themselves from this offence. That is the way the Donatists judged likewise, who excommunicated fallen ones . . . for which reason their churches shrank to a small number. That is the position the Manicheans[K] and others also took, as if the Church were actually in life eternal instead of in the flesh. Men ought not to talk that way about the Church. . . . Whatever is left of sin offends these superspiritual Donatists . . .[L] but it does not offend God seeing that because of faith in Christ he overlooks it and forgives."[19] Here once again it is clear that the Reformers realized well that in the bifurcation an old issue was presenting itself. It may have begun to dawn on them that the hybrid that had come into being "also afterward" was very much like the one that had roamed the earth of yore.

* * * * *

Now that we know something of the matrix out of which the hybrid came "also afterward," we do well to watch the beast in action for a while. Naturally, it took recourse at once to its "other arm": scarcely two years after the fateful confrontation at Zürich, the first martyr of the new rival church, Felix Manz, became a victim of the new hybrid. He was appre-

---

[K] It is doubtful that Luther at this point actually had the followers of Manes in mind. He was probably using the word, as did so many in his day, for *Cathars* in general.

[L] The reader will observe that in this passage Luther, without any inhibition, calls the Anabaptists "Donatists," so convinced was he that the rival church of his day was continuous with the rival church that had come into being in Augustine's day.

"AND ALSO AFTERWARD"

hended for complicity in the new "heresy," was tried, found guilty, and on January 5, 1527, was liquidated. The mode of Manz's execution was novel. For many centuries the empire-church had rid itself of "heretics" by burning them, a mode of execution derived from John 15:6 (via the convenient exegetical form for which the old hybrid, beginning with Augustine, was noted): "Men gather them and cast them into the fire and they are burned." But Felix Manz was drowned. He was placed in a rowboat with his wrists firmly tied together and passed over his cocked knees, and a heavy piece of wood thrust between his bent knees and his elbows. Trussed up in this manner—making swimming impossible—he was rowed to the other side of the Limmat River, thrown overboard, and thus made to perish in Limmat's water. Why death by drowning instead of by fire? The answer to this question may be contained in something that had been said during the confrontation of January 17, 1525. In the course of the argument, those who were averse to christening had brought out the idea (biblical to the core but in eclipse ever since the birth of the original hybrid) that Christian baptism signifies the submerging of the man of sin. They brought this up in their effort to show that a new lifestyle is a condition of genuine discipleship. While Grebel and his companions were making this point, Zwingli had called out angrily, "Let those who talk of going under go under indeed!" It seems that this ejaculation had stuck in the memory of the representatives of the *regnum,* so that they specified death by drowning ("going under") for their first victim.[M] It was perhaps in connection with this remark made at the confrontation that Zwingli himself recommended that "heretics" be put to death by drowning. It seems to have had repercussions

---

[M] The lengths to which Zwingli went in his attempt to get away from the Anabaptists' insistence that baptism has to do with renewal of life is almost unbelievable, as is the callous levity with which he dealt with the matter. For instance, when members of the new rival church said that at the time of their own baptism (their "rebaptism," as their opponents called it) they had experienced "great renewal of spirit," Zwingli shot back that this was "nothing but old wives' tales and prattle of fools" (*"nur altwybisch und närrisch gplerr"*). He also said that "if that is what they defend then many people will not only want to be baptized a second time but repeatedly, if water baptism renewed, strengthened, and comforted the soul every time they were assailed — that would take us back to the manifold lustrations of the Old Testament." When his opponents said that along with their baptism they had become renewed human beings, Zwingli snorted, "Jolly tidings! let's all go for a dip in the Limmat!"[20]

in some rather distant places, for Ferdinand of Austria said that "a third baptism" (i.e., death by drowning) was the best antidote to Anabaptism.[21]

The official grounds for Manz's execution tell the whole story: "Because he has, contrary to Christian order and custom, become involved in re-baptism . . . has confessed to having said that he wanted to gather such as want to accept Christ and follow him, to unite himself with them through baptism . . . so that he and his followers have separated themselves from the Christian Church, to raise up a sect of their own . . . such doctrine being harmful to the united usage of all Christendom and tending to offence-giving, to insurrection and sedition against the government."[N] The gruesome details concerning the mode of execution follow, with the added sentence: "In this way he shall have atoned to the law and to justice . . . his property is to be confiscated by the city government."[22] The last words of Felix Manz were, "Into thy hands, O Lord, I commend my spirit." Perhaps he saw the parallel between what was happening in his case and what had happened to Christ, who was likewise a victim of sacralist thinking, in which deviation from prevailing theological patterns implied sedition and thus called for capital punishment.

The execution of Felix Manz, horrible as it was, was not the end, nor even the ultimate, of the satanism that came with the new hybrid. When the Anabaptist Michael Sattler was put to death for the part he had played in the attempt to replace *Corpus Christianum* with *Corpus Christi*, the sentence read: "Michael is to be committed to the executioner, who is to take him to the city square and there cut out his tongue. Then he is to tie him to a wagon and with a red-hot pair of blacksmith tongs tear shreds of flesh from his body, doing so five times more on the way to the fire. He is to burn his body to powder, as an archheretic."[23] Michael Sattler was a true Christian and a dear child of God; his only fault was that he disliked the hybrid. On the very day that Felix Manz was disposed of in a way not even fit for a rabid dog, another of Grebel's associates, George Blaurock (so named because he usually wore a blue

---

[N] Again, it is the *regnum*, working hand in glove with the *sacerdotium*, that spearheads the liquidation of rival church folk, out of an imaginary fear of "sedition against the government." This should not surprise us, for in "Christian sacralism" loyalty on the level of the state and loyalty on the level of the church are seen as the same thing.

overcoat), was severely beaten for taking part in rival church activities. Two years later, on September 6, 1529, when he was the pastor of a small church of believers in the Tyrol, George was burned at the stake. That little group of believers was once more without a pastor; its previous one had been burned there a mere three months earlier. So it went, throughout various parts of Europe. A contemporary who prided himself in being neutral estimated that by the year 1530, only five years after the bifurcation had taken place, some two thousand persons had already been liquidated for lending a hand in the cause of the believers' church and the composite society. Such were the antics of the new hybrid.

No doubt the rigors practiced against the rival church can be explained in part by psychological considerations. The Anabaptists may have represented a guilty conscience to the magisterial reformers.º The Reformers and the Anabaptists had at the first stood together, but pressures by the *regnum* had caused the former to swing over, while the latter stood their ground. Members of the new rival church twitted the Reformers for yielding, and the magisterial reformers became very touchy about the matter. In assessing the behavior of those who yielded to the *regnum*, we must remember that the alternative was quite certain liquidation. This should make us less dissatisfied with them; for who does not shrink from such an end as that of Manz and Sattler and thousands of others? On the other hand, the courage of those who refused to capitulate to the demands of the *regnum* becomes the more heroic.

If we are to understand Zwingli's course in the matter of christening, we must remember that it was part of a larger concern — the question of the correctness of the *Volkskirche* (a church coextensive with a people). We may say that there were two Zwinglis in this matter, the one a theologian and the other a man of practical affairs. As a theologian, Zwingli saw clearly and confessed openly that christening has no support in the New Testament; as a man of practical affairs he saw as clearly

  ºThere must have been something rankling in Zwingli's bosom, some deep-seated grudge against his erstwhile friends and associates. How otherwise can we explain his deep hatred for them, a hatred that made him speak of and deal with the Anabaptists as though they were veritable demons, though on the previous page he had placed a long list of unevangelized pagans in heaven (Hercules, Theseus, Socrates, Aristides, Antigonus, Numa, Camillus, both the Catos, both the Scipios)?[24]

that to reject christening would not sit right with the *regnum*. It was at the confrontation of January 17, 1525, that the die was cast concerning which of the two Zwinglis would be in the driver's seat henceforward. But prior to the confrontation and the bifurcation, Zwingli had shared with the Grebel party their growing aversion to christening. In fact he may even have been one of their leaders; Manz at least thought so. After outlining his own objections to christening in a note to the City Council of Zürich, he said: "I am sure Master Ulrich understands this matter of baptism the same way we do, knows it even better perhaps — but for a reason which I do not know he does not reveal his views."[25] One wonders whether Manz was really in the dark about Zwingli's reason for not coming out openly against christening, for pulling back at the points where the *regnum* scowled. In any event, Zwingli said in the early days that the issue of christening was not of sufficient weight to justify division. However, he is reported to have said in a sermon that "nothing grieves me more than that I am at present obliged to baptize children, for I know it ought not to be done...." When Zwingli the theologian heard Grebel preach against christening, he said that it was "nothing but the clear Word of God" (Muralt, 184).

But then we see the other Zwingli come on the scene, the practical man of affairs, who backed away from incurring the displeasure of the *regnum* and who was driven by fear of having to do without the politically valuable institution known as christening. It is this Zwingli who says, after granting that christening is not supported by the New Testament, that because of the offense it would give, it would be better to preserve the institution. Word must have got around that Zwingli operated with this "however," for often questions about his position on christening were prefixed by the clause "If you left out of consideration the civil rulers ..." or "If you were able to do so without fear...." When the question came with this prefix, Zwingli's answer was that in such a hypothetical situation he would refrain from the act. Clearly, the final issue for Zwingli was not "What does the Bible teach in the matter?" but "How will it sit with the *regnum*?" Concerning the former question, Zwingli and the emerging rival church saw eye to eye; concerning the latter question, they went in opposite directions. There was a further consideration: Zwingli's salary was paid out of the common treasury; if he incurred the wrath of the civil rulers, his source of income would be cut off. Although he felt strongly enough against christening to say, "Nothing grieves me more than that I am at present obliged to baptize children, for I know it ought not to be done," he added in the same breath: "However, if I terminate it I fear for my prebend" (Muralt, 184).

It is not surprising that after the bifurcation the rival church constituency needled Zwingli for his servile attitude toward the civil rulers and for the swing to the right that resulted from it. One of the leaders in the rival church, Balthasar Hübmaier, threw this at him: "Today he preaches one thing and tomorrow he retracts it all again; to be specific, for years he has preached that infants should not be baptized and now he says they should be" (Muralt, 53). Zwingli was also given the following to think about:

> You used to hold to this same opinion, have written in support of it, have preached it from your pulpit, where hundreds heard it come out of your mouth. And now you make it sound as if they are all liars who allege this of you; yes, you make bold to say that such views never entered your mind. . . . Let me ask you how long you have been of your present opinion . . . ? You had been preaching the Gospel purely and clearly for five years. That was in 1523. . . . You admitted to me that children ought not to be baptized before they have been instructed in the faith. . . . My dear Zwingli, see how your words and your writings and your preachings agree with each other. May God enlighten you, and us all, so that your violence may be removed from devout people.[26]

Shortly after the fateful meeting of January 17, 1525, a change in Zwingli's thinking concerning the delineation of Christ's church started to become clear. In his *Commentaries* (written in March of that year) he began to define the church as a unit that included the whole *Volk*, all who have been christened, or, as he put it, all who "have been given their name in Christ." This included all those who lived within the boundaries of Christendom, including those who did not believe. Zwingli was honest enough in thus defining the church as *Corpus Christianum* to admit that the church so construed is not the church mentioned in the Apostles' Creed. He might, of course, have added that it is not mentioned in the New Testament either; but perhaps that would be asking a little too much of him.

At about this same time the concept of freedom of conscience, which was present in the early Zwingli, disappeared. Zwingli knew the concept of freedom of conscience only in the earliest years of his reformatory career. He had said in his earlier days that no matter how one were to turn and twist he would have to allow Zwingli his freedom in regard to baptism, an outward thing that is not tied to any age level. After the bifurcation he poured out his own wrath — and that of the *regnum* — on those whose policy was simply to make use of such "freedom." Zwingli had said that the question of waiting with baptism depended on whether it could be done "without disturbing brotherly love and unity." When it became apparent that it could not be done without considerable commotion, he withdrew the alternative. Even some of his best friends were unable to change direction as readily as he. One of them, Sebastian Hofmeister, when he heard the news of Zwingli's swing to the right, said: "Our brother Zwingli, if now he wants children baptized, errs from the mark and does not walk in the truth of the Gospel. Of a truth, they will not be able to force me to the baptism of my children. . . . You carry on in a Christian way if you reinstitute the true baptism of Christ which has been so long snowed under. That is what we have decided to do" (Hübmaier, p. 236).

Perhaps there will always remain some uncertainty and disagreement about just how much of an Anabaptist Zwingli was in his early years, before the *regnum* joined the fray. Not everyone will agree fully with a recent investigator, who writes: "It must be admitted that not only Zwingli but also other Swiss and South German reformers, e.g., Oecolampadius, and Capito, originally held views very similar to those of the Anabaptists."[27] However, there can be no doubt or diversity of opinion as to where he (and they) stood after the bifurcation had taken place; he was now squarely in the tradition of *Corpus Christianum*, firmly committed to the idea of a *Volkskirche*. Now he asked: "How could it be that a Church should be baptized in part and not baptized in part, seeing that the whole mass is one people, born the one of the other? It is to become 'one fold and one shepherd,'[p] is it not? How then could it be

---

[p] It is clear that Zwingli was misapplying the words of Jesus here; Jesus had said these things in connection with Jews and Gentiles coming together in one and the same new fellowship, but Zwingli bent them to say something about a single *Volk*.

right not to mark all the sheep with the same mark?"[28] Manifestly, Zwingli now considered baptism to be a sacrament, that is, a ritual whereby an already existing togetherness (that of a people) allegedly becomes a religious togetherness. That is why he argued: "Since all peoples and togethernesses have a distinguishing sign,[Q] God has always[R] given his people their own distinguishing sign too, so that they might not feel it to be a deficiency in their God when they saw others wearing their sign with reference to their idols, and as a consequence get the desire to go after them instead."[29] It is plain that Zwingli by this time had come to look upon baptism as a substitute on allegedly Christian terrain for an institution found already in pre-Christian situations, an institution serving there the same purpose for which baptism had allegedly been introduced. In Zwingli's thinking as it had come to stand now, a child is a proper object of baptism because it is part of an entity held together by such prereligious considerations as those of race, language, geography, and politics. In this theology a child is not considered a candidate for baptism because of its relationship to believing parents but because of its relationship to the *Volk*, which in the fiction of *Corpus Christianum* is said to be "Christian." It is quite apparent that by this time baptism was, in Zwingli's thinking, a sacrament pure and simple, that is, a device whereby an already existing togetherness allegedly becomes a religious togetherness. He could hardly have made it plainer that it was his neighbor's *Swissness* (and therefore his children's) that had put him under the water of baptism. In this new frame of mind Zwingli found himself agreeing with the words of Augustine (which the latter had invented to get out of a difficulty he had imposed upon himself): "Just as in the case of the thief on the cross salvation came to fruition even though baptism was, because of the necessity of the situation, not included . . . so also when baptism is present in the

[Q] It does not seem to have troubled Zwingli as he was saying all this that baptism is hardly a "distinguishing" sign, since it is completely invisible. He does not seem to have asked the question why it pleased God to have his people marked with a nondistinguishing mark. The reason for this divine choice is no doubt to be found in the fact that the "people of God" are a new togetherness, one in which all the older "distinguishing signs" are submerged and rendered meaningless.

[R] This "always" seems to have been inserted here to ward off the Anabaptist argument that even though the old Israel had such a distinguishing sign the "new Israel" does not have one.

case of the child but faith is not, because of the necessity of the situation, salvation comes to fruition."[30]

This kind of thinking seems to have been common to all the magisterial reformers. Bucer,[s] for example, in his rounds with the Anabaptists, who requested of him New Testament validation of christening, pointed to the Great Commission (Matt. 28:18) and then said triumphantly: "There we have abundant command for the baptism of infants. If we are to receive peoples then we have to receive them just as the people of Israel were received. And how was that? This way: 'I will be your God and the God of your seed.' Now I ask of you, are not the children an integral part of a *Volk*, born the one of the other . . . ? Consequently this is our position: just as the Jews were accepted so are we and our children accepted . . . by the device of the sacrament of regeneration."[31]

It should be noted that by this sort of reasoning the whole New Testament advancement over the Old has been lost again. In the Old Testament regime it was the Hebrew child's link with the *Volk* that made it a fit candidate for circumcision as a badge of belonging. However, after Pentecost a new structuring of the people of God emerged. With the conversion of Cornelius, as the apostle James instructed the church (gathered in what is known as the Synod of Jerusalem), God was "making a beginning" in gathering out of the various peoples a people of God unto his name, independent of any consideration of peoplehood. This subtle change in the structuring of the people of God was "amazing and for Jewish sensitivities quite revolutionary although adumbrated in the

---

[s]As with the other magisterial reformers of the first decade, there was a former Bucer and a latter one. He too had said: "If anyone should wish to wait with baptism . . . we would not on that account separate from him nor condemn him; let every man figure it out for himself; the kingdom of God does not consist in eating and drinking and therefore not in water baptism either, but in righteousness and peace and joy in the Holy Ghost."[32] This side of Bucer went into eclipse when it became apparent that the people of the *regnum* had other ideas about the permissibility of "waiting with baptism." Of Bucer too it was said that he "for years has preached correctly and properly about the sacrament — now however he has gone back on this and preaches in a different vein."[33] Bucer was well aware of the Anabaptists' argument that the Christian church has to be an improvement over the older one and that this ideal can best be reached if not everyone is baptized and included in the Christian togetherness but only those who are confessing persons; but the correctness of this early and late does not seem to have registered with him.

Old Testament prophesyings."³⁴ After Pentecost a people of God began to come into being in total disregard of all the biological and historical considerations according to which the people of God had been delineated hitherto; the new boundaries were to be determined by the presence of faith and by it exclusively. This new structuring of the people of God went into eclipse with the Constantinian change; all through the ensuing millennium it was not the child's link with its parents that caused it to be christened, but its link with an allegedly Christian *Volk*. Witness the fact that from the beginning of the change christening took place, if need be, without the parents' cooperation and at times even against their wishes — in what came to be known as *Zwangtaufe* (baptism by force).ᵀ In the theologies that came out of the magisterial reform the vision of the New Testament was not recovered; the conviction persisted that it is the child's link with an allegedly Christian *Volk*

ᵀ*Zwangtaufe* must strike a person as a pretty strange thing. It is that; but in the context of "Christian sacralism" it makes sense. If indeed baptism is a badge of integration with the political unit, there can be no omissions — no more than there can be in the paying of taxes. For example, in 1534 it was decreed in Strasbourg that "no citizen of this commonwealth is to leave his child unbaptized beyond the time of the mother's confinement . . . otherwise the Council will have it baptized and the delinquents will be punished as the case may require." This decree does not seem to have been altogether successful, for in February of the next year it was repeated. Nor was this an isolated instance of *Zwangtaufe*; baptisms performed against the parents' wishes were common. We read: "Our orders are to apprehend the parents, bringing them to me in chains but have the miller's children baptized . . . and delivered into the hands of the guilty man's brother." In one instance, *Zwangtaufe* was performed on the child of an Anabaptist named Schwarzhaus; he told his associates later that as soon as he and the child were back in their own home he had "washed the filth off again" ("den dregk wieder abgeweschenn"). This is not very reverent language, but it was occasioned by those who had made a circus of baptism. Years later, in 1577, it was recorded in a courthouse that "Michel Richter . . . has found his way into the sect and error of the Anabaptists, and in spite of the fact that his errors have been most faithfully pointed out and rebuked he still refuses to have his child baptized. Therefore, we were obliged to baptize said child, the civil authorities approving."³⁵ Philip of Hesse seems to have had some reservations about the propriety of *Zwangtaufe*. He at least asked a committee of theologians (consisting of one Reformed theologian, two Lutherans, and one Catholic) to present him with an advice concerning the matter. The committee was unanimous in saying that unbaptized children should be baptized over their parents' wishes. The recommended punishment varied, ranging from banishment to the death sentence.³⁶

that entitles it to baptism. In the camp of the magisterial reform Plato was quoted approvingly anent the matter; we read: "Plato has said, has he not, that we are born to and belong to the society of which we are a part more than we do to our parents."[37] The very fact that this was said in an attempt to get the Anabaptists out of the magisterial reformers' hair only shows how completely the subtle changes ushered in by the New Testament escaped the magisterial reformers. The eclipse that had begun in the days of the birth of the original hybrid continued on through the Reformation.[u]

By this time Zwingli's theology had become completely flat; he would have nothing to do with the third dimension, the dimension of early and late. Zwingli's final position also came as a reaction to the Anabaptist doctrine of early and late. One of the Anabaptist leaders, Pilgram Marpeck, had written a lengthy Defense, in which he had argued for a recognition of early and late: he said that just as there is a timeless Holy Spirit, one divine being, but with an earlier activity and a later one that began at Pentecost, so likewise is there in God's Word a yesterday and a today, definitely diverse in their outworking. Marpeck argued that if we ignore the early and late, many evils follow, among them a distortion regarding the proper place of the civil power. Zwingli rejected all this with vigor. He would have nothing to do with the idea of an older covenant and a new. He wrote:

> It is evident to all believers that the Christian covenant is nothing but the older covenant established with Abraham — with the sole exception that we Christians have Christ mani-

---

[u]Since then most pedobaptists have stopped basing infant baptism on the child's inclusion in an allegedly Christian *Volk*. Little by little they have gone over to the view that it is the child's link to believing parents that entitles it to baptism. In the thinking of most pedobaptists the people of God is no longer seen as coextensive with the *Volk*. Modern pedobaptists have once more embraced the "amazing and for Jewish sensitivities quite revolutionary" new structuring of the people of God, and thus have distanced themselves from typical reformation thinking. Of one thing we can be sure: since *Corpus Christianum* has been all but unanimously rejected, the controversy over the rightness or the wrongness of infant baptism has lost much of its bite.

> fested whereas they had him only in promise. . . .^v The various types in the Old Testament make this apparent; in the case of Isaac and Ishmael we read of it, and in the case of Jacob and Esau (in Gal. 4), that Esau was the firstborn and was rejected, Jacob moving up into his place; the signification here is that the Gentile people become God's people after the Jews have been rejected. Also this: Jacob had two wives, Lea and Rachel, of whom the one was strikingly prolific but the less-loved one; she represents the Jewish *Volk;* Rachel, who was unfruitful for a time, signifies the Gentile world which was to become the elect people of God, so taking the place of the Jewish *Volk.*

This is tricky hermeneutics, and it shows how desperate Zwingli was for biblical support of his idea that the New Testament thinks in terms of a covenant with a *Volk.*

Zwingli appropriated for his purpose the old *Lo-ammi* passage of Hosea: "This shows plainly that the Church consisting of a Gentile *Volk* has become the people of God, in the place of the Jewish *Volk.*" Again it is crystal clear that for Zwingli church and *Volk* are coextensive. Zwingli also made grateful use of "many shall come from the east and from the west" (Matt. 8:11), glossing very conveniently *die Menge* as the *Volk.* In Zwingli's *Schweitzerdeutsch, die Menge* means "the mass" or "the totality"; therefore, it would be hard to say in plainer terms that the structuring of society had not been changed. It would be difficult indeed to draw up a more daring defense of *Corpus Christianum* than that contained in this gloss.

If we should wish for still more evidence of the medieval cast of Zwingli's final position, we may look at a letter he wrote to the King of France, whom he wanted to stir up to do his "duty" by sustaining Protestantism and suppressing the Catholic "heresy."

> Since the visible Church comprises rebels and criminals, men who are without faith and who do not care about being ex-

^vZwingli (as well as the other magisterial reformers) seems not to have noticed that in the book of Hebrews the difference between the old covenant and the new is not that of promise and fulfillment; it is a matter of replacement, a new covenant that is put in the place of an older one. Hebrews speaks of a covenant that was abrogated and a new covenant put in its place, one in which it will no longer be necessary to say to a covenant-member "Know the Lord," since all will be knowing him already.

communicated,[W] even if done to them again and again, therefore the magistrate is needed to constrain the impudence of sinners. Since there are shepherds in the Church (by which, according to Jeremiah, is meant the princes) it is obvious that a Church without a magistrate is a defective and mutilated Church. Far from objecting to the magistrate . . . we teach that he is necessary unto the perfecting of the ecclesiastical body. . . . Just as men cannot exist unless body and soul be joined together, the body forming the more humble part, so cannot the Church exist without the magistrate, although the latter's concern is with the less exalted, the less spiritual things.[38]

Then, having gone this far in his admiration of the hybrid, Zwingli threw all restraint to the winds, urging the magistrate to violence in the area of religion:

Why should not the Christian magistrate destroy icons and abolish the mass, especially if he acts with the consent of the Church? This does not mean that he is to cut the throats of the priests if it is possible to avoid such cruelty. But if it is not possible, then we would not hesitate to imitate even the harshest examples, provided that the Spirit gives the same certainty which he gave those heroes of old. For, let me say this in passing, I know of bishops who will never cease to give trouble unless and until they meet up with an Elijah who puts them to the sword. In the meantime let us spare them if charity demands it because they still give ground for some hope. But if this charity commands us to kill them for the well-being of the body, then it is better to pluck out a blind eye than to run the risk of losing the whole body.[39]

By this "whole body" Zwingli meant, of course, the entity which we have called the *Corpus Christianum*. For the final Zwingli the "Christian municipality" was identical with the "visible church." The final Zwingli was not only ready to put up with the abhorrent hybrid, he was prepared to fondle the blundering beast. Just as Augustine had managed to evade the Donatists, Zwingli now managed to evade the Anabaptists by the device of a church both visible and invisible. Zwingli was fully aware that the two camps that had developed did not represent a new situation: he saw the close parallel that ex-

---

[W] No doubt this remark about excommunication was thrown in to offset the Anabaptist doctrine that in matters of religion there should be no punishment over and above excommunication, a doctrine which Zwingli obviously assumed the king had heard.

isted between the conflicts that had accompanied the birth of the original hybrid and the conflicts he was experiencing in connection with the birth of the new one. That is why he spurred the magistrates on in an effort to stamp out the rival church, with words such as these: "Don't give up; the Anabaptists are not going to win out; their cause is not of God, for it did not succeed a thousand years ago either."[40] The parallel between the rise of Constantinianism in the fourth century and the rise of neo-Constantinianism in the sixteenth is uncannily close: in both a period of correct thinking went before; in both the *regnum* led the way and the *sacerdotium* chimed in, hoping by so doing to escape the cross; in both instances a rival church then arose in protest. The similarities can be extended even further: in both instances a lunatic fringe of the rival church appeared (known as the *Circumcelliones* in the days of the early hybrid and as Münsterites in the days of the later one); in both instances those who assisted at the birth of the hybrid had to reverse their earlier convictions, Augustine in his *Retractationes* and the magisterial reformers in theirs.

We should not conclude that the bifurcation was occasioned by divergent views on the correctness of infant baptism. That would be too narrow a simplification; the issue was that of the rightness or the wrongness of "Christian sacralism," an issue in which infant baptism was immediately involved. One could also say that the central issue was that of *Corpus Christi* versus *Corpus Christianum*, or of the composite society versus the unanimous one. One could also say that it was a matter of salvation via the preached Word over against salvation via submission to sacrament. One could add the question whether a definitive life-style is a necessary feature of discipleship. And the issue could be put in many other ways. As a matter of fact, Zwingli had kowtowed to the *regnum* in regard to the other "sacrament"[x] before he did so in connection with

---

[x]In the matter of the Lord's Supper, with the christening issue, political considerations made the *regnum* of Zürich oppose Zwingli in the reforms he was proposing. City Hall checked Zwingli in this matter, saying: "To no one, least of all to the preachers, is it permissible to declare ancestral principles and institutions null and void. . . . By so doing the Holy Church, the holy fathers, the councils, the pope, the cardinals and bishops, and so on, will be mocked, disdained, made suspect, and then disobedience to the authorities, disunity, heresy . . . will ensue." This may

christening; and the people who were to peel off because of the christening question had rebuked him for it.

We have seen how Zwingli urged the use of the sword in support of the "right" religion. It was to be foreseen that this would lead to civil war, since some of the cantons of the Swiss federation went Protestant and some remained Catholic. Bloody conflict between the two "other arms," each doing its alleged duty, was therefore inevitable. In the summer of 1535, a mere decade after the new hybrid of the Reformation had risen to its feet, tensions between the two Christendoms rose to such heights that civil war broke out. On October 11 of that year, in a battle fought at Cappel, the Protestant forces met defeat. After this blow to the Protestant cause, Zwingli was no longer on hand to tell the *regnum* what was "of God" and what was not; his body was found slain on the field, his hand still clutching in death the musket he had shouldered in the service of the new hybrid. This was truly a horrible way for a career that had held such great promise at the outset to end. But the pit into which Zwingli had fallen was of his own digging: he had taught the *regnum* of the Protestant cantons that its duty was to suppress, by force of arms if need be, every religion but the "right" one; meanwhile, other men of the cloth were teaching the *regnum* of the Catholic cantons the same "wisdom." Since no one was able to settle for all parties concerned which was the "right" religion, civil war was the inevitable outcome.

Zwingli's last days were horror-filled. A few months before his death on the battlefield he had asked to be relieved of his office; but the *regnum*, to whom he had been so useful, was loath to let him go and persuaded him to stay on. In a sermon preached in those final agonizing days, Zwingli had said: "A chain has been forged and it is all complete, one that will cut off the head of many a devout Züricher."[41] A little later the hybrid held in its grisly maw the body of Ulrich Zwingli.

* * * * *

As we have already said, what happened at Zürich was in no way unique or confined to that area. The magisteriliza-

---

look like a hodgepodge of ideas, but it is not a hodgepodge at all; the quarrel was a coherent one. It all revolved around the question of whether or not the hybrid should be destroyed.

tion took place elsewhere, as did the bifurcation. In many other places there was first a wavering concerning the propriety of infant baptism, followed by a more rigorous attitude. That the matter of baptism played such an important role should not surprise us: the preservation of the old order depended on the preservation of christening, and the possibility of introducing a new order depended on its termination. As the Anabaptists saw things, christening was a supporting pillar of the Constantinian system, and as such its preservation militated against a true Christian church. They never tired of saying, "Wherever government and church are together, as in Berne, there can be no true church."[42] The reformers knew this too, and for a while they tried for the termination of christening; but when the *regnum* entered the picture and bared its teeth, the price went up, and many thereupon went magisterial. Zwingli was indeed one of the first to change direction, and some of his coworkers were quite perturbed at the news of his change. One of these, as mentioned above, was Sebastian Hofmeister. Had he stuck with his guns, he would have come over to the camp of the new rival church. Since he did not end up there, we must conclude that Hofmeister too pulled in his horns.

At Strasbourg the sequences were the same as at Zürich. Bucer, the Strasbourg reformer, said at the outset: "If anyone wishes to wait with baptism . . . we would not on that account separate from him nor condemn him." Because the reformers at Strasbourg were known for their leniency in the matter, quite a few people who were in trouble elsewhere for their rejection of christening came to Strasbourg to live. When the attitude of the *regnum* brought about a hardening there also, these were understandably disappointed. One of them, Conrad Haug, said: "The preachers here have been preaching for two years now that people are to be left free in the matter. . . . Capito and Bucer have assured us upon our arrival here that christening is not grounded in Scripture and will therefore be discontinued within a year; upon this I and my wife and children have come here to live." Another, Karl Meisinger, said: "I don't want my child baptized, because Capito said to me six years ago . . . that christening is a nothing and must go." However, Strasbourg followed the lead of Zürich and issued a series of codes — promising "punishment as the case may require" for anyone who left a child unbaptized "beyond the mother's confinement."

In these edicts the local *regnum* was merely following the supreme ruler, the emperor. He decreed in 1535:

> All those, be it male or female, who are found to be infected with the said condemned sects of rebaptizers ... whatever their class or condition; all who indulge in or adhere to, or aid in this, will incur the forfeiture of body and goods, and be put to death without delay. That is to say, by fire in the case of those who remain obstinate and persist in their evil opinions and designs, or who have borne or assumed the name of "prophets" or "popes" or "bishops"; all other persons who have been rebaptized or who have secretly and advisedly sheltered another or others of these said Anabapists, after having renounced their evil sentiments and opinions and being in a state of true contrition and remorse, these will be put to death with the sword if they are men[y] and by the pit[z] if they are women.[43]

In the face of such odds the reformers at Strasbourg also pulled in their horns, just as they had done at Zürich and elsewhere. They made room in their theology for the coercing *regnum:* to keep the peace they went magisterial. Presently we find Bucer saying that "magistrates are duty-bound not to tolerate anyone who assails or openly reviles the doctrine of the Gospel ... a man who refuses to be indoctrinated in the things that pertain to the doctrine of Christ is also not to be tolerated." The fact that he said all this in the face of representatives of the rival church only makes his defense of the hybrid and its ways all the more emphatic. One of his associates, Adam Krafft, added this: "He who is coerced today may come of his own accord tomorrow and will then thank his magistrate for forcing him to come. . . . Thus did the king of Nineveh. . . . The imperial edict of Nebuchadnezzar teaches all Christian magistrates that they do indeed have the duty of coercing to the faith."

As had been the case at Zürich, a heavy contributor to the bifurcation in other places was the matter of a definitive life-

---

[y] It is not surprising that the emperor prescribed death even in the case of the truly penitent. In "Christian sacralism" this is inevitable. For, at the bar of the *regnum* penitence does not stay the hand that metes out punishment. Penitence has a different meaning in the court of the *sacerdotium*, where it stops the process.

[z] The expression "by the pit" signifies death by being buried alive. This had been the common way of getting rid of female "heretics" during the centuries before the Reformation.

"AND ALSO AFTERWARD"

style. When the reformers went magisterial, it became impossible to say that true Christians are known by their way of life. That was bad enough, but when the magisterial reformers thereupon began to defend the latitudinarianism, those who were already breaking step with them found in this matter a weighty argument for going their own way. It is a fact that the magisterial reform did little or nothing to clean up the moral swamp the Reformation had inherited; some argued that in this respect things had become worse than they were. Balthasar Hübmaier, who became one of the leading spokesmen for the new rival church, wrote about this situation in these words:

> Yes, the old saying is being fulfilled "It goes from bad to worse, things are not getting better but worse. . . ." This punch in the jaw we have to endure from the side of the worldly ones, God have mercy on us. For we have to endure this because we keep excusing ourselves. For everybody nowadays wants to be a good Christian and soundly evangelical, by taking a wife, eating meat in lent, no longer bringing sacrifices, never fasting, never praying — but all we see is boozing, gourmandizing, blasphemy, usury-lifting, lying, cheating, swindling, violating, dispossessing, forcing, compelling, stealing, robbing, fire-setting, gambling, dancing, flirting, loafing, harloting, fornicating, raping, tyrannizing, garroting, murdering. . . . Yet (O the pain of it) all this transpires under the cover of the Gospel. And when you say to that kind of evangelical, "It is written, brother, cease from evil and do the good," they shoot back at you, "It is impossible for us to do good — all things are included in the decrees of God and thereby unavoidable." They think that by this device their sins become permissible.[A] And if you continue, "It is written, he that does evil shall go into fire that is not quenched," they quickly find an apron of fig leaves with which to cover their blasphemy, as they say, "It is written that faith alone saves us, not our works." With that kind of subtlety they manage to be and remain soundly evangelical.[44]

These are not exactly honeyed words; it is straight shoot-

[A] Reference is, of course, to the doctrine of the divine decrees as incorporated in most of the theologies that came out of the magisterial reformation. Augustine had made grateful use of this concept of the decrees because it helped him in his effort to keep the *Corpus Christi* from being discernible. The magisterial reformers may have been drawn to it for the same reason. It is interesting, to say the least, that the rival church, which had no need of the idea of an invisible church in contrast with the visible one, did not incorporate the doctrine of the decrees in their theological system.

ing. The interesting (and immensely significant) fact is that no one in the camp of the magisterial reformers offered to disprove these scathing assertions; in fact, they granted that the description was true to fact. They did argue at great length that the church of Christ is not defined in terms of life-style. Or they began to say that the Anabaptists' demands for a definitive life-style implied perfectionism.[B] Or they used the hackneyed argument that the Anabaptists' moral rectitude was bait, used by the devil, to attract a lot of fish. Now that we can look at the whole matter from some distance, it becomes clear that what Hübmaier said was not only timely but soundly correct. People were being taught only two of the three pivotal doctrines: 1) that we cannot save ourselves, 2) that it is by faith that we are saved; but the third doctrine, that salvation is not simply a matter of pardon but includes renewal, was being slighted. Hübmaier argued that under cover of these two half-truths all evil, unfaithfulness, and unrighteousness had gained the upper hand completely. He said that the camp of the magisterial reformation had failed to learn the lesson that faith without works is dead. The best rejoinder Luther himself was able to come up with was: "Doctrine and life are to be dis-

---

[B] The slur of "Perfectionism" had been used against people of the rival church ever since the days of Augustine. It was also cast in the face of the rival church in Reformation times. Calvin repeated it over and over. However, it was entirely unfair from the beginning. No Anabaptist claimed to have achieved the perfect life; in fact, they said over and over and in the plainest of language that they needed forgiveness often. Menno Simons, for example, confessed that "all my righteousness is nothing but a filthy rag." He added: "Think not that we boast of being perfect and without sin. Not at all. As for me, I confess that often my prayer is mixed with sin and my righteousness with unrighteousness."[45] Dirck Philips, another Anabaptist leader, argued that Christians are to be holy even as God is holy and that this must be understood to mean, not that Christians can or may become as holy as God is holy, but that they are to seek holiness with all earnestness, as Paul the apostle did when he said that his whole aim was to know Christ and the power of his resurrection." When Zwingli charged Hübmaier with perfectionism, the latter replied that the accusation was a monstrous injustice. On one occasion when Zwingli charged those of the rival church with perfectionism, Hübmaier said: "You do us wrong. If we spoke that way we would be mad indeed. . . . O God, what can such revilings mean! Ascribe not to us sinners a guilt for that which we hold no less in abhorrence than you do." Out of this conflict came the distinction between "living in sin" (which the child of God can *not* do) and "falling into sin" (which he can do and does). The distinction is indispensable if one is to be true to the biblical givens.

tinguished, the one from the other. With us conduct is as bad as it is with the papists. We don't oppose them [the Anabaptists] on the issue of conduct. Hus and Wyclif, who also made an issue of conduct, were not aware of this. . . . To treat of doctrine is to grab the goose by the neck."[46]

There is a chorus of testimony to the excellent life-style that prevailed among those who had chosen for the rival church. A great many people testified that it was this drawing card that had made them join it.[c] They kept up a continued appeal to the civil powers to stop taking the magisterial reformers' word for things. Two men who were in prison for their Anabaptism wrote to the landgrave Philip of Hesse, in whose territories they were jailed:

> Very well then, one man has as much to lose as the other . . . but Paul writes in Second Corinthians 5, "We must all appear before the judgment seat of Christ in order that each may receive according to the way he has lived, whether it be good or bad," or as Christ has it, "He who keeps my commandments the same is he that loves me . . ." or as the apostle puts it, "He who says he knows God but does not keep my commandments is a liar and the truth is not in him." That is why Paul says in Romans 2:5-16: "But thou, O man, by your hard and

---

[c]There is also a chorus of testimony that it was the failure of the magisterial reform in the matter of life-style that was driving people into the arms of the Anabaptists. One Anabaptist, after saying that he had "obtained much instruction from the writings of Luther, Zwingli, and others," went on to say: "However, we were aware of a great lack in the matter of repentance, conversion, and the true Christian life. It was on these things that my heart was set. I waited and hoped for a year or two, since the minister had much to say about amendment of life. . . . But I could not close my eyes to the fact that the doctrine which was being preached . . . was not carried out; no beginning was made toward true Christian conduct . . . true repentance and Christian love were not in evidence. . . . Then God sent his messengers, Conrad Grebel and others, who had surrendered themselves in the doctrine of Christ by conversion. With their assistance a congregation was formed in which repentance was in evidence by newness of life in Christ."[47] Even voices from the camp of the magisterial reform had to admit the reason for the swelling of the rival churches. Katharina Zell, the wife of the magisterial reformer, said to a roomful of preachers: "Better give yourselves the fault for it that in doctrine and life we are the effective cause that they separate themselves from us." She added, for good measure: "He who commits crime the magistrate should punish, but his business is not to coerce and play the boss in matters of faith, as you seem to think. This belongs to the heart and the conscience. . . ."

impenitent heart you are storing up wrath for yourself on the day when God's righteous judgment will be revealed, who will render to every man according to his works" — *works* it says, not according to a man's imagined or trumped up faith, but each man after his works, namely praise and honor and life everlasting to him who with patience in good works seeks after life eternal; to him however who is contentious and does not obey the truth — what is it God will give him? All one and the same, as the false apostles are saying? Paul says, "Not at all, but wrath and fury, tribulation and distress, to every soul of man that doeth evil. . . ." Those who in our times try with God's help to do these things, these the false teachers call hypocrites and they compare them with the man who stood in the temple boasting of his piety, in order that . . . no man may learn what the obedience of faith is. . . . What, O what, has become of the testimony of Christ in Matthew 12:36, "I tell you that every man shall give an account . . . of every idle word, in the day of judgment"! And the false teachers say, "If a man says that he believes that Christ has paid for him, has suffered in his place, has made atonement for him with God, let him live as he pleases, his sins are forgiven and blotted out, even though it doesn't look it." If however one takes a good look at their congregations, at the children they have begotten by their word, that is the way you will find it. Therefore we humbly pray Your Excellency to examine the Scriptures and judge our witness, our word, our conduct, in its light.[48]

Philip, if left to himself, was inclined toward toleration and leniency; but he was constantly being advised by the magisterial reformers, who were on his payroll, to bear down hard on the Anabaptists. He was torn between the two theologies that had drawn away from each other in the bifurcation, one school of thought that embraced the hybrid and one that detested the beast.

* * * * *

The initial measure of ambiguity in Zwingli's career, one that made the heirs of the older rival church look hopefully in his direction, and then a return to "Christian sacralism" as the result of involvement by the *regnum,* and then a bifurcation that resulted in the assembling of a new rival church — all this was also found in the career of Martin Luther. Luther too began at a place far to the left of his final position. Early in his career Luther was not the ardent pedobaptist he later became. He said in his earlier days that "there is not sufficient evidence from Scripture that would justify one in beginning infant baptism at the time of the early Christians after the apostolic period."[49] However, he added that "so much is evident that in our times no one may venture with a good conscience to reject or abandon infant baptism which has so long been practiced." Why, we are led to ask, did Luther add this remark about the venerability of the institution of christening? Was it perhaps because he sensed it that the *regnum* would not take to the idea that christening be terminated?

In those early days Luther said some things that were bound to cheer the hearts of all who were inclined toward the views that prevailed in the old free church tradition. In those early days (in 1523, two years before the eventful meeting held at Zürich), Luther wrote: "In matters of faith we have to do with a free act, one to which no one can be coerced. . . . Heresy is something spiritual; it can neither be bruised with iron nor burned with fire nor drowned in water; only the Word of God can overcome it. . . . The secular authorities should keep hands off, should busy themselves with their own affairs and let everyone believe this or that as he can or chooses; force must not be used in this area of life."[50] In that same year Luther said, "The soul's thoughts and reflections are revealed to no one but God; therefore, it is impossible to compel one with physical force to believe this or that. Another kind of compulsion does it; physical force does not."[51] This was surely music to the ears of the older "heretics."

In those early days Luther likewise manifested a profound dissatisfaction with the concept of *Corpus Christianum*. He saw very well that the word "church" had come to cover a lot more area than it does in the New Testament, and this caused him to toy with the possibility of two kinds of worship services — one attended by the *Corpus Christianum* and the other by the *Corpus Christi*. (It is interesting to note that Luther himself wanted to preach in the *Corpus Christi* assembly while a vicar officiated at the other gathering.) This ambition to recover the believers' church of the New Testament came to clear expression in Luther's *Deutsche Messe*, composed in 1526; in it he wrote: "They who seriously want to be Christians and want to confess to the Gospel in word and deed, these ought to have their names inscribed in a book and assemble in a house by themselves for the purpose of prayer, the reading of Scripture, the administration of baptism, the reception of the sacrament, and to engage in other Christian cultal acts . . . but I neither can nor may as yet set up such a gathering, for I do not as yet have the people for it. If, however, the time comes that I must do it, so that I cannot with a good conscience refrain from it, then I am ready to do my part."[52]

Are we to suppose that Luther had in mind a believers' baptism, one involving adults, who were among those who "seriously want to be Christians"? Was he thinking of a sort of second baptism for these? If so, Luther was at this point very close to the position of the Anabaptists. Was he thinking of restricting the sacrament (which in his parlance refers to the Lord's Supper) to the smaller gathering? We know that at this time he said that "the sacrament ought not to be broadcast among the populace as the paptists do." If this was what Luther had in mind here, he also stood very close to the position of the Anabaptists in this matter. In the *Deutsche Messe* he wrote of introducing church discipline in the smaller assembly; was he thinking of a *Corpus Christi* kept "pure" by discipline? If so, he was once more saying precisely what the Anabaptists were saying. The talk about "refraining" indicates that Luther was hanging back from taking a step that he knew he should take. The reason for his hanging back, says he, is that he did not as yet "have the people for it." However, it is more than likely that his main reason for dragging his feet was that he knew the step would not meet with approval by the *regnum*.

This early Luther also comes to expression in his celebrated *Grünendonnerstagpredigt*. In it he argued that if people were obliged to come to the sacrament rather than having it brought to them, "then you would see how few are Christians and how few would go. It should be feasible to do what I would fain do: assemble those apart who truly believe, in a separate place. I have wanted to do this for a long time but it has not been possible as yet; for we have not preached and agitated for it enough as yet. . . . We ought not to scatter the sacrament over the entire populace as the papacy has been doing."[53]

To his friend Nicolas Hausman Luther confided in 1523: "I have long contemplated prescribing a way of conducting the mass and of holding communion, but so far we have been unable to achieve this objective. I do have the intention, at a future date, not to let anyone partake when communion is served save those who have been interrogated and have given

"AND ALSO AFTERWARD"

satisfactory answers touching their faith; the rest we will exclude."54

In these early days Luther said that in the larger gathering "Christians and non-Christians sit together." One wonders how a person who has been christened can be called "non-Christian," and how people who are all members of *Corpus Christianum* can be thus divided into two mutually exclusive groups. But there were in the early Luther's thought system these and related ambiguities.D This earlier Luther went into oblivion with a swing to the right. And, as in the case of Zwingli, it happened in connection with a brush with the *regnum*. Luther's "kidnap" experience showed him that he needed the support and good will of the *regnum* if he as a person, as well as the Reformation as a cause, was to survive. The Luther that came out of Wartburg (to which the men of the *regnum* had whisked him for his survival) was not the same Luther that had gone into it. It was during his stay in the hideout that Luther went magisterial — with all the trimmings and implications.

This development gave Luther's cause a secure future; but it also led to a sizable exodus, to a "going forth from us of Anabaptists, Sacramentarians and other Faction-folk," as he himself put it. By going magisterial Luther lost some adherents on whom he had counted, and the loss grieved him. It should be remembered that as soon as the news of the nailing up of the theses had reached the far corners of Europe, Luther had received visitors at his door, official delegates from the existing rival church to the south and east. Luther liked what they said so well that he immediately agreed to write an introduction to a statement of faith they had just planned to put out, no doubt emboldened by the news concerning the theses. He wrote to his friend Spalatin enthusiastically about these visitors: "The Picards have sent some delegates to see me, to discuss their faith with me; it all looks quite good to me, except that they

---

DAn important difference is apparent, however, between Luther's thinking at this point and that of the rival church. Luther was thinking of a both-and situation, the rival church of an either-or; Luther wanted a church consisting of *Corpus Christi* plus a church consisting of *Corpus Christianum*, whereas the rival church wanted *Corpus Christianum* scuttled. In other words, Luther was ambiguous while the rival church was not. At the time Luther thought he saw a chance to be true to the New Testament without repudiating the hybrid; they saw no such chance.

use some barbarous phrases instead of the biblical ones. . . .[E] Whether they think correctly in the matter of faith and works[F] I am not sure, I rather doubt it."[55] History was to show that Luther and his visitors would clash with each other concerning the need for a contrasting life-style. When Luther went magisterial he made it impossible for himself to preserve the New Testament emphasis on "fruits bespeaking an inner change."

Thus Luther's swing to the right cost him dearly in terms of support from those who stood in the tradition of the old rival church. When it became apparent that Luther was making his peace with a new version of *Corpus Christianum,* a groan of disappointment arose from the camp of those who had looked hopefully in the direction of Wittenberg. Two things stand out in the charge with which those in the rival church tradition now began to rebuke Luther. One was that he had once more (as in the days of Constantine) welded the cross of Christ to the sword of the *regnum;* the other was that as a result he was letting down the bars in the matter of behavior patterns. The two accusations join hands in the following declaration, which emerged from old rival church circles:

> These two, Luther and Zwingli, have exposed all the knavery and tricks of the papal harlot, much as if they were out to smash it with thunderbolts; but they have not raised up a better holiness in its place, but have attached themselves to the worldly powers, having put their confidence in the help of man, and it has gone with them as with a man who as he patches an old kettle only makes the hole bigger; they have raised up a people utterly callous in sin.[56]

Other voices from those quarters said that although Luther had at the outset been in possession of the spirit of God, he had now become a veritable devil, the very antichrist. In addition, Luther had "fallen back to the beast," that is, back to the

---

[E] Just what these "barbarous phrases" were is not known, although it would be very interesting to know. Members of the rival church are known to have been partial to a text other than the Vulgate, and this may have caught Luther's ear. It is quite certain that as Luther worked at his translation of Scripture he leaned heavily upon "heretical" translations already in existence; it has been argued that he simply copied over whole pages from the "Picard Bible," a procedure for which his enemies in the Catholic Church rebuked him.

[F] It is apparent that Luther had already sensed that his heavy emphasis on salvation as pardon did not sit quite right with these visitors.

Roman school of thought which he was now defending, so that the kingdom of God which had previously come near to him was once more cast away. Still another complaint went this way: "This their doctrine Luther and Zwingli defend and sustain with the sword, a matter they have in reality learned from the father and head thereof, the antichrist, although they know right well that the weapons of the Christian are not physical but mighty before God. . . . Christ says to his disciples, 'If any man wishes to follow me . . . let him deny himself and take up his cross and follow me'; he doesn't say 'the sword,' for it has no place at all next to the cross, the two comparing as do Christ and Pilate, being as compatible as a sheep and a wolf."G In their complaints against Luther, these seceders summarized their position on the marriage of cross and sword:

> We say with truth on our side that the magistracy is not commanded with so much as a single word to rule in matters of faith or to play the master there — even though there are many in our day who cry out as they give the sword into the hands of the civil ruler in order to judge in matters of the faith — and they seek to justify this by referring to the Judges and Kings of Israel. They do this without firm grounding in the truth, even if we were to grant that the rulers in Israel were commanded in some fashion to punish idolatry and other such things. We allow this lapse seeing that it was a servile people of the Law, with whom everything was done by compulsion, its religion included. . . . Now however in the free-preaching Gospel of Christ all compulsion has been terminated, since it is not right, neither with force nor by constraint, to saddle anyone with the faith or to punish unbelief by means of the magistracy . . . which indeed some have acknowledged who now fight against it vehemently, this however because they were then the only ones who fought against the abominations, until that moment when others came up, persons who opposed their false constructions even as they opposed the papacy. Then misery and distress followed; they forgot their former teachings, turned their tongues around and constrained the civil power to pro-

―――――
GIt has become something of a legend that the so-called left wing of the Reformation abandoned the magisterial reformers because the latter did not go far enough. However, it is clear that what those in the old rival church tradition had against the mainline reformers was that they had completely changed direction, had abandoned their former position for a new one. The criticism was that just as in the days of Constantine the Christians had shirked the cross by accepting the flirtations of the *regnum*, so the magisterial reformers were evading the cross by kissing the hand of the *regnum*.

tect and sustain their false faith; they began to affirm the very thing against which they had written and contended, as, for example, that the magistrate must keep hands off in regard to the matters of faith.⁵⁷

It was but human for Luther to be hurt by this chorus of criticism for his return to "Christian sacralism." And it was but human for him to begin paying back in kind. Soon he was speaking of the Picards — the very people with whom he had once been taken in — as "those heretical Picards who crawl into their conventicles . . . to raise up a sect apart." In another place he refers to them as "those spiritual Jews and miserable heretics, who flee from evil Christians, to go off by themselves as they creep into conventicles. Oh those blasphemers and Christ-betrayers! The children of God do not flee from the fellowship of the evil ones. . . ."⁵⁸ The chorus of reproach issuing from the older rival church was augmented by many voices from the new. These rebuked Luther for not having been brave enough to reinstitute the believers' church of the New Testament. He had said that he didn't "have the people for it as yet," but his critics ascribed Luther's hesitation to fear of the consequences. The fact that members of the rival church did what Luther said could not be done, and did it with nothing less than phenomenal success, must have been a bitter pill for Luther to swallow.

Now that Luther had returned to "Christian sacralism," there was no longer any ambiguity in his position. As with Zwingli (and with Augustine long before), Luther's swing to the right required some *Retractationes*. Now he retracted his earlier assertion that "heresy is something spiritual" and that "only the Word of God can overcome it," and certainly his teaching that "the secular authority should keep hands off, busy itself with its own affairs and let everyone believe this or that as he can or may."ᴴ Now Luther was firmly in favor of

---

ᴴIt was a good thing for Luther that he did not continue to talk as he had once talked; it might have cost him his cloth, if not his life. During these years a Protestant minister, Anton Engelbrecht, was unfrocked in the Strasbourg area "because he refuses to sustain sound teaching concerning baptism . . . and puts forth a new and perverse Anabaptist error, namely, that the magistrate must leave everyone to his own devices in matters of religion." Nor was Engelbrecht the only Protestant pastor to lose his cloth for saying that the Anabaptists were not completely wrong,

a "right" religion sustained, propagated, and enforced by the sword of steel; now he lauded the practice which he reported to Leonhard Beyer, a parish priest at Zwickau, and recommended to him: "By the authority and in the name of the Most Serene Prince we usually frighten and threaten with punishment and exile all those who are negligent in religious matters and do not come to the sermons. This is the first step. If they do not improve their ways we then instruct the priests in charge to set a time limit, a month or so, that they may listen to reason. After that, if they remain obdurate they are excluded from the community and all contact with them ceases. . . ."[59] Now he said that "heretics who dare teach matters contrary to the faith as it is clearly founded on the Scriptures and professed by all Christendom . . . should not be tolerated but punished as blasphemers. . . . Moses laid down in his law that such blasphemers and all false teachers should be stoned."[60]

Now that Luther had gone magisterial, he was able to put his name to a *Recommendation* submitted to Philip of Hesse, who, progressive thinker that he was, was questioning the "duty" of the magistrate to put heretics to death. In this piece drawn up by Luther, Bugenhagen, and Creutziger, we read:

> Every person is duty-bound to prevent and suppress blasphemy, each according to his status. By virtue of this commandment princes and civil authorities have the power and the duty to abolish unlawful cults and to establish orthodox teaching and worship. Concerning this point Leviticus applies: "He that blasphemeth the name of the Lord, let him be put to death." . . . Princes must not only protect the goods and the physical being of their subjects but their most essential function is to promote the honor of God, to repress blasphemy and idolatry. That is why in the Old Testament the kings . . . put false prophets and idolaters to death. Such examples apply to the function of the princes.[61]

From these quotations it is clear that Luther's theology had gone completely flat. The changes dictated by the New Testament had been obscured: Paul prescribed *excommunicatio* for a sin (that of incest) for which the Old Testament regime

---

that if the Anabaptists harbored erroneous ideas the same was true of John Calvin. In these years Adrian van Haemstede was deposed (and banished) for his "errors."

had prescribed *exterminatio* (in the sense of liquidation). Luther had turned the clock back in this matter — beyond Paul — to the Old Testament dispensation and its prescriptions.

The early Luther had talked about introducing some kind of church discipline whereby at least the contemplated *ecclesiola* in the *ecclesia* could maintain certain standards.[1] This fine plan also went into the moth balls as a result of the swing to the right. His theology, which had from the start shown an imbalance in favor of salvation as pardon at the expense of salvation as renewal, hardened significantly. To a friend and fellow worker who was trying to work out some kind of church discipline Luther said: "I was glad to hear of your zeal . . . for Christian discipline"; but he added that "in this sad time . . . to introduce it is a thing I don't dare to try." Then he added, in language that is so typical of the man: "You know, you have to let a peasant do his bit of boozing and a drunken guy will wet a haycock down."[62]

The final Luther, the man who had earlier talked of holding a worship service for "true" Christians exclusively, was now unambiguously opposed to any gathering for religious worship save that espoused by the *regnum* and geared to the *Volk* in its entirety — as opposed as Plato had ever been. It was this final Luther who wrote:

> Conventicles are in no case to be tolerated . . . these are the thieves and murderers of whom Christ spoke in John 10:8, persons who invade another man's parish and usurp another man's office, conduct not commanded them but forbidden to them. And a citizen is obliged, if and when such a sneak-thief comes, before he listens to him or lets him teach, to inform his civil magistrate as well as the pastor whose parishioner he is. If he fails to do this then let him realize that he behaves like one unfaithful to his magistrate and acts contrary to his oath, and,

---

[1] The concept of church discipline is an embarrassment in every sacral system, so it was an embarrassment to the magisterial reformers. In their embarrassment they took recourse to the argument, used for example, at the Bern Confrontation in 1531 and 1538. This argument was that the discipline set forth in the New Testament was only an interim arrangement intended for the era between the loss of the right of the sword in New Testament times and the recovery of it with the Constantinian change; after that church discipline was "no longer needed" since the church had again received the power of the sword! Thus it comes as no surprise that in the case of Zwingli, from the year 1526 on the concept of church discipline disappears.

as a despiser of the pastor whom he is obliged to respect, acts against God. Moreover, he thereby becomes himself guilty and has become a thief and a rogue along with the sneak-thief.... They must neither be tolerated not listened to, even though they seek to preach the pure Gospel, yes, even if they are angelic and simon-pure Gabriels from heaven.... Therefore let everyone ponder this, that if he wants to preach or teach let him exhibit the call or commission that drives him to it or else let him keep his mouth shut. If he refuses this then let the magistrate consign the scoundrel into the hands of his proper master — whose name is Master Hans [a euphemism for the hangman].[63]

Nor was this mere *theory* as to how leaders of conventicles should be dealt with, merely a brief eruption from Luther's ebullient soul. It was a piece of theology well thought through and plainly stated, with its practical and legal implications. "Meetings in private houses and forests are to be prevented with all diligence, no matter what is read or preached in them, nor how good it may be in itself, these gatherings have not only a dimension of schism in regard to the church but also a dimension of sedition with reference to society, and give occasion to all sorts of disobedience and immorality — for which reason they must not be tolerated."[64] The concept of the conventicle was well defined: "They who conduct conventicles are persons who without license and permission by the *regnum* make bold to preach, likewise such as preach in unusual places and the wrong ones."[J] Under constant pressure from the magisterial reformers, Philip of Hesse declared that whoever violated the preaching office by assuming it without a call would be banished in perpetuity upon pain of capital punishment if ever he came back. Nor was this mere theory: agents were constantly circulating with their eyes on abandoned buildings, caves, or clearings in forests, for the purpose of bringing to the police people who conducted or attended conventicles. We read of a raid in the vicinity of a little place called Bacha: "As the gates were being closed for the night we conducted a search at

[J]There are many cases on record of persons in possession of a legal "call" by the *regnum-sacerdotium* combination who went to the conventicles of the rival church, in some cases even conducted them; the last phrase in this official statement seems to have been added in order to include this kind of Nicodemite of the cloth.

suspected places; and we found one Melchior Rinck[K] together with twelve others . . . gathered together; we were able to ascertain that there had been preaching. . . . They were put in prison."[65]

Since the theology of one who begins to think in terms of *Corpus Christianum* must necessarily become sacramental (because sacrament makes a pre-religious togetherness into a religious togetherness), it is no wonder that Luther's final theology was sacramental. Sacramental theology conceives of grace as something that works automatically, that is, not contingent on human response to an overture; we find Luther supporting such sacramentalism. He looked upon the teaching sustained in the rival church that believing decision is required as altogether objectionable. It is apparent that the final Luther knew the hybrid for the mixed up beast it was, knew of its origin in the distant past with Augustine (whose name was attached to the order to which Luther had belonged), knew its ways, and knew that there was a rival church that disliked the hybrid's ways—but Luther supported it nonetheless. What had happened in the German Reformation was described in these words by a French historian: "The German Christianity which had set out to free the Christian religion from paganism ended up by itself returning to the central principle of antiquity, namely, the close union of priest as well as cult with the civil municipality."[66]

* * * * *

It remains to take a look at that segment of the Reformation for which John Calvin set the pace. Calvin was unlike the rest of the reformers in that he did far less of an about-face: with him there was not such a clear swing to the right as there was with the other reformers. Some would argue that this otherness of the Genevan reformer was due to his logical mind. But it is rather to be ascribed to the simple fact that Calvin appeared on the scene too late to share in the ambiguities of the earliest moments of the Reformation. His career began *after* the die had been cast; the bifurcation had already

---

[K]Melchior Rinck was a well-known Anabaptist leader, also known as "the Greek" because of his proficiency in the language of the New Testament.

occurred.ᴸ However, the side chosen by Calvin in the controversy concerning *Corpus Christi* versus *Corpus Christianum* is not in doubt: he stood squarely with the magisterial reformers. In fact, it can be said that he was the most magisterial of all.

Let us look first at Calvin's doctrine of the church: in setting forth his views on the church in the *Institutes*, the first thing he wishes to make plain is this:

> The Scriptures speak of the Church in two ways; sometimes when they speak of the Church they mean the Church as it really is before God, the Church into which none are admitted but those who by the gift of adoption are the sons of God and by the sanctification of the Spirit are true members of Christ . . . often too by the name Church is designated the whole body of mankind who by baptism are initiated into the faith; by partaking of the Lord's Supper profess unity in true doctrine and charity, agree in holding the Word of the Lord and observe the ministry which Christ has appointed for the preaching of it. In this Church there is a large admixture of hypocrites who have nothing of Christ but the name and outward appearance, ambitious, avaricious, envious, evil-speaking men, some of impure lives moreover.

A much simpler way of saying this would be that the church both is and is not *Corpus Christi*, is and is not *Corpus Christianum*, and that society both is and is not composite, is and is not unanimous. Calvin does not recognize a church that is not the front side of the state (or vice versa). It is clear that Calvin wanted to retain the everybody-embracing church and at the same time stay out of trouble with the New Testament. He found himself in the same dilemma into which Augustine had

---

ᴸThis does not mean that Calvin was not influenced by the pre-Reformation rival church in any way; it is altogether likely that he too owed a debt to it. In his biography of Calvin, Beza says that "he received his first impressions of true religion from Olivetan." Olivetan, who was Calvin's cousin, had been active in the Waldensian church, was even a Waldensian pastor, according to some. The first Bible in French translation printed at Geneva was the work of Olivetan. Also, while Calvin was engrossed in Seneca (from whose grasp he never fully escaped) while a student in Paris, he lived with Etienne de la Forge, another Waldensian. Calvin acknowledged (to Czerwenka, a delegate sent to Strasbourg from the Bohemian rival church) that he too "was at one time a Waldensian." Perhaps the rival church, against which Calvin raged, represented his bad conscience in that it reminded him of his own switch from a Picardian past to the magisterial reformation, a step to which his contact with the Renaissance mentality had taken him.

worked himself a millennium earlier. And Calvin made grateful use of every device Augustine had invented to get out of his self-imposed difficulty. Calvin also took refuge in the device of a visible-invisible configuration of the church; in fact, Calvin offered to fix the ratio between the two "churches" by referring to "a small and contemptible number hidden in a huge multitude, a few grains of wheat hidden in a large pile of chaff." Following Augustine, Calvin also made abundant use of the concept of election in eternity to bolster the idea of a church that was indiscernible, "as it really is before God." Like Augustine, Calvin fought with all his might against the idea that the church is discernible — in the life-style of its members.

Calvin did not object to having the church defined as *Corpus Christi,* provided that in the next breath it was defined as *Corpus Christianum* — a clear case of trying to blow hot and cold at once. As the German theologian Wernle has pointed out, there were in Calvin's mind "three concepts of the church, each of which spoke its piece to him: 1) the invisible church of the elect, 2) the visible church held together by Word and sacrament, 3) the church of the saints with its criterion of the inoffensive life and the employment of discipline to keep it free of offence."[67] And it is understandable that a contemporary scholar, Arthur Cushman McGiffert, comes to the conclusion that "Calvin's doctrine of the Church was a composite of many and diverse and inconsistent elements, and because of this, confusion concerning the meaning, the place, and the purpose of the Church has since his day reigned almost everywhere in the Reformed wing of Protestantism."[68] (One finds it difficult to disagree with this, except to say that it is not necessary to single out "the Reformed wing of Protestantism," since the same confusion reigns in all other "wings" of the Reformation.)

It has been said that it is the conception of a free church consisting of freely committed and practicing believers, as opposed to the inclusive state church of the Catholics and most Protestants, that formed the basic doctrine of the Anabaptists. If this is true, then we know what Calvin's attitude toward the new rival church was bound to be — utter disagreement.

In 1527, the Anabaptists held a secret conference at Schleitheim (near Schafhausen), where they drew up a brief credal statement, which Calvin somewhat later undertook to refute item by item.ᴹ The Schleitheim statement contained among other things a definition of the church, the issue that was central in the bifurcation which had taken place. It was no doubt written in order to keep the heirs of the old rival church from being influenced and drawn away by the both-and definition advanced by the magisterial reformers. Schleitheim defined the church as "a fellowship of the saints, namely, of all believing and regenerate Christians and children of God, born again from above by the Word and the Spirit." Calvin "refuted" this statement at some length, offering as a substitute for its definition of the church "that mass among whom the Word of God is purely preached and the sacraments administered according to the institution of Christ." Later, the Belgic Confession (Article 27) defined the church as "a holy congregation of true Christian believers, all expecting their salvation in Jesus Christ, being washed by his blood, sanctified and sealed by the Holy Spirit." Significantly, Calvin did not feel the need to refute this definition, so very similar to the one drawn up at Schleitheim. Both of them are excellent definitions of the church as *Corpus Christi,* and the Anabaptists would have been altogether in agreement with the Belgic Confession's definition. Why, we must ask, did Calvin "refute" Schleitheim and give at least tacit approval to the Belgic Confession? The answer is very simple: the Belgic Confession gives what is virtually a second definition of the church in Article 29, this time defining the church as *Corpus Christianum.* In this second definition the church is said to be that place where "the pure doctrine of the gospel is preached. . . ." Clearly, it was because the Schleitheim confession defined the church as *Corpus Christi* alone that Calvin got on his high horse about it; for

---

ᴹThe very fact that a need was felt so early in rival church circles — a mere three years after the bifurcation — for a conference and the issuing of a credal statement poses an insoluble problem to all who begin the story of the Reformation at 1517. The postscript to the seven articles reads as follows: "Beloved . . . these are the articles about which some of the brethren have erred until now, things that have not been understood in the same way, so that many weak consciences have been troubled and the name of God greatly dishonored, for which reason it had become necessary for us to come to unity. To God the praise!" The problem concerning which the meeting was called was that those of the old rival church had sensed a new danger, posed by the emerging magisterial reform. Schleitheim is plainly slanted against the magisterial reformers; small wonder Calvin made it his business to refute it!

he had no objection to defining the church as *Corpus Christi* so long as it is defined as *Corpus Christianum* in the next breath.^N

The Schleitheim confession also contained a definition of the state, one that likewise elicited Calvin's ire because it went in opposite direction of his own. For Calvin the divinely intended function of the state was "not merely . . . to enable men to breathe, eat, drink, and be warmed . . . but it is that no idolatry, no blasphemy against the name of God, no calumnies against his truth, nor other offences to religion, break out and be disseminated among the people. . . ." Calvin's view of the state was that of Seneca, so that he declared: "Wherefore no man can doubt that civil authority is, in the sight of God, not only sacred and lawful, but most sacred, and by far the most honorable of all stations in mortal life."[69] It is no surprise that he took great pains to "refute" Schleitheim at this point especially. It had said: "The sword is an ordinance outside the perfection of Christ; princes and rulers are ordained for the punishment of evil-doers and for putting such to death. Within the perfection of Christ excommunication is the ultimate in punishment, physical death being not included in it." This excellent formulation avoids saying that the *regnum* is of the devil; it avoids likewise making the *regnum* an institution of redeeming grace. Schleitheim proceeds on the tacit assumption that grace is progressive, that the state is the creature of preliminary (conserving or "common") grace and the church the creature of subsequent (redeeming or "special") grace. The Schleitheim conception of the state and the neat distinctions made in it contain insights that are amazing in the light of the times. It is true, one might perhaps wish that Schleitheim had used some other expression than "the perfec-

---

^NManifestly, both the old evangelicals and the new drilled their own definition of the church into the minds of their followers. When Hans Kuchenbäcker, an Anabaptist, defined the church as "a fellowship of the saints, consisting of believing twice-born Christians and children of God, born from above by the Word and the Spirit," those who followed the magisterial reformation "corrected" the man's "error" thus: "When we talk about the church . . . then we mean that mass among whom the Word of God is preached and the sacraments administered after the institution of Christ; wherever these two features are present there we are not to question that God most certainly has among the big pile of called ones his little heap of truly believing ones, be they as few or as many as may be the case."[70]

tion of Christ" for *Corpus Christi;* but that raises the question of what expression could have been used instead. The word "church" had to be avoided, for that term was standard for *Corpus Christianum;* nor could the Low German word *gemeynte* be used, because that word was in common use for parish, the local segment of the church-state combination.[o] It was necessary, therefore, to coin a new term, one not already freighted with unwanted connotation.

In the light of Schleitheim — and of countless other utterances issuing from Anabaptist circles, all saying that the magistrate is "of God" — it is most discouraging to note that the magisterial reformers constantly said that they were "against government," as the Belgic Confession continues to say of them to this day. Rather than deliberate character assassination, perhaps this persistent charge that the Anabaptists were anarchists was an honest (but frightful) inability to understand what the Anabaptists were saying. So intertwined were church and state in the thought system of the magisterial reformers that anyone who said the sword had no place in the church's affairs was understood to be saying that it has no place in society. People had to distance themselves first from the Constantinian heritage before they would be able to perceive what the Anabaptists were driving at.

As mentioned above, Calvin wrote a "refutation" of Schleitheim's definition of the *regnum* (or, as it was called in those days, the "magistracy"). In the course of his attempted refutation, he quoted I Corinthians 12:21, where we read: "The eye cannot say to the hand, nor the head to the feet, 'I have no need of you.'" It would be difficult to tip one's hand more conclusively than Calvin does here: for his quoting of this text in this argument shows clearly that he considered church and state to be two parts of the same body, related to each other as the eye to the hand or the head to the feet. All this was said by Calvin to prove that the sword is not an "ordinance of God outside the church," as the Schleitheim statement contended. Calvin and his adherents quoted a second passage — I Corinthians 12:28 — in support of "Christian sacralism." The Anabaptists had challenged the magisterial reformers to find

---

[o]In some areas of the southern United States a county is called a *parish;* here the word, which once connoted simultaneously an ecclesiastical unit and a political one, has lost its former connotation and retains only its latter one.

a passage in the New Testament that speaks of the magistracy as something within the church. Although this was impossible to do, since the New Testament contains no such passage, Calvin was not stumped; he came up with the text: "God has set some in the Church, first apostles, secondarily prophets . . . after that . . . governments" (vs. 28). This hermeneutics is surely open to serious challenge, for it makes "government" a *charism* within the Christian church, in the same category as and on a par with such "gifts" as "miracle-working" and "tongue-speaking." The "governments" of this passage have to do with offices or functions in the *sacerdotium*, not in the *regnum*, as Calvin would have us think. Calvin found still another New Testament text (he knew that those of Schleitheim would yield to no other) with which to "refute" the rival church's conception of the state: it was the passage in which he says "Paul" (Calvin was mistaken; it actually was Peter) wrote against "despising governments," which he said the Anabaptists were guilty of. However, the Anabaptists regularly spoke of the *regnum* as a thing instituted by God, and it is hard to see how this adds up to a "despising."

In all this Calvin was but working out the principles stated in his *Institutes* concerning the *regnum*:

> Civil government is designed as long as we live in this world, to cherish and support the external worship of God, to preserve the pure doctrine of religion, to defend the constitution of the Church. . . . No government can be happily constituted unless the first object be the promotion of piety. . . . All laws are preposterous which neglect the claims of God and merely provide for the interest of men. Therefore as religion holds the first place among all philosophers and as this has always been regarded by the universal consent of nations,[p] therefore Christian princes and magistrates ought to be ashamed of their indolence if they do not make it the object of their most serious care.

It comes as no surprise that since Calvin closed his eyes to the early and late of Scripture, he stumbled into the same spurious early and late into which Augustine had stumbled before him. Calvin spoke of the pre-Constantinian times as an

---

[p] The assumption seems to be that the New Testament has nothing to teach us which "all nations" and their "philosophers" did not already know and practice. Our guess is that Seneca was one of the "philosophers" Calvin had in mind here, from whom he had derived much of his concept of the state.

era "in which the dignity of the Church still lay hidden." In his attack upon Schleitheim, Calvin argued: "We serve the same God our ancestors served; we have the same law and rule which they had. . . . It follows therefore that we ought not to expel from among us the institution of civil justice nor drive it out of the Christian Church."[71] It has been said that of all the Reformers none understood the Anabaptists less than did Calvin.[q][72] He writes as though the Anabaptists were out to "expel from among us the institution of civil justice," although no one among them had so much as hinted at any such thing. The Anabaptists did insist that the sword of the magistrate has no function in the church; but Calvin was so engrossed in "Christian sacralism" that he was unable to grasp the difference between expelling the sword from church affairs and expelling it from civil affairs.

In view of all this, it is not surprising that Calvin was firmly opposed to the conventicle, to all worship not done under public auspices. In this matter he stood with Plato's *Laws*. In the matter of the conventicle he lectured the rival church severely, so severely that they winced and complained that he was too severe with them. In a couple of tracts with which Calvin made his debut in the Low Countries in 1543 (the area in which he was determined to gain his greatest victories), he scolded all evangelicals who did not agitate for a magistrate-supported cult of religion but were satisfied to meet in conventicle. What displeased Calvin was not so much the lack of fortitude he thought he saw in the conventicle-goers, nor even their Nicodemitism — though he rebuked these too. What irked him primarily was that the conventicle made reform espoused by *regnum* that much less likely. The conventicle was seen by Calvin as an obstacle to the magisterialization of the reform. The final counsel given in these tracts is: "If all those whom our Lord has enlightened would with one accord and all together have the fortitude rather to die, leave everything behind, than to profane themselves with wicked superstitions, then He would come to their assistance with means which we do not know as yet[73] . . . . " The "means" Calvin had in mind was the conversion of the princes and their

---

[q]The fact that Calvin did not know the German language must have contributed to his failure to understand Anabaptism; he was dependent on secondhand information concerning it.

officers, to the tearing down of idolatries and the restoration of the true worship of God.

In the light of what we have observed in Calvin thus far, it is not really surprising that he endorsed the notion that it is the duty of the *regnum* to put heretics to death. He wrote: "Whosoever shall now contend that it is unjust to put heretics and blasphemers to death will, knowingly or unknowingly, incur their very guilt. This is not laid down on human authority; it is God that speaks and prescribes it as a perpetual[R] rule for the Church." The burning of Servetus was the logical outcome of this thinking.

On the other hand, the rival church had said at Schleitheim that the ultimate punishment for heresy is expulsion from the gathering of the faithful, adding (for good measure and to make the point unmistakably clear) that that does not include "physical death." Acting on these insights, it had introduced church discipline in the form of excommunication — with no more said, no *civil* penalty. For Calvin, as for all who hold to "Christian sacralism," church discipline was a knotty problem. When the *regnum* and the *sacerdotium* together constitute a single entity, a person expelled from the latter cannot remain in good standing with the former; exclusion from society must then follow. In this view, *exterminatio* and *excommunicatio* are implied in each other. Perhaps Calvin had not yet been able to work the idea of church discipline into his system.[S] Although the Belgic Confession spoke of the exer-

[R]The word "perpetual" is no doubt introduced here to offset the Anabaptist idea that although death for heresy was enjoined in the Old Testament it was not intended for the New.

[S]There is not much doubt that the concept of church discipline in the form of an *excommunicatio* without *exterminatio* was first worked out in the circles of the rival church and from there was later appropriated by the mainline reformers. Calvin spoke of the Anabaptists as "ingrates" who had pilfered their idea of church discipline "from us." If by "us" he meant his own person, it is clearly a false accusation; for in 1527 (the date of Schleitheim) Calvin was a lad in his teens. Moreover, Grebel, in a letter to Thomas Müntzer, had already spelled out a well-articulated doctrine of church discipline in 1524, when Calvin was a lad of fifteen. Even if we take the "us" to refer to the camp of the magisterial reformers in general, the charge Calvin made still cannot be taken seriously; for in 1527 (not to say 1524) nobody in the camp of the magisterial reformers had written a word pointing in the direction of an *excommunicatio* that did not imply *exterminatio*. Furthermore, when the mainline reformers came across church discipline as practiced among the Bohemian Brethren, they were amazed, almost entranced. The ascription of "ingrate pilferers" is totally un-

cise of discipline as one of the "marks" of the true church, the French Confession, written at virtually the same time and having Calvin's approval, did not mention any such "third mark."

In any event, the liquidation of Servetus tells us plainly how flat Calvin's theology was. Here was a man who was said to be — and certainly was — off the beam in certain areas of theology. If he had been a member of the rival church, he would have been read out of the fellowship, period. But in Calvin's mind Servetus was a member of *Corpus Christianum,* and that implied that discipline in his case would not stop short of *exterminatio*. To be sure, Servetus was guilty of heresy; but in Calvin's thinking the old legal identification of heresy with sedition (in vogue since Theodosius) still stood. That is why Calvin was able to plan Servetus' *exterminatio* for an infraction in the area of theology; he wrote beforehand of the ill-fated Spaniard: "If ever he comes to the city and my authority then counts for aught, I will never let him get out of the city alive."[74] That is how Calvin came to make the matter of Servetus pending not in the court of the *sacerdotium* (where it belonged) but in the civil court of the *regnum* (where it did not belong). Some have tried to make something of the fact that, late in the trial of Servetus, Calvin put forth an effort to have the man destroyed in some other way than by fire. However, the fact is that Calvin was not opposed to *exterminatio* in the case of Servetus, merely against the proposed mode. Death by fire had been the punishment for heretics for more than a millennium, and Calvin, realizing that death for heresy was becoming questionable in the public mind, would have preferred execution by a means in which the sedition aspect rather than the heresy aspect of the man's deliction would stand out. In Calvin's mind, the one still implied the other — heresy implied sedition.

The burning of Servetus was accepted as right and proper throughout the ranks of the magisterial reformers. Melanchthon congratulated Calvin for the part he had played in the frightful event: "To you the Church owes now and always will owe a debt of gratitude. . . . I affirm that your magistrates did the

---

acceptable: it is simply impossible that the Anabaptists "pilfered" from anybody in the camp of the magisterial reformers in 1527 or 1524; there was nothing to pilfer in the matter of church discipline.

right thing when they put the blasphemer to death."[75] Although approval was not entirely unanimous in the camp of the magisterial reformers, criticism came mainly from rival church circles. For example, while Servetus was on trial, there was an Anabaptist living in Switzerland — where he had gone to escape the magisterial reformers — under the assumed name of Jan van Brugge (his real name was David Joris). He tried to restrain the *regnum* of Geneva in the Servetus affair with these words:

> Noble, wise, prudent Lords, consider what would happen if every liberty were granted to men's opponents to kill heretics. How many men would remain on earth if each had the power over the other according to their mutual definition of heresy? Turks and Jews consider Christians to be heretics and Christians treat each other as such. Papists and Lutherans, Zwinglians and Anabaptists, Calvinists and Adiaphorists, all excommunicate each other. Must men hate and kill each other because of differences of opinion? Therefore, leave the sword to one side; if some person entertains wicked or erroneous opinion then pray for him and provoke him to love, to peace, to unity. . . . In regard to this Servetus, if he is a heretic in God's eyes then do not you inflict any bodily torture upon him but make the necessary admonitions, and, at the worst, banish him from the city if he remains obstinate and disturbs the peace by his doctrines. . . . No one is permitted to go beyond that.[76]

When "Jan van Brugge" penned this brave letter, he was taking the considerable risk of having it lead to his detection. What such detection of a former leader in the rival church would have entailed may be discovered from the fact that several years later, after the tired refugee was dead and buried and his true identity was uncovered, his body was exhumed, dragged through the streets, and then burned to ashes.

However, it was not the rival church alone that expressed disapproval of the Servetus execution. Far from it. Very soon after the news of the burning had traversed Europe, a book published anonymously appeared on the market, roundly condemning the Servetus affair. Genevans guessed that it was the work of Sebastian Castellio, a Renaissance figure who had authored the very influential *Conseil à la France Desolée,* one of the earliest treatises advocating freedom of conscience. However, far from taking to heart the arguments advanced in this anonymous publication, Calvin, with Beza as his faithful helper, put out a lengthy argument defending heretic-burning in general and the Servetus execution in particular. There were also many voices from within the Protestant camp, from some of the older men who had not as yet made their peace with magisterialization and all that went with it. One of these was Pieter Bloccius, a native son of the Low Countries who had served in the *kruiskerken* (as some Protestant churches called themselves while they were still "under the cross"). He wrote:

> That heretics are to be killed Christ has nowhere taught.... So demented are many men in our times that they call Christians Castellionists for urging, with Christ, that the tares must be allowed to stand. Matthew, who wrote this, must have been a Castellionist! They who recommend that heretics be put to death show that they are not truly regenerate, men who would be more blessed if they would seek out a hundred passages from the New Testament dealing with love. He who persecutes heretics seeks only to destroy.... The Greek and Latin poets have sternly rebuked blood-guzzlers such as Pharaoh and Caligula ... and now men who belch forth books advocating the killing of heretics want to pass for Christians; this you have not learned from Christ, who rebuked his vengeful disciples.[77]

Apparently such reprimanding voices were by no means rare, and it is clear that Calvin fretted because of them. In a letter addressed to a friend on October 5, 1554, he complained: "If you but knew the tenth part of how I have been hurt by these shameful calumnies, you would, kind as you are, groan beneath the burden of grief by which I am tried. Dogs bark at me from all sides. I am being called a heretic. Whatever of slander they can invent is hurled at me. Actually the unfriendly ones and the critical in our own camp attack me even more fiercely than do they of the papal company. Surely I have not deserved this at the hand of the Church!"[78]

As time went on, however, more and more people rallied to Calvin's defense, especially in the Low Countries. Holland was about to begin the Eighty Years War, and magisterialization as well as the attending issues of liberation from Spain served to engender the kind of fanaticism needed to see the war through to victory. During the war the book which Bloccius had said was "belched forth" by "demented" persons was given a new lease on life in Dutch Calvinistic circles. It was republished in a Dutch translation by one of the leading ministers of the Dutch Reformed Churches, Johannes Bogerman, a man whose popularity can be deduced from his election to chair the Great Synod of Dordt two decades later. Bogerman, who had been an ardent Anabaptist-hunter in his previous charge (at Sneek), had no sooner arrived in a new charge than he began to urge the local *regnum* to do its "duty" with respect to the Catholic and Anabaptist "heretics" in the city. As a consequence, an edict was published in 1601 forbidding the holding of conventicles, with fines spelled out which were heavy enough to break the back of any rival church in the city.[79] All the punishments prescribed in this edict were civil in nature — fines, confiscations, banishments, the blocking of inheritance rights, etc. — in a word, all the kinds of punishment meted out by the *regnum,* for which Augustine had built up the argument in the days of the original hybrid.

The new hybrid found the Dutch landscape to its liking; it thrived there for a long time to come. It liked the taste of the flat theology that became regnant with the Eighty Years War. It flourished on that theology virtually up to modern times, so that one is led to wonder whether it ever left the country. Little more than a century ago a booklet was written by a clergyman named Wormser, with an introduction by Groen van Prinsterer, in which we are told: "The entire Dutch nation is baptized — behold, a fact about which there is no argument . . . therefore teach the nation to understand and value properly its baptism and church and state are out of trouble."[80] Nevertheless, there were things in the soil and air of Holland that would in time force the hybrid to retreat to higher ground. The venerable spirits that censured the burning of Servetus never became extinct. The influence of the rival church was sure to be felt. The New Testament was now in everyone's hand, and its division of labor teachings were sure to work themselves out. Most important of all, the public opinion before which Calvin had winced was not easily muted; the time was to come when no one, not even the most die-hard, would any longer defend the liquidation of Servetus. The time was to come when the Reformed Churches would begin to feel uncomfortable in the presence of Article 36 of the Belgic Confession, so uncomfortable that they would reject officially its teaching that it is the *regnum's* duty to "prevent all idolatry and false worship."

Calvinists of unquestioned pedigree have addressed themselves to the question of the reason for this change, the cause behind the hybrid's lagging spirit. The late Professor A. A. Van Schelven, long a professor of church history at the Free

University of Amsterdam (an institution that is still at least officially Calvinistic), has said: "In the light of history the matter stands this way: the Calvinistic life and world view has been an active agency toward toleration and separation of Church and State only if and when it was driven to it, when it was cross-pollinated by anabaptistic and humanistic ideas."[81] When we remember the two sources from which most of the disapproval of the Servetus affair emanated — the "Castellionists" and the rival church — it will be hard to disagree with Van Schelven's conclusions.

In a recently published symposium by contemporary Dutch scholars, Dr. W. Nijenhuis writes: "Calvin's views concerning the magistracy leave no room for toleration in the sense of freedom of religion. The promotion of the true religion, belonging as it does for Calvin to the task of the civil ruler, implies the punishment of the heretic, as Calvin showed most plainly in his celebrated sermon on Deuteronomy 13." One of Nijenhuis's colleagues in the symposium says: "I can see it no other way than that the theocracy, or bibliocracy, in Geneva . . . constitutes a high point in intolerance." He adds: "Calvin did not condemn the intolerance of the papacy because it was intolerant; he opposed it because the papacy had departed from the true religion. . . . Neither Lutheranism nor Calvinism nor Zwinglianism have contributed to the development of toleration in Europe; rather, the beginnings of that development lie with the so-called stepchildren of the Reformation."[82]

Students of the Reformation will also find it increasingly difficult to disagree with the conclusions to which William Warren Sweet has come:

> There is a widespread notion among Protestant groups that separation of Church and State, and thus religious liberty, was one of the products of the Reformation . . . that religious liberty was but the logical development of the principle held by all the reformers. Just where this notion arose is difficult to say, and no reputable historian of our own times would endorse it. . . . The fact is that the rise of Protestantism was accompanied by an unprecedented outburst of violence.[83]

Anyone who takes it upon himself to dispute this statement will do well to address his criticism solely to the word "unprecedented"; then he has a case. For although the later hybrid did bring with it considerable violence and oppression, it did not do so in an unprecedented way. The original hybrid still holds the record for violence. It must be granted that when the Reformed Churches performed major surgery on Article 36 of their Belgic Confession in order to reverse its thought, they reversed their evaluation of the hybrid and thereby rejected not simply an unhappy formulation but an entire theology, that of the magisterial reform.

Episode Two

A full century after Conrad Grebel had his troubles at Zürich, on the opposite side of the Atlantic other infants were being left unbaptized, and another *regnum* made it its business to do something about it; when that did not work out as desired, another banishment took place, another *exterminatio*. The scene was the Massachusetts Bay area in the New World. The hybrid had managed to get across the ocean; manifestly, it had not changed its complexion in the migration to a new shore. We shall now trace some of its antics in the New World. Since Roger Williams, the clergyman who founded the colony that is now the state of Rhode Island, played a leading part in the episode we are about to trace, we shall concentrate on him in very much the same way we concentrated on Grebel in the Zürich of a century earlier. It must be borne in mind, however, that Williams, like Grebel, was not on his own; he too had his associates.

When the massive Christendom of medieval times broke up into a collection of smaller Christendoms during the Reformation, one of the by-products of the resulting nationalism was colonialism, the planting of "colonies" on foreign soil. Each such colony had its "right" religion, the "right" religion of the mother country. Although there was increased toleration in these new Christendoms (the mother countries), brought about in large part because of the cross-pollination of which Prof. Van Schelven spoke, a colony was usually less tolerant than was its mother country. This was to be expected: for if the sacral premise is allowed to stand — that consensus on the religious level is the prerequisite of civil quiet — then unanimity on the religious level is even more necessary in the colony than at home; if political stability is needed anywhere it is needed in a colony.[T]

The colony which the Dutch planted in the New World under Pieter Stuyvesant is a good example of such reduced toleration in a colony. Although the mother country was at this time tolerating considerable diversity in the matter of ultimate loyalties, this was not true of its colony. Only people of the "right" religion were admitted to Nieuw Amsterdam; the governor tried to keep out "all unbelievers and Jews." Even Lutherans were less than welcome, though some seem to have gotten in anyway, for the records of the *regnum* occasionally report — with some glee — that a "Martinist" had converted to the "right" religion.[U]

[T]Such reduced toleration for a colony was in vogue until recently. When the people of the Secession of 1834 in Holland were looking for a place to go in order to escape the hardships that were being imposed on them for leaving the "right" church, their request for permission to go to the Dutch East Indies was denied them because, as it was put: "You are causing civil disturbance at home, what will it be if we let you go to Java?"

[U]The "right" religion of the Netherlands was also exported to South Africa, where *regnum* and *sacerdotium* were in cahoots from the start. The salaries of governor and *dominee* were paid out of the same treasury; citizenship and church membership were implied in one another. As the colony expanded, churches were organized outside the political boundaries of the Cape Colony, and by decision of the civil authorities these were excluded from membership in the ecclesiastical structure of the *Nederduits Gereformeerde Kerk*. When some Moravians came to conduct a mission to the natives, the *regnum* gave them a very rough time. As late as 1837, the leading man of the law for the people of the *trek* swore an oath to "defend and protect the Christian confession as provided for in Article 36, as well as that which goes with it, the Catechism and the liturgical formularies of the Dutch Reformed Church. I will admit no one to any office in my government, neither in an ecclesiastical nor in a civil role, unless he is a member of the aforesaid Church." Although the tendency toward greater toleration and even freedom of religion is now in evidence in the Republic of South Africa, the relation between *regnum* and *sacerdotium* is that of the magisterial reformation. Church and state are in theory separate, but they are in actuality very close, closer than in any other "Calvinistic" land. The *Nederduits Gereformeerde Kerk* is essentially a *Volkskirche*, a situation that Prof. Schippers of the Free University of Amsterdam has called "a monstrosity with which we are stuck" in the Reformed Ecumenical Synod tie. Because of this "monstrosity," the Reformed churches of South Africa find it almost unthinkable to criticize or oppose the policies of the *regnum*.

In the English-speaking "colonies" planted in the New World the same reduced toleration was in evidence, as the banishment of Roger Williams indicates, although there was plenty of intolerance born of sacral presuppositions in the mother country as well. England had an unusually vigorous rival church in pre-Reformation times. For example, think of Lollardism: already in the days of Chaucer almost anywhere in England one could "smell a Loller in the wind." Recall too that medieval England was always full of "hedge-priests," unordained, uncommissioned men of religion; these "hedge-priests" were perhaps ministers of a rival church. However, when the Reformation came to England, it was magisterial from the start; it was at least as magisterial there as it was anywhere on the continent — perhaps more so. This may be explained, in part at least, by the fact that in England the Reformation was promoted by King Henry VIII for his own private reasons. Therefore, anyone who wished to work for church renewal in Eng-

---

No doubt this anachronistic situation exists because those factors which Van Schelven said caused the Calvinism of Holland to become more tolerant (i.e., "humanism" and "Anabaptist" cross-pollination) did not find their way across the equator and thus had little or no impact on South Africa. The effects of its ideological isolation manifest themselves on every hand in that troubled country. The language of Article 36 of the Belgic Confession, for example, has never given the Reformed churches in South Africa pause. Everyone knows about apartheid in South Africa; what is not generally known, however, is that it was sacramental thinking that gave the impetus to apartheid. Sacrament, especially *die nagmaal* (Afrikaans for the Lord's Supper), serves to bind together in religion what is already together on other planes (race, language, geographic origin); and it was this function of sacrament that stood in the way of people of two different races ("European" and "brown") going to the same *nagmaal*. In 1855 some forty-five "Europeans" petitioned the consistory of Stockenström, a hitherto "brown" congregation with which some "Europeans" worshiped (because there was no "European" congregation in the vicinity as yet), for permission to have the Lord's Supper served to them at a separate serving within the same worship service, in order "not to be an offense to each other." The consistory turned down this request, as was to be expected, for it was "brown." The matter was thereupon appealed to the Classis of Graaf-Reinet; being largely white, they decided "to recommend to the honorable consistory of Stockenström, in order to satisfy the prejudices and the weaknesses of some, to serve the *nagmaal* at two or more servings for the new [white] members after it has been served to the old [brown] members." Here we have the *Volkskirche* in action. The only slightly decent thing in the picture is that the "Europeans" who couldn't digest the idea of a people of God drawn from all peoples said they would be satisfied if they were served *after* the others.

land had to compare notes with the head of the *regnum*. The English Reformation was thus predisposed by its very nature to be magisterial. This would explain how it happened that of all Reformation churches the Church of England remained closest, both in its polity and its theology, to the pre-Reformation pattern; Anglicans scarcely accept the label of "Protestant," prefer rather to be known as "English Catholics" (especially in the "high church" wing). The Church of England is geared more closely to *Corpus Christianum* than are other Protestant churches; it is extremely sacramental in its theology and comes closest to being a *Volkskirche;* in it *regnum* and *sacerdotium* are closely allied — if not in practical reality, certainly by law.[v]

Since we will be dealing with the English colonies in the New World, it is necessary first to take a close look at the mother country's sacralism. It would be impossible to be more firmly committed to the idea of *Corpus Christianum* than were the spokesmen for the established Church of England. For example, Richard Hooker compared church and state to two sides of a right triangle, of which either side is the base, depending upon how one holds the triangle. Speaking of church and state, he taught that "no person appertaining to the one can be denied to be of the other also." As is usually the case, Hooker's ideas on baptism tell the story. Of christening he said:

> Children are signed with this mark: "one Lord, one faith, one baptism," Ephesians 4:5. In whom these things are, the Church doth acknowledge them for her children; only them she holdeth for aliens and strangers in whom these things are not found. For want of them it is that Saracens, Jews and Infidels, are excluded out of the bounds of the Church. Others we may not deny to be of the visible Church, as long as these things are not wanting in them. . . . If for external profession they be

---

[v]English history is full of seeming contradictions: in spite of the above evidence of magisterialism, the free church (recall that by "free" we mean "not tied to the apron strings of the *regnum*," neither helped nor hindered by it) is to a large extent an English creation. The world owes the final victory of the idea of separation of church and state to the English-speaking people. The reason for this, to the best of my knowledge, has not been adequately accounted for. Perhaps it is because England was geographically and ideologically at the perimeter of the empire all through history. Also, the Christianity that was first brought to the Islands came not from Rome but from the eastern Mediterranean (for example, the British initially observed the Easter date of the Byzantine world).

Christians then are they of the visible Church of Christ and Christians by external confession they are all, whose mark of recognizance hath in it these things which we have mentioned, yea, although they be impious idolaters, wicked heretics, persons excommunicable, yea, cast out for notorious improbity.[84]

It was by means of the visible-invisible trick that Richard Hooker (like so many before him and after him, ever since Augustine) was able to classify as "Christians" people who were "impious idolaters, wicked heretics, persons excommunicable" — all as the result of a dogged determination to keep the hybrid on its feet. Hooker does not offer to explain what "external profession" can possibly be: surely if it is merely external it is not profession, and if it is really profession it is not external. Hooker must be classified as either pre-Christian or post-Christian, for he puts the idea of a composite society far from him. Karl Barth has called views like those of Richard Hooker a "new Judaism," and who can quarrel with that?[w] But if Karl Barth is right in calling "Christian sacralism" a "new Judaism," then we will have to call just about everything that came out of the magisterial reformation by that name.

In the context of Richard Hooker's theology, it is not at all surprising that in order to hold public office in the England of his day one had to be a member in good standing of the church — the "right" one. It was possible to be excommunicated in England then, but there were heavy civil penalties attached to such excommunication. This was true even in the first "step" in such excommunication: unless a man under the first "step" of censure humbled himself and obtained absolution — for which a fee was collected — all Christians (which meant everybody in the societal enclave) were forbidden to communicate with him, buy from him, or sell to him, an arrangement calcu-

---

[w] Judaism is, of course, strictly sacral; in it the spiritual community and the political community are one. This sacralism comes to classic (if somewhat ludicrous) expression in a recent article written by Rabbi S. M. Lebrman of Jerusalem (in *Barkai*, a Jewish periodical published in the Republic of South Africa). He quotes with enthusiasm one Rabbi Hisda, who wrote: "Just as the malodorous *galbanum* was included in the temple incense as per Exodus 30:34, so must sinners be included in the worshipping community." Extending this bizarre interpretation, he informs his readers that the Hebrew word *ṣbr* (meaning "assembly" or "congregation") is in reality a contraction of three words: *ṣ* from *ṣaddiqim* (meaning "righteous") plus *b* from *benonim* ("middle-of-the-road persons") and *r* from *resham* ("wicked ones").

lated to bring about economic ruin. If such a man did not submit to the "keys" of the church within forty days, its court could report him to the crown and he would be imprisoned and ultimately subjected to *exterminatio* either in the etymological sense or in the derived sense of expulsion from the realm. This was, of course, medieval to the core — though it was at the same time in line with the thinking of the magisterial reformation.ˣ

Typical of the thinking in England during the seventeenth century, typical of the hybrid as it flourished there, is a statement Edmund Calamy made in a sermon preached for the benefit of Parliament in 1644: "If you do not labor according to your duty and power to suppress the errors that are being spread in the Kingdom then all these errors are your errors and these heresies your heresies; then you are the Anabaptists . . . and 'tis you then that hold that all religions are to be tolerated."[85] Robert Baylie, a member of the Westminster Assembly, put the same dogmatic sacralism in these words: "Liberty of conscience and toleration of any and all religions is so prodigious an impiety that this religious parliament cannot but abhor the very meaning of it. Whatever may be the opinion of . . . Mr. Williams and whatever some of that stamp may say, Mr. Burroughs, upon many unanswerable arguments, has exploded that abomination."[86] The "Mr. Williams" referred to was none other than Roger Williams, whose experiences with the hybrid in the New World we are in the process of tracing. Apparently he was already inclined toward the thought system of the rival church before he went to the New World.

From these remarks by Robert Baylie we learn that the magisterial reformers in England were not the only ones engaged in the fight against entrenched Catholicism, that there was also a non-Catholic opposition party known as the "Anabaptists." Manifestly, the reform movement had bifurcated in

---

ˣJohn Calvin contributed his bit to the viability of the hybrid in England of that time. He urged the youthful King Edward to emulate the example of Israel's King Josiah, urging him specifically to "root out all papist superstitions completely."[87] Not much came of Calvin's meddling: Edward died soon after (1553) of tuberculosis at fifteen years of age. Thereupon Bloody Mary came to the throne, and being a fanatic Catholic, she tried to do to the Protestant cause what Calvin had urged Edward to do to the Catholic one.

England just as it had on the continent. We must take a quick look at the English rival church, which was important enough to warrant Robert Baylie's warnings addressed to Parliament, for it had much to do with subsequent history, and it offers a perspective of the climate in which Roger Williams lived and worked. The reader may have received the impression that the rival church in general and Anabaptism in particular was a continental phenomenon — which is far from true.

Although it is commonly agreed that the origins of Anabaptism were on the continent, it was represented on the British Isles quite early. When a group of Anabaptists were apprehended on the continent in 1538, a letter was found on one of them indicating that their leader, Peter Tesch, was planning to visit the Anabaptists in England. The landgrave of the area saw to it that Henry VIII was duly alerted to the alleged danger posed by these Anabaptists in his domains. It was Philipp Melanchthon who drew up the letter for the landgrave; and Melanchthon had previously warned the king in his own name. According to Melanchthon in these letters, Anabaptism had originated in Flanders, a rather unusual representation that might be explained by the fact that many of the Anabaptists in England were Flemish refugees. Moreover, it is hard to say just where the cradle of Anabaptism was, since it was heavily indebted to movements that antedate 1517. Perhaps, if the truth were known, Anabaptism was as much a product of Flanders as of Switzerland or southern Germany.

Earlier still, in 1531, an Englishman named William Barlow was already warning his countrymen against the Anabaptist rival church. Interestingly enough, he called it "the Thyrd faccyon of the Reformation," no doubt meaning thereby that Anabaptism was third after Calvinism and Lutheranism. He was apparently apprised of the bifurcation that had occurred. In 1534 a native of Flanders named Bastian was arrested in England for spreading Anabaptist ideas and literature. On May 25, 1536, some twenty-five Anabaptists were arrested in England, and fourteen of them were burned at the stake in June of the next year. It has been estimated that more Anabaptists were burned in England during the reign of Henry VIII than Lollards executed during the previous century; and that as many as eighty per cent of Bloody Mary's victims were

Anabaptists.ʸ And there are more instances of rival church congregations that were discovered and their leaders burned. Thus, the rival church and its principles were rife in England in the early years of the Protestant Reformation, and they must have contributed to the rise of free church movements there.

Continental Anabaptism reached England in another — though related — way. A great many Englishmen who had gone to the Low Countries were influenced by the rival church there and brought back its ideas upon their return. Many of these people had gone to Holland because they had dissent in their blood already, some to escape from imminent danger because of their separatist ideas; they came back firmer in their convictions and bolder. One of them was Mark Leonard Busher, who wrote the treatise "Religion's Peace, a Plea for Liberty of Conscience" (1614), which has been called the earliest known publication advocating complete religious freedom. In it the idea is advanced that freedom of conscience requires that "no civil favor be granted or withheld by the whim of the king — it is a God-given right of man and is essential to the very nature of. Christianity." Busher fled to Holland for the sake of conscience and was a member of an Anabaptist group at Kampen.

Another English Anabaptist, Robert Browne (for whom the separatist group known as Brownists was named), held the following views of the function of civil rulers:

> Yet may they doo nothing concerning the Church, but onlie civile, and as civile magistrates, that is, they have not that authoritie over the Church, as to be Prophetes or Priestes, or spiritual Kings, as in all outwarde Iustice, to maintain the right welfare and honor thereof, with outward power, bodily punishment, and civil forcing of men. And therefore also because the Church is in a common-wealth, it is of their charge, that is, concerning the outward provision and outward iustice, they are to look to it; but to compell religion, to plant churches by power, and to force submission to Ecclesiastical government by lawes and penalties belongeth not to them.[88]

ʸThe presence of so much Anabaptism in England a mere decade after Grebel's collision with the *regnum* at Zürich indicates earlier presence and conditioning. As we said when discussing the rise of Anabaptism on the continent, beginning the English Reformation in 1517 presents some formidable psychological difficulties: how could polarities of such severity develop in a mere decade? It is likely that English Anabaptism also had roots in much earlier times. Lollardy may very well have been to the rival church in England what a movement like sacramentarianism was to the rival church on the continent.

When Robert Browne began to gather about him groups of disciples at Cambridge, London, and Norwich, he was expelled from England. He crossed over to the Netherlands, where he published at Middelburg several works setting forth his principles: "Reformation Without Tarrying for Any," "Order for Studying the Scriptures," and "Life and Manners of All True Christians." The last composition displeased the established church in England so much that the death penalty was prescribed for anyone found guilty of possessing a copy, a measure that elicited Sir Walter Raleigh's remark in Parliament that it would be impossible to punish them all.

Francis Johnson, a Puritan clergyman who was seeking to answer the separatist argument put forward in a book by Barrows and Greenwood (entitled "Plain Refutation"), was himself converted to the rival church ideas he had set out to refute. While Johnson was in prison for this in 1593, his little band of followers left for Holland. A contemporary, Henoch Clapham, wrote of that little settlement: "About thirteen years synce, this Church through persecution in England was driven to come to these countreyes. A while after they were come hither divers of them fell into the heresies of the Anabaptists (which are too common in these countreys). . . ."

John Smyth and Thomas Helwys likewise came to the Low Countries because of "leftist" convictions and were confirmed in "Anabaptist" ideas there. Smyth had been a good Puritan, teaching that the magistrate had the duty to cause all men to worship the true God, or else punish them with imprisonment, confiscation of goods, or death "as the qualitie of the case requireth"; but later he and his flock "shooke off this yoake of antichristian bondage, and as ye Lords free people, joyned themselves (by a covenant of the Lord) into a Church estate, in ye fellowship of ye gospell, to walke in all his wayes, made known or to be made known unto them, according to their best endeavors, whatever it should cost them, the Lord assisting them." The resulting rival church met in two sections, one at Gainsborough under the leadership of Smyth and the other at Scrooby under John Robinson. Both had such rough going that they went to Holland in 1608, where Smyth came to the conviction that not covenanting but adult baptism is the tie that binds believers together. John Robinson described the change that had come over his former associate in these words: "Mr. Smyth, Mr. Helwys, and the rest, haveing utterly dissolved and disclaymed their former Church state and ministry, came together to erect a new Church, by baptism; unto which they ascribed great virtue, as that they would not so much as pray together before they had it. And after some streyning of courtesy, who should begin . . . Mr. Smyth baptized first himself[z] and next Mr. Helwys and so the rest, making their particular confessions."[89]

Later, around 1612, John Smyth drew up a confession of faith which consisted of 102 articles, a confession that shows strong Anabaptist influences. Its 82nd article reads as follows:

> We believe that the magistrate is not by virtue of his office to meddle with religion or matters of conscience, to force and compel men to this or that form of religion or doctrine, but to leave the Christian religion free to every man's conscience, and to handle only civil transgressions, injuries and wrongs of man against man, in murder, adultery, theft, etc. . . . for Christ only is king and lawgiver of the Church and Conscience.[90]

Thomas Helwys went back to England, where he published a tract entitled "The Mistery of Iniquity." In it the Church of Rome is identified as the first beast of the book of Revelation and the Church of England as the second beast. Helwys argues that "God hath given to the King an earthly kingdome with all earthly power, against the which none may resist but must in all things obey, willingly, either to do or suffer; Christ alone is King of Israell and sitts upon David's throne, and the King ought to be a subject of his Kingdome; none ought to be punished either with death or bonds, for transgressing against the spirituall ordinances of the New Testament, such offences ought to be punished onely with spiritual sword and censures." In an address to King James I, to whom Helwys sent a copy, he said:

> Heare, O King, and dispise not ye counsel of ye poor, and let their complaints come before thee. The King is a mortall man,

---

[z]Most readers will consider it bizarre for any man to baptize himself, as John Smyth did. It is bizarre — but not without some sort of precedent. We read in Genesis 17 that Abraham and all his house were circumcised on one day, and it is generally assumed that Abraham performed the ritual on himself first and then on the rest. John Smyth was apparently convinced that it was time to begin a new sequence — just as Abraham had — and this may have given him the idea of self-baptism. Smyth was manifestly so certain that baptism in its traditional form and meaning was out of tune with Scripture that a reinstituting of Christian baptism was needed.

and not God, therefore hath no power over ye immortall soules of his subjects, to make lawes and ordinances for them. If the King have authority to make spirituall Lords and lawes then he is an immortall God and not a mortall man. O King, be not seduced by deceivers to sin so against thy poore subjects who ought and will obey thee in all things with body, life, and goods; or els let their lives be taken from ye earth. God save the king![91]

We see then that there was considerable movement back and forth of rival church ideas between England and the continent; and there was also sustained suppression of these ideas and oppression of those who held them. As we shall see now, the rival church ideas — as well as the suppression of them — were exported to the colonies in the New World.

It is possible that the "Pilgrim Fathers" sailed from Leyden to the New World partly because it had become apparent to them, as they moved about in Dutch society, that if the revolutionary ideas of the rival church in Holland and England were to have a chance to work themselves out and succeed, it would have to be in a new environment suitable for the purpose. This would have to be an environment uncluttered by a long heritage of "Christian sacralism," where it would be possible to move beyond the climate which the magisterial reformers had left them. At any rate, a very significant indication that these pilgrims were thinking along these lines was the farewell speech with which their leader addressed them as they embarked in the *Mayflower* in 1620:

> If God reveal any thing to you by any other instrument of his, be as ready to receive it as ever you were to receive any truth by my ministry; for I am verily persuaded, the Lord has more truth yet to break forth out of his holy word. For my part, I cannot sufficiently bewail the condition of the reformed churches, who are come to a period in religion and will go at present no further than the instruments of their reformation. . . . The Calvinists, you see, stick fast where they were left by that great man of God, who yet saw not all things. This is a misery much to be lamented, for though they were burning and shining lights in their times, yet they penetrated not into the whole counsel of God, but were they now living, would be as willing to embrace further light as that which they first received. I beseech you remember, it is an article of your church covenant, that you be ready to receive whatever truth shall be made known to you from the written word of God. . . . I must

> also advise you to abandon, avoid, and shake off the name of *Brownists;* it is a mere nickname, and a brand for making religion, and the professors of it, odious to the Christian world.[92]

What "more truth" was Robinson thinking of when he said this, and what "further light" did he have in mind? It is apparent that he was thinking of something that would go beyond the "truth" prevalent in "the reformed churches" of his acquaintance in Holland; it is also apparent that he was thinking of a truth that would go beyond that body of thought to which Calvin had given shape (Calvin, who "yet saw not all things"). Robinson's parting advice to drop the name Brownist seems to show that he was thinking of a forward movement to which the name "Brownist" had been attached in malice, a theology which Robinson wanted his followers to keep even as they rejected the odious name attached to it. The words of their revered leader were still in the Pilgrims' ears as they drew up and signed the Mayflower Compact. Had their leader's prophetic words sensitized his followers for a structuring of society that would go beyond that of the Reformed Churches and beyond him who had given them the form which they had in Holland? It is not fanciful to suggest that this "new light" was the legacy of the rival church. It has been perceptively suggested that the English Puritan "left" can be understood only when we realize the depth of the inspiration it drew directly from the Swiss, German, and Dutch Anabaptists.

In John Robinson we find a very high esteem for Calvin coupled with a keen sense of disappointment in him, as well as an ardent desire to move forward from the place where Calvin had left them. It is especially noteworthy in this study that we find the same dual appraisal of Calvin in Roger Williams, who said of Calvin and Beza that "these excellent men endeavor (as James speaks) to bring forth from the same fountains sweet water and bitter, which is monstrous and contradictory" (*Complete Works,* IV, 264—hereafter *C.W.*).[A] The

---

[A] Williams was merely anticipating what A. C. McGiffert has said, that "Calvin's doctrine of the Church was a composite of many and diverse and inconsistent elements and because of this confusion concerning the meaning, the place, and the purpose of the Church has since his day reigned almost everywhere in the Reformed wing of Protestantism."[93] Those who designed the monument to the reformers that graces the city of Geneva today brought in one man from the New World — Roger Williams. Were he and the other dignitaries in this monument simultaneously made alive, they would soon be

immediate cause for this complaint was as follows: Williams had made grateful use of Calvin's assertions set forth in his commentary on Romans 13:4, which were very much in line with Williams' own thinking. In Calvin's commentary Williams had found, in his own words: "This whole discourse concerneth civill Magistrates, and therefore in vaine doe they who exercise power over consciences, goe about from this place to establish their sacrilegious tyranny." Williams said he had read also the following in that commentary: "Paul hath not respect unto the whole law, he speaks only of those duties which the Law commands toward our neighbors." Williams had made equally grateful use of Beza's words concerning that passage: "Since the Apostle in this place discourseth of the duties of men one toward another, I thinke this terme *law* ought to be restrained to the second table."

All this was of course grist for Williams' mill. However, Williams' antagonist John Cotton, in his polemics against Williams, pointed to Calvin and Beza's *Defensio* (in which they had defended the burning of Servetus). There the Genevans had sung a different song regarding the Romans passage: they had argued (again in Williams' words) that "this one thing sufficeth me, that by the coming of Christ neither was the State or the Civill government changed, nor was anything taken away from the Magistrate's office. Goe to then, that which Paul teacheth that he beareth not the Sword in vaine, ought it to be restrained to the one kind only? They themselves with whom I have to deal confess that the Magistrates are armed of God to punish open crimes, so that they abstaine from matters of religion, that so ungodliness may run riot by their connivance. But the Holy Ghost crieth out against this in many places." Beza had also said, according to John Cotton: "The Magistrate is God's Minister, who beareth the Sword to take vengeance on them that doe evill . . . wherefore one of these must needs be, if the Magistrates should have no just power over Hereticks, either that Hereticks are not evill doers (which is so grosse that I think it needs no Refutation) or else that Pauls speech is to be restrained to a certain sort of evill deeds,

---

in a deep argument on the question of what to do with the hybrid. Williams would urge that it be "put to sleep," and the rest would want it listed among the protected species. Roger Williams realized two centuries before the Reformed churches did, that Article 36 of the Belgic Confession is in error.

"AND ALSO AFTERWARD"

to wit, such as they call corporall sinnes, of which distinction of evill deeds I shall dispute more largely hereafter."[94] This, of course, was grist for Cotton's mill. It is thus no wonder that Williams said Calvin and Beza were "bringing forth from the same fountains sweet water and bitter." The trouble was simply this: the Genevans operated with two mutually exclusive concepts of the church.

Surely Roger Williams must have owed many of his insights to the rival church tradition as it ran through Anabaptist circles in Holland. We have no evidence that he was ever in the Netherlands in person, but it is significant that he put forth a sustained effort to master the Dutch language. That may well have been because so much of the rival church literature was in that language, literature which he seems to have devoured. Williams must have learned Dutch quite thoroughly, for we know that he taught it to others.[B] This means that virtually the entire literature of Dutch Anabaptism (which was voluminous) was accessible to Roger Williams in the original. In any event, very soon Williams had to hear all the charges and reproaches that had been thrown in the face of the rival church over the years. One of the "heresies" laid to his charge was the old slur about "refusing the oath." It has been suggested that Williams' aversion to the oath was a result of his boyhood experience of serving as messenger in the courts, where he had a chance to witness the utter flippancy with which oath-taking was handled, so that he very early rebelled against the oath as such. But it is more likely that Williams' opposition to the oath entered his mind along with the rest of the rival church heritage. Had not the Waldensians and the Anabaptists after them refused the oath? The "heretics" saw that to swear an oath is to engage in a deeply religious act, one for which not every person is to be considered capable; they thought that to ask it of all comers was to close one's eyes to the composite nature of human society. For this reason they rejected the practice. Moreover, the reader will recall that the oath had been for centuries part of the equipment with which the empire-church sought to liquidate the opposition: since very early

---

[B] In a letter to Governor Winthrop he wrote: "It pleased the Lord to call me for some time, and with some persons, to practice the Hebrew, the Greek, Latin, French, and Dutch. The secretary of the Council, Mr. Milton, for my Dutch I had him read me more languages."

times every adult male was required to promise under oath to report any "heretic" as well as any "heretical" goings-on. It was thus inevitable that the people of the rival church traditionally looked upon the oath as a device of the devil.[c]

Rival church circles in the New World were also belabored with the charge that they "would have no magistrate," which, as we have noted above, was ancient but entirely unfounded. People of sacral thought habits see church and state as two aspects of a single entity; for that reason they interpret the demand that the sword be lifted out of the affairs of faith as a demand that it be lifted out of human society. The age-old axiom that civil tranquillity is impossible unless the populace sees eye to eye in matters of man's highest loyalty was etched so deeply in their souls that it was solemnly asserted in the New World as late as 1656. Some of the colonies decided to exclude "all Quakers, Ranters, and notorious heretics"; when the Roger Williams people in Providence indicated that they refused to go along with this, saying that freedom of conscience was their "most prized possession," the Massachusetts Bay commissioners replied that this teaching "tends to the very absolute cutting down and overthrowing of civil government among you." This was the very same doleful tale the earlier Anabaptists had been obliged to listen to. It was common for a complaint against Roger Williams and his adherents, after listing all their faults and failures, to end with some phrase about "no magistrates." We read: "A sister of Mrs. Hutchinson . . . being infected with Anabaptistry . . . Mr. Williams was taken (or rather emboldened) by her to make open profession there-

---

[c]Unless we keep clearly in mind the very important part which the oath played in the fight to keep the hybrid alive and well, we will not understand the weight which people on both sides of the issue of "Christian sacralism" placed on it. The Heidelberg Catechism devotes a whole Lord's Day (37) to the question of the propriety of the oath — more space than it devotes to the article in the Apostles' Creed having to do with the Holy Spirit! Calvin at one time said many favorable things about Pierre Alexander, a native of Flanders, but then added that he had *"une lourde fault"* (a weighty defect): he taught that the oath is forbidden in the New Testament, a "fault" so serious in Calvin's mind that he said it disqualified Alexander for the position for which he was being considered. Many a "heretic" sealed his own doom by saying that the oath was out of order. Why, we must ask, were people so worked up about the question? Our courts allow a man to detour the oath, allow him instead to "solemnly affirm" (a provision that dates from the demise of the hybrid and was written to meet the consciences of the heirs of the rival church).

of, and accordingly was rebaptized by one Holyman.... Then Mr. Williams rebaptized him and some ten more. They also denied the baptizing of infants, and would have no magistrates." This was a false accusation, just as it had been earlier in connection with the continental Anabaptists. How false it was may be gathered from Williams' response to the charge: "I should be far yet from unsecuring the peace of a City, of a Land (which I confesse ought to be maintained by civill weapons and which I have so much cause to be earnest with God for); nor would I leave a gap open to any mutinous hand or tongue, nor with a weapon left in the hand of any known to be mutinous and peace-breakers." Williams was plainly the victim of a cliché as old as the original hybrid when he was accused of anarchism.

Roger Williams was not given to anarchy; he had a very high view of the *regnum*, saw it as a creature of God's grace — albeit not of his redeeming grace. He did attack the idea of a "Christian" state. Church and state, said he, are like two different ships; in the church-ship the prince is only a passenger, without special powers on the ship and obliged to obey the ship's laws. However, in the state-ship the magistrate is in command. Whether such a magistrate was himself a Christian or otherwise, his functions were the same — that is, purely civil. No doubt a Christian prince should and would perform his duties through the fear of God in a more enlightened way, and with a more demanding conscience;[D] but it remained a fact that "the Christian pilots power over the soules and consciences of his sailors and passengers is not greater than is that of the Anti-Christian...."

> All civil states, with their officers of justice, in their respective constitutions and administrations, are proved essentially civil, and therefore are not judges, governors, or defenders of the spiritual or Christian state and worship.... It is the will and

[D]Roger Williams was not blind to the benefits that accrue to a whole society because of the presence of a believing element in that society, benefits that accrue through a kind of osmotic action. He was aware that such benefits had accrued in Calvin's Geneva, much as he disagreed with Geneva's "Christian sacralism." Williams wrote: "The Ordinances and Discipline of Jesus Christ, though wrongfully and prophanely applied to naturall and unregenerate men, may cast a blush of civility and morality upon them as in Geneva and other places (for the shining brightnesse of the very shadow of Christ's Ordinances casts a shame upon barbarisme and incivility)" (*C.W.*, III, 225).

command of God that, since the coming of his Son,[E] the Lord Jesus, a permission of the most Paganish, Jewish, Turkish, or anti-Christian consciences and worship be granted to all men in all nations and countries; and they are only to be fought against with that sword which is only, in soul matters, able to conquer, to wit, the Sword of God's Spirit, and the Word of God. (*C.W.*, III, 75)

In this entire argument Williams was but repeating what Helwys had said before, as early as 1612. In his *A Short Declaration of the Mystery of Iniquity,* Helwys had rejected the concept of the "Christian" magistrate:

All earthly powers are one and the same in their severall dominions . . . our Lord the King is but an earthly King and he hath no authority as a king but in earthly causes, and if the king's people be obedient subjects, obeying all human laws made by the King our Lord the King can require no more; for man's religion to God is betwixt God and themselves; the King shall not answer for it, neither may the King be judge between God and man. Let them be heretics, Turks, Jews or whatsoever, it appertains not to the earthly power to punish them in the least measure.

As we have seen earlier, the rejection of Christendom always implies the rejection of christening; in this Roger Williams ran true to form. As early as 1633 he was already on the way toward the repudiation of that sacramental performance on which *Corpus Christianum* depended. In that year an elder in the Plymouth colony felt it his duty to warn against Williams, "lest he run the same course of rigid separation and Anabaptism which Mr. Smyth the se-baptist at Amsterdam has done." On May 1, 1639, Hugh Peters, writing for the Salem church (with which Williams was then connected) to the church at Dorchester, declared: "We thought it our bounden duty to acquaint you with the names of such persons as have had the great censure passed upon them in this our church, with the reasons thereof . . . Roger Williams and his wife. . . . These wholly refused to hear the Church, denying that it, and all the churches in the Bay, to be true Churches, and (except

---

[E] This "since the coming of his Son" indicates that Williams (as well as Helwys) was committed to the early and late concept of the rival church; he too was aware that in the Old Testament the policy concerning the matter in hand was not to be repeated in the New Testament dispensation.

two) are all re-baptized" (*C.W.,* IV, 55). Manifestly, Williams had by this time picked up a pronounced dislike for the hybrid; indeed, he had submitted to believer's baptism during the previous month of March. Mr. Chauncy (later to become president of Harvard) lamented the fact that, "in the government of Plymouth, to our grief, not only the pastor of the congregation waiveth the administration of baptism to infants but divers of his congregation have fallen in with him." It was at approximately this time that Williams wrote his penetrating tract "Christening Maketh Not Christians," which seems to have gained many people to his views.

We have seen how the *regnum* at Zürich rose to the defense of the politically valuable institution of christening; thus it should come as no surprise that the *regnum* of the Massachusetts Bay area did not sit idly by at the news of what was happening to the old rite. So great was the consternation that it passed a law, dated Nov. 13, 1644, reading as follows:

> It is ordered and agreed that if any person or persons within the jurisdiction shall either openly condemne or oppose the baptism of infants, or, go about secretly to seduce others from the approbation or the use thereof, or, shall purposely depart the congregation at the administration of the ordinance . . . and shall appear to the Court wilfully or obstinately to continue therein after due time and means of conviction, every such person or persons shall be sentenced to banishment.[95]

In other words, such a person would become the object of *exterminatio* in the derived sense of the word. At about this same time the Virginia colony enacted a law that "every person who refuses to have his child baptized by a lawful minister shall be amerced 2000 pounds of tobacco — half to the parish and half to the informer."[F] The old notions woven into "Christian sacralism" were coming to expression once more: if a person is to be put out of the church he cannot be allowed to stay in the commonwealth; one who refuses to make his child a part of *Corpus Christianum* cannot himself remain a member of the society.

It could have been predicted that with such laws on the

[F] It may interest the reader that at this same time a law was enacted providing that "the man and the woman committing fornication shall pay each 500 pounds of tobacco." Apparently, fornication was held to be but half as bad as a break with christening!

books and such convictions in the hearts of men there would be court action. There was. In July 1635, Williams was summoned to Boston to answer charges brought against him in the General Court. Interestingly enough (although not at all surprisingly, since we know that the rejection of christening was but a single facet of a much broader issue), the charges did not center on the matter of christening. The charges were: "First, the teaching that the magistrate ought not to punish the breach of the first table, otherwise than in such cases as did disturb the civil peace." The local clergymen had been asked to be at the trial, no doubt to satisfy the ancient provision that, before the *regnum* can act against the "heretic," he must be declared such by the *sacerdotium*. These, almost to a man, declared Williams to be guilty and deserving of banishment from the colony for maintaining "that the civil magistrate might not intermeddle even to stop a church from heresy and apostasy." The only comforting thing in the whole sorry account is that at the news of Williams' banishment the whole town of Salem was "in an uproar, for he was esteemed an honest, disinterested man, and of popular talents in the pulpit."[G] But that was not enough to stay the sentence. Williams was thrust out of the colony into the cold of a bleak New England winter, with wife and child. The New World hybrid had claimed new victims on the ancient charge of heresy-sedition.

One of the points at which all flat theology must run aground is the matter of discipline. It must either abandon the whole idea of discipline and carry anyone on its rolls, even the most profligate, or it must take the evildoer in hand; but if it does the latter, *excommunicatio* will not suffice — *exter-*

[G]There is every reason to think that it was not just the banished man's "talents in the pulpit" that endeared him to many people in the area. There seem to have been quite a few — more or less cryptic — Anabaptists in the settlements. We read in John Cotton's writings that "there be Anabaptists . . . tolerated to live not only in our jurisdiction but even in some of our churches." Winslow, in his *Briefe Narration* of 1646, as he speaks of Anabaptists and the laws against them in Massachusetts, says: "Certain men desiring some mitigation of it, it was answered in my hearing: 'Tis true we have a severe law, but we never did or will execute the rigor of it upon any; and we have men living amongst us, nay, some in our churches, of that judgment." As had been the case with the Reformers in general, so it was apparently with Williams: he found followers before he made followers (*C.W.*, IV, 416).

minatio must follow. Williams saw through the fallacy of the old sacral argument. He asked John Cotton reproachfully: "Why was I not yet permitted to live in the world, or Commonweale (of Massachusetts), except for this reason, that the Common-weale and Church is yet one, and hee that is banished from the one must necessarily bee banished from the other also." Williams was also well aware of the harmful effect flat theology has always had on the concept of discipline. He saw that failure to perceive the early of the Old Testament and the late of the New was responsible for the disarray into which the matter of church discipline had fallen. With his usual clarity of insight, he called attention to the fact that in I Corinthians 5:13 Paul takes the Old Testament disciplinary action that was to end in *exterminatio* and alters it to end in *excommunicatio* and no more. Williams said: "The same word used by Moses for putting an evil-doer to death in physical Israel, by sword, stoning, etc., is used here by Paul for spiritual killing or cutting off by excommunication." Only a person committed to progressive grace could have noticed Paul's far-reaching transvaluation.

Fortunately for Williams, and even more for his family, he was on good terms with the surrounding Indians. They took him and his dependents into their wigwams until spring came. This hospitality shown by the Indians for the homeless Williams reflects another feature in the tensions that had developed. We have seen above how the concept of Christendom precludes mission in the New Testament sense of the word, and inversely how the recovery of such mission requires a foregoing repudiation of *Corpus Christianum*. Roger Williams had abandoned the concept of *Corpus Christianum*; therefore, he could develop a sense of mission.

In this development Williams not only stood alone but also had the clergymen of the day to buck. They continued to see the citizenry and the people of God as identical entities. For example, John Cotton, one of the stronger preachers of the time, in his disputations with Williams argued:

> The dispensing of the Word in a Church-State (that is, by Church-officers to Church members united together in the Church-State) is indeed an expression of familiar and deare Communion between Christ and His Church, as between the husband and his spouse, between a mother and the child, and, between the shepherd and his flock; but suppose Pagans and

Indians should ordinarily frequent our Church assemblies (as they are wont to doe in hearing the Word) doth he, Roger Williams, think that there is the like spirituall and familiar Communion between Christ and them as between Christ and his Church? (*C.W.*, II, 215)

In Cotton's view church and state are a single entity, best expressed in the symbol "Church-State"; all individuals who are not a part of the citizenry are somehow outside the concern of Christ. As if a believing Indian were further from the "Communion" with Christ than an unbelieving Englishman! As if being an Englishman were an asset in the things of God and being an Indian a liability! Williams thought radically otherwise about these matters.

In the course of his argument Cotton had referred to the Indians as "heathen." This drew from Williams an eloquent repudiation of that word: Williams said it was the correlative of the (to him thoroughly objectionable) word "Christendom." "Heathen" is a "Christian" equivalent of *Goyim*, used in the Old Testament for all non-Jewish, or Gentile, peoples. The word "heathen" harks back to the dispensation when a person's membership in a population group was an asset — and nonmembership a liability — in the things of the spirit. In Williams' thinking, total human society does not consist of "Christians" (called that because they are part of a christened population group) and "heathen"; it consists of believers and nonbelievers. In this matter Williams showed remarkable originality and insight, born of his discovery of the three-dimensional grace. For the word "heathen" is an invention that was put on the market to satisfy a need that dates back to the birth of the original hybrid. It stands for an unchristened population group: there are no "heathen"[H] in Christendom, only

---

[H]The word "heathen" originated in medieval times regarding the people known as gypsies. These roving bands of unchristened people were notorious for taking things that did not belong to them. As with all groups that are basically sacral in their thinking, the gypsies did not consider taking things from nongypsies to be theft; theft for them was to divest a fellow gypsy of his belongings. This kind of spin-off from sacral thinking was common in medieval morality, where plundering non-Christians was not considered the same as plundering christened ones. The same duplicity occurs in the medieval rationale regarding slave-holding: to enslave a person belonging to an unchristened group was not considered wrong; only to enslave a fellow "believer" was wrong. The same argument ran in the sacralism of medieval Arabs: they engaged in slave-trading without com-

outside of Christendom. "Heathen" are those who surround *Corpus Christianum*.

No one should be surprised that, with their religious leaders speaking about the Indian neighbors as did John Cotton, the common people were quite devoid of concern for the souls and the general well-being of the natives of this new land. In his introductory paragraph to "Christening Maketh Not Christians," Williams said he had "oft heard both the English and the Dutch . . . say 'These Heathen Dogges, better kill a thousand of them then that we *Christians* should be endangered or troubled with them. . . . They have spilt our Christian Bloud, the best to make riddance of them, cut them all off and so make way for *Christians*.' "

Williams, to whom the expression "Christian Bloud" was unintelligible (as it should be for all clear-thinking people), not only thought differently about the Indians than did the rank and file and his critic John Cotton; he also behaved differently toward them. Early in his career he wrote in a letter: "My soul's desire was to do the natives good." He went in and out among them, even striking up an acquaintance with Chief Massasoit. To him they were not "heathen" but fellow human beings. In another letter he witnessed: "God was pleased to give me a painful [i. e., pains-full] and patient spirit, to lodge with them in their filthy, smoky holes, even while I lived at Plymouth and Salem, to gain their tongue." As a matter of fact, he did acquire a working knowledge of the local Indians' dialect, so that among his literary relics is a handbook of the language intended to help others who would "do the natives good." When it is recalled that a full century and a half later, in 1792, William Carey (often called the pioneer in the recovery of mission) had to ask searching questions and argue at length "whether the Great Commission given by our Lord to his disciples be still binding on us," we realize how far ahead

---

punction, for they restricted their operations to *kaffirs* ("unbelievers"). Because gypsies stole, they were ordered to spend the nights outside the towns. Fortunately for them, every municipality had its "commons," an unproductive heath on which nothing but heather grew. Thus the gypsies were associated with the heath and came to be known as "heath-people" or "heathen." Since these "heathen" were unbaptized, the word "heathen" was later extended to denote any unbaptized population group. Thus the very word "heathen" is the progeny of the hybrid. It continues to be in use wherever the hybrid has not been expelled.

of his time Roger Williams was in the matter of mission — all because he had repudiated flat theology and the *Corpus Christianum* view of the church. We may also say that it was because he had learned to know the hybrid for the mongrel creature it is.

Williams' assessment of the Constantinian change is quite clear: he had no use for it. This is apparent from such passages as the following:

> All may see how since the Apostacie of Antichrist the Christian world (so called) hath swallowed up Christianity, how the Church and Civill State, that is the Church and the world, are now become one Flocke of Jesus Christ, Christ's sheepe and the Pastors of them, all one with unconverted, wilde and tame beasts and Cattell of the world and the civill and earthly governours of them. (*C.W.*, III, 174)

In another place Williams wrote:

> I acknowledge the Ordinances of the Magistracie to be properly and adequately fitted by God, to preserve the civill State in civill peace and order; as he hath also appointed a spiritual Government and Governours in matters pertaining to his worship and the consciences of men, both which Governments, Governours, Laws, Offences, Punishments, are Essentially distinct and the confounding of them brings the whole world into combustion. (*C.W.*, I, 51)

Unlike the magisterial reformers, who to a man considered the Constantinian innovation to have been a great boon to the church of Christ, Williams, along with the rival church of early times and late, considered it to have been a disaster. Wrote he:

> The poor servants of Christ, for some hundreds of years after the departure of the Lord enjoyed no other power, no other Sword nor Shield but spirituall, until it pleased the Lord to try his children with Liberty and ease under Constantine (a sorer Tryall then befell them in 300 years persecution) under which temporall protection, munificence and bounty of Constantine, together with his temporall Sword, drawne out against her spirituall enemies, the Church of Christ soon surfeited of the too much honey of worldly ease, authority, profit, pleasure, etc. (*C.W.*, IV, 384)

In another place he had this to say about the Constantinian change:

> Then began the mysterie of the Churches sleepe, the Gardens

> of Christ's Churches turned into the wilderness of Nationall Religion and the world (under Constantine's Dominion) to the most un-Christian Christendomme. (*C.W.*, IV, 442)

Williams' evaluation of the Constantinian formula concluded that "the unknowing zeal of Constantine and other Emperours, did more hurt to Christ Iesus his Crowne and Kingdome, then the raging fury of the most bloody Neroes. . . . Babel or confusion was ushered in, and by degrees the Gardens of the Churches of the Saints were turned into the Wildernesse of whole Nations, untill the whole world became Christian or Christendome" (*C.W.*, III, 184). We witness here a thinker who had left the magisterial reformers' lofty appraisal of the hybrid far behind.

Roger Williams had also moved far beyond the concept of toleration; he was a proponent of freedom of conscience, which is quite a different thing. The word "toleration" actually implies intolerance, for it is the correlative of establishment; only in the context of a "right" religion can one speak of being tolerant. Freedom of conscience, on the other hand, implies that no religion or ultimate loyalty has the right of way and thus that no "other" religion has to be "tolerated." Williams wanted freedom of conscience, not toleration. This is apparent from the fact that, even though he had little sympathy for Roman Catholicism as such, calling it "antichrist" and "the great whore" (as non-Catholics commonly referred to it in his day), he wanted freedom of conscience for them as well, along with all other groups.

> I confess in this plea for freedom to all consciences in matters of worship, I have impartially pleaded for the freedom of the consciences of the Papists themselves, the greatest enemies and persecutors (in Europe) of the Saints and the truths of Jesus, yet I have pleaded for no more than is their due and right, and (whatever else shall be the consequent) it shall stand for a monument and testimony against them and be an aggravation of their former, present, or future cruelties against Christ Jesus and all that uprightly love him, his true Disciples and followers. (*C.W.*, IV, 47)

Roger Williams and his followers were able to escape the flat theology of the Reformation and its implications because they had learned to see that the Christian church stands closer to the New Testament than to the Old. He had noticed how seldom those who fancied the hybrid drew their arguments from the New Testament. Speaking of Catholics and magisterial reformers, Williams wrote: "Nor one nor other seldome dare to plead the mighty Prince Christ Jesus for their Authour, yet both (Protestant and Papist) pretend they have spoke with Moses and the Prophets, who all, say they (before Christ came) allowed such holy persecutions, holy Warres against the enemies of the holy Church" (*C.W.*, III, 58).

The distinction of early and late in the theology of Roger Williams stands out clearly:

> Where do you find one footstep, Print or Pattern in this doctrine of the Son of God, for a nationall holy Covenant, and so consequently . . . a Nationall Church? Where find you evidence of a whole Nation, Country or Kingdom converted to the Faith and of Christs appointing of a whole Nation or Kingdome to walk in one way of Religion? If you repair to Moses, consult with Moses and the old Covenant or Testament, we aske, are you Moses or Christs Followers? or do you yet[1] expect the comming of the Son of God to set up the Christian Israel, the holy Nation, the particular Congregation of Christian Worshippers, in all parts of the world? (*C.W.*, II, 264)

Perhaps nothing Williams wrote sets forth more clearly the procompositism cast of the man's mind than the famous "Shipletter" (as it has come to be called), a composition written to dispel certain widespread rumors that in newly founded Providence there "was no civil rule" — a charge which the rival church had heard from Reformation times. In this "Shipletter" he wrote:

> There goes many a ship to sea, with many hundred souls in one ship, whose weal and woe is common, and is a true picture of a commonwealth, or human combination or society. It hath fallen out sometimes, that both papists and protestants, Jews and Turks, may be embarked in one ship; upon which supposal I affirm, that all the liberty of conscience, that ever I pleaded for, turns upon these two hinges — that none of the papists, protestants, Jews, or Turks, be forced to come to the ship's prayers or worship, nor compelled from their own partic-

---

[1] This "yet" takes us back to the notion, found already in Augustine's writings and recurring in medieval thinkers and the writings of the magisterial reformers, that the people of God was destined to include the whole human race. This prospect had occurred to the author of Revelation, who thought of it as the reign of Antichrist. Williams had thought of it too and had rejected it. He wonders whether his opponents were still thinking that the future holds such a final worldwide church in store.

ular prayers or worship, if they practice any. I further add, that I never denied, that notwithstanding this liberty, the commander of this ship ought to command the ship's course, yea, and also command that justice, peace and sobriety, be kept and practiced, both among the seamen and all the passengers. If any of the seamen refuse to perform their services, or passengers to pay the freight; if any refuse to help, in person or in purse, toward the common charges or defence; if any refuse to obey the common laws and orders of the ship, concerning their common peace or preservation; if any shall mutiny and rise up against their commanders or officers; if any should preach or write that there ought to be no commanders or officers, because all are equal in Christ, therefore no masters nor officers, no laws nor orders, nor corrections nor punishments — I say, I never denied, but in such cases, whatever is pretended, the commander or commanders may judge, resist, compel and punish such transgressors, according to their deserts and merits. (*C.W.*, IV, 278f.)

In this "Shipletter" Williams not only draws the blueprints for the composite society but also clears himself once more of the charge, hoary with age, that one who breaks with *Corpus Christianum* is guilty of "rejecting the magistracy." In it he also rejects the teaching contained in Article 36 of the Belgic Confession a full century before the Dutch churches began to doubt its theology — that one who, like the Anabaptists, rejects the sacral society is an anarchist. The question arises here whether Williams knew the Belgic Confession, whose teachings he plainly rejects. He may very well have been acquainted with that confession either in its original French or in its early Dutch translation. Moreover, the Belgic Confession had been brought to England by the *vluchtelingsgemeenten* (the refugee churches) that flourished there, with the old cathedral "Austin Friars" as headquarters. In addition, the Belgic Confession had already been "englished" in 1644[96] (before the "Shipletter" was written) expressly to satisfy the need for a concise statement of faith which members of the "refugee church" could give to their neighbors who asked about their faith.

Thus it is apparent from the writings of Roger Williams that he was committed to the idea of progressive grace; the state was for him the creature of God's grace, but not a product of his redemptive grace, as he made clear in many expressions: "I shall humbly suggest . . . as the greatest causes, fountaines and tap roots of all Indignation of the most High, against the State and Countrey: First, that the whole Nation and Generations of Men have been forced (though unregenerate and unrepentant) to pretend and assume the name of Christ Jesus, which only belongs, according to the Institution of the Lord Jesus, to truely regenerate and repenting soules. Secondly, that all others dissenting from them, whether Jewes or Gentiles, their Countrymen especially (for strangers have a Libertie), have not been permitted civill cohabitation in this world with them, but have been distressed and persecuted by them" (*C.W.*, I, 361). This line of thought was so manifestly correct even to Williams' archenemy John Cotton that the latter said that the two points were "worthy of due consideration and attention. I would rather say amen to them, than weaken the weight of them." However, thereupon Cotton, as was the inevitable custom of all who sustained the hybrid, said that in the really weighty matters of the faith the civil ruler had the duty to suppress ideas out of keeping with the "right" religion (*C.W.*, I, 361, n. 22), thus supplying us with another example of the both-and theology that had been fashioned in the days of the first hybrid's birth. It was yet another example of blowing both hot and cold, of "sweet water and bitter from the same fountain."

When the Salem church was trying to engage Roger Williams to be its pastor, the men of the local *regnum*, running true to form, were worried because they knew about the man's rejection of *Corpus Christianum* theology. Therefore, they enacted a law prohibiting anyone from being admitted to the freedom of that body politic who was not a member of one of the churches within the limits of the municipality. It speaks for itself that Williams disliked the law, not so much because it was sure to impose a hardship upon his own person as because of the principle involved: that membership in a church of the "right" religion was a prerequisite for citizenship. He argued that by this law the "door of calling to the magistracy was shut against natural and unregenerate men, though excellently fitted for civil office," and also closed to "the best and ablest servants of God, except they be entered into Church estate." This, he added, was "to pluck up the roots and foundations of all common society in the world, to turn the garden and paradise of the Church and state into the field of the civil state of the world, and to reduce the world to the first chaos and confusion."ʲ

Williams not only did not ask government favors for his constituency, but he also chided those Protestants who "ride the backs and necks of Civill magistrates as fully and as heavily (though not as pompously) as ever the great Whore sat the backs of Papist Princes" (*C.W.*, IV, 430). Along with the members of the rival church of pre-Reformation times, Williams saw the post-Constantinian world as a time of decay, in which people "disdain'd to serve a poore despised Christ, a carpenter, one who came at last to the gallows . . . and therefore have they framed to themselves rich and Lordly, pompous and Princely, temporall and Worldly Christs, instead of the true Jesus Christ." Here we hear the argument, heard from the "heretics" throughout medieval times, that the pomp and pride of the post-Constantinian times were features of the fallen church — just as humility and simplicity are the necessary qualities of the true church. Ostentation, the medieval "heretics" had insisted, had rubbed off on the church at the time of the birth of the original hybrid. Williams had evaluated the principle known as *cujus regio ejus religio* (to whom the region belongs politically, his religion rules), which had led Frederick of the Palatinate to order out of his domains all who would not accept the Heidelberg Catechism (which he had commissioned to be written) as their creed; and Williams realized what a farce it makes of religion. The history of his own native England gave him all the laboratory proof he needed. Of that history he wrote: "Who knowes not how easie it is to turne, and turne, and turne againe whole Nations from one Religion to another? Who knowes not that within the compasse of one poore span of 12

ʲThis expression "the first chaos and confusion" is interesting, and somewhat confusing. Does Williams mean the "confusion," the "flowing-together," that characterized the Old Testament regime, in which *regnum* and *sacerdotium* were indeed "confused"? Or does he mean thereby the chaos of the prediluvian world, into which God introduced the creature of his preliminary grace, the state? Either interpretation makes sense, but my guess is that Williams meant the latter. He saw, very correctly, that the civil leaders of Salem were committed to a position that precludes the very idea of a God-intended, and thus God-pleasing, *regnum* in those areas where the gospel message and its program of redemptive grace has not yet come. In either case, we again see that Williams' theology was sketched on the grid of progressive grace.

yeares revolution,^K all England hath become from halfe Papist, halfe Protestant, to be absolute Protestant; from absolute Protestants to absolute Papists, from absolute Papists to absolute Protestants?" (*C.W.*, III, 325f.)

We who are so accustomed to the things for which the intrepid Roger contended are likely to allow the boldness and courage of the man's thought to escape us. He pleaded for all this in the face of deeply entrenched sacralism, which had just put the following regulation on the books of the Massachusetts Bay *regnum*: "Whosoever shall stand excommunicate for the space of six months, without labouring what in him or her lyeth to bee restored, such a person shall be presented to the Court of Assistants, and there proceeded with by fine, imprisonment, or further, etc. . . ."[97] Williams knew that banishment awaited him; yet he carried on.

Since Roger Williams had learned to dislike the hybrid, it was inevitable that he would attack the idea of a cult to which people were driven. He wrote in criticism of involuntary attendance at the shrine: "Never did the Lord Jesus bring into his most holy worship for he abhorres (as all men, yea the very Indians doo) an unwilling Spouse, and to enter into a forced bed; the will in worship, if true, is like a free Vote, *nec cogit nec cogitur;* Jesus Christ compells by the perswasions of his Messengers to come in, but otherwise with earthly weapons he never did compell nor can be compelled. The not discerning of this truth hath let out the bloud of thousands in civill combustion in all ages, and made the whore drunke and the Earth

---

^K Williams' reference to "one poore span of twelve yeares" is to the period (1547-59) during which the "right" religion had been that of Henry VIII, then that of Edward VI, then of Mary Tudor, and finally of Elizabeth I. It was a period in which people were ordered to change their ultimate loyalties as they changed their shirts. Nor was this the only instance of "turne, and turne, and turne again." This also occurred in the Palatinate, where Frederick laid the Heidelberg Catechism upon all his subjects, ordering those who did not comply to leave his territories (an act that was in violation of the Treaty of 1555, and for which he was taken to task at the Diet of Augsburg); when Frederick died in 1576, his son, Louis VI, reintroduced Lutheranism as the "right" religion and likewise told all who refused to go along with the change to quit the country; in 1583, when the throne went to Frederick IV (as yet a child under the tutelage of his uncle, John Casimir), Calvinism was once more imposed on the people. It is easy to see what becomes of authentic Christianity when men thus play politics with the faith.

drunk with the bloud of the Saints, and witnesses of Jesus" (*C.W.*, VII, 38).

As we have seen throughout this study, wherever the hybrid exists, the question of the conventicle is sure to come up. Medieval Christendom's proscription of the conventicle had a long tradition in the England in which Williams had been brought up. In the year 1569, for example, when a conventicle was discovered there, its leader and twenty-four of his followers were arrested and jailed until they promised not to meet in conventicle again. In Roger Williams' thinking, the relationship of church and state was such that the conventicle was not only permissible but represented the only *right* kind of assembly. It was the cult done under public auspices that was wrong. He wanted all religious gatherings to be free, that is, neither helped nor hindered by the *regnum*. How radical and intolerable this was bound to appear in colonial America may be gathered from the treatment meted out to one Obadiah Holmes for his behavior. This man had left the established church and had joined the fellowship of a small rival church that consisted of persons who had broken with christening. He was haled into court "for continuing a meeting upon the Lord's Day from house to house"; but he fled to Newport to escape the wrath of the *regnum*. In July of the next year he came to the town of Lynn to visit an aged and sick member of their little fellowship. During this visit a companion of Holmes named Clarke preached at a conventicle. The men were arrested for this and brought to trial in Boston. Holmes was sentenced to pay a fine of thirty pounds "or be well whipt." He refused to pay the fine and therefore suffered the whipping: it was not lightly done, the servant of the *regnum* "striking him with all his strength (yea, spitting in his hand three times as many affirmed) with a three-corded whip, giving him therewith thirty stroakes." The governor later testified that the flogging had been done "in such an unmerciful manner that in many days, if not some weeks, he could take no rest but as he lay upon his knees and elbows, not being able to suffer any part of his body to touch the bed on which he lay." One witness, a Mr. Palfrey, testified that "the poor sufferer had such inward peace that in a manner he felt it not." No doubt Holmes was convinced that he was walking in the footsteps of the apostles, who after similar treatment were "rejoicing that they were counted worthy to suffer dishonor for the name."

Just before this particular horse-whipping, John Cotton, minister of the "right" religion in the area, had preached a sermon (in connection with the "threat" which Williams and his ilk were posing) in which he repeated the age-old sacralist axiom that there must be unity acquired through a common sacrament if there is to be civil tranquility. In this sermon Cotton had said that "denying infant baptism would overthrow all; it is a capital offence and they are soul-murtherers." Very probably it was this sermon, with its unveiled reference to those who were rejecting the sacrament of christening, that prompted the men of the *regnum* to publicly flog Obadiah Holmes — an excellent citizen and an obedient subject in all things that pertain to the office of the magistrate.[L] His only fault was that he no longer loved hybrids and had begun to believe authentic Christianity yields a composite society.

We who take for granted the kind of society for which the rival church of those days agonized should not forget how radical the position appeared in the eyes of the establishment. Nor should we be surprised that the ideas believed and propagated in the rival church came to be accepted very slowly, syllable by syllable, and often unwillingly. Decades later some of the best minds in the New World still looked upon Roger Williams as a hopeless "crank," and his ideas a petulant brainstorm. In 1702, Cotton Mather, acknowledged to have been one of the best thinkers — certainly one of the most influential preachers — in New England, looked back at the events of which we have been speaking and wrote: "In the year 1654 a certain windmill in the Low Countries whirling round with extraordinary violence by reason of a violent storm then blowing, the stone at length by the rapid motion became so intensely hot as to fire the mill, did set a whole town on fire. But, I can tell my reader that about twenty years before this there was a whole country in America like to be set on fire by the rapid motion of a windmill in the head of one particular man."[98] Mather's man with the windmill in his head was none other than Roger Williams. One can somewhat understand the inability of Williams' contemporaries to assimilate his ideas in a fortnight (although it is hard to accept that a man of John

---

[L]In any event the people in England held John Cotton responsible for the whipping. Shortly after the news of it had reached England, John Cotton received a letter from England informing him that "these rigid wayes have lay'd you very low in the hearts of the saynts."

"AND ALSO AFTERWARD"

Cotton's mental caliber should have thought Williams a "haberdasher of small questions"). But it is difficult indeed to comprehend why a man like Cotton Mather, so long after, should be as yet completely blind to the profundity and correct simplicity of Williams' principles. History was to show, however, that the ideas of Roger Williams were anything but "small."

After his banishment from the Massachusetts Bay Colony, Williams bought a sizable piece of land from the Indians[M] and founded on it a settlement in the signature of his "small" ideas, a municipality where a man's religious loyalty (or lack of it) did not give him either a pull or a push in the civil area. This experiment with outright freedom of conscience was destined to become a pilot venture. It gave the precedent for that separation of church and state provided by the First Amendment of the Federal Constitution, which was presently drawn up to secure the composite society for which the rival church had agonized since times out of memory.

* * * * *

Although the ideas propounded by Roger Williams did not greatly impress even some of the best minds in the New World, they did draw the attention of European observers. These seem to have sensed the epoch-making potential in Roger Williams' ideas and the pilot venture at Providence. They sensed the radical implications of Williams' fight for societal compositism. For example, a German historian by the name of Gervinus wrote:

> Roger Williams founded in 1636 a small new society in Rhode Island upon the principles of entire liberty of conscience. . . . The theories of freedom in Church and State . . . were here brought into practice in the government of a small community.

[M]The fact that Williams purchased land from the Indians brings into focus other aspects of the man's strength. Manifestly he did not share in the prevailing notion that just as the children of Israel had pushed the natives out of the land of promise, it was the right and calling of the colonial sacralists to dispossess the Indians. His convictions on this point were another thorn in the flesh of the establishment. He had said at one time that the King of England did not have any land in the New World to give away by charter; the legal owners, said he, were the red-skinned natives. This position, of course, was very unwelcome in his day and was listed as one of his "small" and unacceptable ideas.

> It was prophesied that the democratic attempts to obtain universal suffrage, a general elective franchise, annual parliaments, entire religious freedom, and the Miltonian right of schism, would be of short duration. But the institutions have not only maintained themselves here, but have spread over the whole Union. They have superseded the aristocratic commencements of Carolina and of New York, the high Church party of Virginia, the theocracy of Massachusetts, and the monarchy, throughout America; they have given laws to one quarter of the globe, and dreaded for their moral influence, they stand in the background of every democratic struggle in Europe.99

Georg Jellinek, long-time professor of history at Heidelberg and a recognized authority on American origins, had this to say of Roger Williams and his "small" ideas:

> The idea of legally established unalienable, inherent, and sacred rights of the individual is not of political but of religious origin. What has sometimes been held to be a work of the Revolution was in reality a fruit of the Reformation and its struggles. Its first apostle was not Lafayette but Roger Williams, who, driven by a powerful and deep religious enthusiasm, went into the wilderness in order to found a government of religious liberty, and his name is uttered by Americans even today with deepest respect.100

Earlier, the German historian Lezius had had this to say of Williams and his convictions:

> The Protestant concept of the State . . . was not favorable to the idea of toleration. To a modification of the Protestant concept of the State, one which would encourage toleration, did the Anabaptists force the promoters of a State-Church; by so doing they have, as they suffered and contended, performed an unspeakable service . . . one for which they have not as yet, not by a long way, received the thanks which is their fair due at the forum of history. . . . On German soil these non-back-fighting Anabaptist Christians did not achieve much in the way of correcting the errors of the Reformation. . . . The situation was quite different in England, and here the free-churchism of the Anabaptist reformation fought through to a great victory for toleration by means of a modification in the concept of the State. . . . The separation of Church and State is not the product of the *Aufklärung* [Enlightenment] but is the ripe fruit of the free Church idea of the Anabaptist Reformation.101

Not all historians would agree with Lezius' sweeping assertion that "the separation of Church and State" as exempli-

"AND ALSO AFTERWARD"

fied in America is not the product of the Enlightenment but "the ripe fruit of the free Church idea of the Anabaptist Reformation." There can be no doubt that men like Thomas Jefferson had read the Encyclopedists, and it would be very strange indeed if they had not taken over some of those ideas. But there can also be no doubt that the Revolution in America differed in important respects from its French counterpart. One of these differences is that in the American Revolution one does not find the bitter hostility toward the church that was so much a feature of the French Revolution. Even today it is unusual to find an American damning the church. There are, to be sure, plenty of Americans who ignore the church completely; but few Americans have deep-seated resentment toward the church, as is so often the case in other countries. The church has not required them to support an institution in which they are not interested; it certainly hasn't asked the *regnum* to force people to support it by tax levies, as it so commonly did in lands where *Corpus Christianum* lingered on.

Recently a German scholar has said, as he viewed the wreckage caused by the Nazi rampage: "What a pain it is for anyone who knows Church history that we treated the gentle Anabaptists the way we did! At that time the best spiritual forces of the Reformation emigrated out of the Churches of the Reformation."[102] He was referring to the fact that it was due to the lingering sacralism in Germany as fed and nourished by the magisterial Reformation that the Nazis were able to swing into power virtually without any resistance from the churches. The Nazi minister of propaganda declared early in the Nazi takeover: "The *Volk* is not a subsidiary concern of the Church but is its *chief* concern; a fellowship of the total people the Church must be, not a separate fellowship with its own separate structurization; concern for its own separate fellowship has often deflected the Church away from its real God-given assignment and restricts it in the matter to this day." Very few persons in Germany saw where this view was going to lead, for they were accustomed to hearing language like that: they were used to a close church-state partnership as worked out in the magisterial Reformation, and they saw nothing sinister in the proposed idea of a religious togetherness that coincided with the political togetherness — until it was too late to head off the monstrous hybrid and its attendant evils. It was not until the formation of the *Notpfarrerbund* (emergency pastors' association), which then became the *Bekenntnisfront* (the confessional front) under pastor Niemoeller, that the concept of the composite society again came into view. Since that time many German thinkers have come to the conclusion that Constantinianism has had its day, although there are also those who in desperation are giving blood transfusions to the hybrid.

We have pointed out that because the ideas prevalent in rival church circles since very early times were successfully suppressed on the continent, it was not until the French Revolution broke that the hybrid received its mortal wound in those parts. The French Revolution ushered in many of the ideas for which the rival church had agonized, but it did so in a mood altogether different from that of those who had in earlier times pioneered for separation of church and state, as well as for all the many corollaries of three-dimensional theology. It was also different from the mood of the American revolutionaries. Thomas Jefferson, for example, was and remained altogether appreciative of America's religious heritage, especially of those religious ideas that had been nurtured in the Anabaptist segment. In a letter to the Baptist Association of Danbury, Connecticut, he declared: "Believing with you that religion is a matter which lies solely between man and his God, that he owes account to none other for his faith and for his worship, that legislative powers of government reach actions only, and not opinions, I contemplate with sovereign reverence that act of the whole American people which declares that their legislature should make no law respecting an establishment of religion, or prohibit the free exercise thereof."[103] This attitude of friendliness to the churches was characteristic of the promoters of the American Revolution.

In this letter to the Baptist Association, Jefferson was referring to the First Amendment of the Federal Constitution, from which he was plainly quoting. The genesis of this First Amendment is, of course, a part of the story being told in this study, the story of the ups and downs of the principle of compositism. When the thirteen colonies came together for the purpose of federation, most of them still had a "right" religion. Thus, the question came up concerning which religion would be the "right" religion of the federal government that was to be fashioned. This led to a hopeless deadlock, for each of the units wanted its faith to be the faith of the resultant whole. After much discussion, some wrangling (and, it is said, some prayer), it was decided to create a central government which would show neither favor nor disfavor toward any of the ultimate loyalties to which groups of citizens might hold. It was this that led to the writing of the famous First Amendment. Without the position set forth in it, the federation would have been quite impossible. We can also say that had it not been for the precedent of the "toleration State," Roger Williams' Rhode Island, the First Amendment would have been very unlikely. The experiment at Rhode Island had, at least, given the lie to the old sacralist notion that if there is to be quiet on the public square there must first be unanimity at the shrine. Societal compositism was secured by legal enactment of the First Amendment, and in doing so this amendment marked a new departure in the structuring of human society, in that it presupposed compositism in the area of people's highest loyalty. In all of this we can see the final fruition of ideas long held and nourished in the rival church. For, as Ernst Troeltsch has said of the American innovation: "Here the stepchildren of the Reformation have at long last lived to see their great hour in the history of the world. . . . Here the medieval concept of culture was brought to its end and in the place of the medieval constraint culture of the State-Church combination came the beginning of modern free-from-the-Church culture of the individual man."[104]

The principles of the rival church bore fruit in yet another area in the New World — the termination of slaveholding. Rhode Island, the place where those principles were first put to practice, is known to have played an important part in emancipation.[105] This reflects that colony's affinity with old rival church ideas and ideals, which included a repudiation of slaveholding. Henri Bullinger, Zwingli's successor at Zürich, said in a letter dated 1560, that "it is an old tradition among Anabaptists[N] that . . . there should be no slaves, that it is morally wrong for one man to own another man."[106] It should

---

[N]The question must be asked how Bullinger could speak, in 1560, of an "old Anabaptist tradition," when Anabaptism as commonly thought of was but one generation old. He was probably using the term loosely, as many did in his day, to denote pre-Reformation "heretics," perhaps the Waldensians.

not come as a surprise that the rejection of the sacral formula for society led to a rejection of slaveholding. Sacralism creates a climate that accommodates itself very readily to involuntary servitude because it uses coercion instead of voluntarism in the area of men's highest loyalty. For this reason sacral societies have regularly sheltered the institution of slavery. Examples of this go back to ancient times. Egypt of the Pharaohs was sacral, and it enslaved Israelites; Israel itself was sacral, and it had its Midianites as "hewers of wood and drawers of water." The theoreticians of sacralism have regularly defended the enslavement of persons and groups not bound by the sacramental bond that held their own society together. The doctors of medieval "Christian sacralism" taught that Saracens and other "heathen" are properly subjected to perpetual and involuntary servitude. The Islamic world, which is sacral in its thinking, considered it permissible to enslave *kaffirs*, that is, non-Mohammedans.[o] The Spanish *conquistadors* in our Southwest also acted on the medieval teaching of their church that it is proper to enslave unchristened persons.[p]

* * * * *

All churches in the New World, even those whose European counterparts are still close to the format of "Christendom," seem to accept with gratitude what the new structuring of society gives them. For example, a spokesman for Lutheranism, Theodore Meyer of the Missouri Synod, said: "The freedom of the Church, lost under Constantine, was not even regained in the Reformation. The Church of Germany — and of all Protes-

---

[o] It is a matter of record that the slave trade which brought waves of black people to the New World was launched by Arab traders, men whose religious indoctrination taught them that slavery was morally permissible. Arab pioneering in that nefarious business is reflected in the fact that in much of Africa a black person is to this day called a *kaffir*, an Arab word meaning "infidel."

[p] The "christianization" of the Indians of the Southwest was speeded up by the doctrine that it was permissible to indenture a "heathen" but not permissible to do so with a christened person. This gave the Indians the choice of going to the gold mines, where life was unbelievably cruel, or to the baptismal font. Anyone who has crawled in those narrow tunnels of the ancient gold-mining activities will not find it difficult to understand that many chose the latter alternative.

tant countries of Europe — became, and to this day has remained, a part of the State's machinery. Not until the United States of America was established did the world see a land in which this right and natural and Scriptural relation between Church and State exists: separation."[107] Father John Cogley gives a Roman Catholic viewpoint:

> We have no Church-State problem in the classic sense. Our system of separation, so it seems to me, is as close as any people can come to resolving the inescapable difficulties in trying to give to Caesar what is Caesar's and to God what is God's. . . . It works. The rights of the Church are scrupulously observed in the American courts; the needs of the State are recognized and honored by the Church. I cannot think of any place on earth where it is easier for a man to fulfill his religious duties than in the United States — to give God what is His. Nor can I think of a place where the State asks so little of what the religious man cannot give. When it does, the religious man can make a conscientious appeal and the State will listen. . . . Where is the Church in a healthier condition?[108]

It is, of course, true that it is still good Roman Catholic doctrine that the sword of the *regnum* be used to advance the "right" religion (Catholicism); but it is certainly also true that most American Catholics would demand that this "right" doctrine be repealed rather than that the American formula be rejected.

The thought system of the rival church has in our day received a sweeping endorsement from the late Karl Barth. Realizing that the German Nazi movement would have been impossible without the background of "Christian sacralism," he began to question the legitimacy of the whole Constantinian formula. Barth saw that Constantine had been "the creator of the Christian *Volkskirche*," which Barth thereupon rejected forthrightly. He found it deplorable that "when Constantine elevated Christianity to the status of the religion of the State . . . and when the terrain of the Church was made to coincide with that of peoplehood, then many thought they saw in this development the reinstitution of the Old Testament dispensation and at the same time the fulfillment of the New Testament prophecy of Revelation 20."[109] Barth soon saw that the whole Constantinian venture was a grand mistake. He wrote:

> Do I err if I think that the real and determining ground for the baptism of infants was, with the Reformers and since that day each time again, quite simply this: men could not bring themselves then, not in any case or at any cost — nor can they now, in any case or at any price — to let go of the idea of an evangelical Church in the format of *Corpus Christianum,* the image of a *Volkskirche?* A *Volkskirche,* as a State Church and Church-of-the-masses, this the Church can no longer very well be if it breaks with infant baptism. *Hinc, hinc, illae lacrymae!* [Whence, whence all these tears!] Does not that concern which reveals itself here perhaps have its primitive form in that fact to which Luther upon occasion confessed, namely, that there would not be so very many baptized ones if and when people had to *come* to baptism rather than be *brought* to it? We are not unmindful of the practical and actual difficulty involved in the decision that looms up here; but we wish nevertheless to ask whether this is a legitimate worry. Is it not always the case, and so also here, that it is advisable to take a careful look at those things which we hold to be indispensable in any event and at every cost? Are we then really so sure of the intrinsic correctness of the Constantinian system, the present configuration of our *Volkskirche?* Is our conscience in the matter then so good, that we can and may be determined, come what may, to hang on to it — even at the price of inflicting, by a misconstructed baptism practice, endless wounds and sickness upon the Church . . . ? Where, pray, is it written that the Christian Church is not to be a minority, perhaps a small minority? Would she not be more useful to her surroundings if she were a *healthy* Church instead? What does it really profit the Church to continue to be a Church-of-the-people rather than a Church-for-the-people . . . ? What is needed is very simple: a baptism to take the place of christening, one that is justifiable also from the side of the person receiving the baptism. He must, if things are to be right, pass from the status of a passive object of baptism to the status of a choosing and freely confessing . . . partner of Jesus Christ.[110]

There can be no doubt that Barth rejected *Corpus Christianum.* However, one might wish that he had worked out and stated as clearly just what he would carve out to take its place. There does not seem to be a simple formula whereby two institutions, one born of God's conserving grace and one of his redeeming grace, work smoothly together. The termination of *Corpus Christianum* does not solve all problems; in fact, it raises some new ones. As Hendrik Kraemer has pointed out, ever since *Corpus Christianum* has eroded away, the foremost problem of the church has been its relationship to the world.

Clearly, for Karl Barth the hybrid was not at all the lovely creature prevailing opinion had held it to be for a millennium or more; for him it was an ill-bred mongrel, the uncouth beast against which the rival church had agitated since the day of its birth. It is no wonder that two factions holding such widely divergent views were constantly at odds with each other: what the one called an upward movement the other called a fall; the one group's angel was the other's devil; what the one blessed the other cursed. The success of either evaluation of the hybrid depended on the suppression of the other view. However, it can perhaps be said today that most Protestants (and even some contemporary Catholics) are trying to maintain a position somewhere in between — not ready to endorse "Christian sacralism" any longer but not quite prepared to reject it. There are those who try to continue the both-and construction invented in the days of Augustine, a church that is both *Corpus Christi* and *Corpus Christianum*, both visible and invisible. People find it difficult to continue to embrace the hybrid, but difficult also to open fire on it. It is doubtful that such halting between two opinions can continue indefinitely.

In any event, it is still difficult to disagree with what Walter Hobhouse said early in this century: "Long ago I came to believe that the great change in the relations between the Church and the world which began with the conversion of Constantine is not only a decisive turning point in Church history but is also the key to many of the practical difficulties of the present day, and that the Church of the future is destined more and more to return to the condition of things somewhat like that which prevailed in the ante-Nicene Church; that is to say, that instead of pretending to be coextensive with the world it will confess itself to be the Church of a minority, will accept a position involving a more conscious antagonism with the World, and will, in return, gain in some measure its former coherence." Q 111

 Q In reference to the expression "former coherence," it may be pointed out that there is a connection between the discarding of Constantinianism and the espousal of ecumenism. The ecumenical movement did not begin until the concept of "Christendom" had begun to erode. One gets the impression that the fragmentation of the church was occasioned not so much by theological as by pretheological differences; it was rising nationalism rather than theological diversity that caused the Reformation to divide into various streams. The ecumenical movement does not result so much from theological accommodation as from the lessening of some of these pretheological differences. It is clearly significant that the so-called younger churches, which do not have a Constantinian heritage, are the churches most ardently committed to ecumenism. The more a given denomination is still held together by prereligious principles of inclusion, the less it feels for ecumenism. For instance, in the Reformed Churches of South Africa the prereligious ties are still very much in evidence, perhaps more so than in any other denomination; these churches are at the same time the least interested in ecumenicity.

POSTSCRIPT

In this study we have examined the actions and interactions of two religious traditions. On the one hand is the pre-Christian tradition, which needs unanimity and thus enforces conformity; on the other hand stands authentic Christianity, which needs diversity and therefore feeds the idea of the composite society. Basic to the difference between the two is a divergent view of man. In authentic Christianity, with its *Corpus Christi* view of the church, man is seen as a being who, since he exists "in God's image," has a sort of sovereignty: God deals with him in a way decidedly different from the way he deals with the rest of his creatures. In this view, God does not deal with man "as with sticks or stones" — to borrow an expression authentic Christianity has devised for the purpose — but as a person. For this reason language plays such an important part in this religious tradition, since language and personal relationship are mutually dependent on each other. On the other hand, the rest of the religious traditions of mankind see man as of a piece with the other creatures. Here language is not so much an exchange of propositions as a sort of emotional stimulus, much like that of a mother cat as it licks its kittens. Language as a matter of subjects and predicates is held in abeyance; sacrament and sacramental manipulation take its place. Salvation by sacrament goes hand in hand with a much lower view of man than is held by those who believe in salvation by response to the Word.

In view of these deeply rooted differences, it is not surprising to note that societies that have been molded by sacramental systems (i.e., pre-Christian societies) fall prey very readily to totalitarianism. The view of man in sacral or sacramental societies is identical to that in totalitarian systems. There is a close similarity between a *regnum* that manipulates the rank and file through a "praesidium," and a *sacerdotium* in which an *ecclesia docens* manipulates the laity through the use of sacramental elements. Therefore, it is not by chance that the concept of the dignity of man, the idea of self-determination, the granting of the right to opt, and all the other features that are part of the democratic vision were engendered on a terrain which had somehow managed to clear itself of the hybrid. Democracy, considered both ideologically and historically, is the progeny of the "heretic"; which is to say that it has its religious roots in authentic Christianity. The birth of America coincided with the expiration of the hybrid there. The republic that came into being two centuries ago was in virtually every way the answer to prayers that had gone up in conventicles held since time immemorial. In the United States there is no longer a rival church — for the quite simple reason that there is no longer an established church.

In this book we have dealt with history. It is not the historian's task to predict the future; that job he can safely leave to the prophet. Yet, during times like these, one cannot help trying to look ahead. Then the question will arise whether the hybrid is really as dead as it appears to be, or whether it is perhaps just playing dead. We have seen that the beast is tough, that it can adjust to great changes in topography and climate, can cross oceans and span continents. Therefore, the question is: will it heal itself of its deadly wound, rise to its feet once more, and prowl the earth again? All figurative speech aside, is the concept of the composite society safe and secure upon the earth? Totalitarianism, with its harsh demands for sameness, is widening its scope. There may be talk about "letting a hundred flowers grow"; but such talk, as we have had occasion to learn to our dismay, turns out to be just another demonic device intended first to locate dissent and then to suppress it, in an all-out effort to insure the starkly monolithic society.

Even in the free world the idea of diversity is on the defensive. Alikeness is the prevalent concept in pulpit and classroom alike. Propelled by such a predilection for sameness, John Dewey, said to be "the father of American education," says in *A Common Faith* that "historic Christianity is committed to the distinction of sheep and goats, the saved and the lost. . . ." He adds that unless such differentiations are somehow scuttled, the American dream of democracy cannot come true. The exact opposite of this thesis is, of course, more nearly correct: namely, that since the essence of the American dream is the composite society, the realization of the American dream is contingent on the perpetuation of the "sheep and goat" configuration, a situation in which there is room for widely diverse ultimate loyalties. The corollary of that configuration is the assumption that the *regnum* must not involve itself in these ultimate loyalties but must manage to carry on its own proper agenda on the plane of people's lesser loyalties. What John Dewey pleads for in *A Common Faith* is the return to a "right" religion, which, as history teaches us, invariably becomes wretchedly "wrong."

It is in keeping with the mood of coming to the end of this study that we glance at the last book of the Bible. In it we encounter a prophet who lets his eye range over what is to occur on the earth in the last days. What does he see? Cosmic victory for Christ? Hardly that: the battle of the ages is still raging as fiercely as ever. Does he see a continuation of pagan sacralism, which hustles off to a lonely island those who, like the writer of the Apocalypse, pose a problem to the monolithic society? Not that either, for in the final scene that John envisions, paganism has disappeared from the earth. What the lone visionary on Patmos does see is a world directed by a pseudo-Christ, known as Antichrist. It is a world bound together by a sacramental tie, visibly identifiable by the sacramental sign on the hand and the forehead of the rank and file. This sacramental sign assures uniformity in thought and deed. Without this final badge of massive sameness, it will be impossible either to buy or to sell, that is, impossible to live. And John sees a "remnant," a minority that rejects the common sacramental symbol, trying to be faithful to the Lamb in a monolithic society. Just as there was a divinely determined *terminus ad quem* in the days of the original hybrid, so in these final days there will be a God-given *terminus,* lest the abrasion suffered by the "remnant" prove to be "too much even for the elect." Then "Curtain!" After the final curtain there will be an ultimate compositism -- two camps "with a great gulf fixed" between them.

As long as there are sons of God upon the earth as well as daughters of men, congress between them is always a possibility. And thus there is the possibility of the engendering of a final hybrid — "and also afterward."

APPENDIX

The following fragments of medieval poetry indicate that the quality of life-style practiced by the medieval "heretics" was clearly distinguishable from that of their neighbors. These fragments also record some of the terms of opprobrium used against these conscientious believers. In my translations I have tried to reproduce rhyme and meter in English where it occurs in the original language.

The first selection is from the Waldensian tract entitled *La Nobla Leçon*. In it the following verse occurs:

S'il en est un bon	If there is a good man
qui aime et craigne Jesus Christ,	Who loves and fears Jesus Christ,
Qui ne veuille maudire,	Who can't be made to curse,
Ni jurer, ni mentir,	Nor swear, nor lie,
Ni commettre adultere,	Nor commit adultery,
Ni occire, ni prendre a autrui,	Nor kill, nor take from others,
Ni se venger de ses ennemis —	Nor avenge himself of his enemies —
Ils disent qu'il es Vaudes	They say he is a Vaudes[A]
Et digne d'etre puni.	And deserves to be punished.

The following passages from the versified *Life of the Duchess Iolanthe* (*Het Leven van Grafin Iolande van Vianen van Bruder Herman* [ed. J. Meyer; lines 3882f.]). In this narrative poem we read of a person who draws back from the prof-

---

[A] I have left the word "Vaudes" untranslated. It could be translated as either "sorcerer" or "Waldensian." It matters not, for the medieval "heretics" were often accused of dabbling in the black arts, an accusation the Waldensians were also used to hearing.

ligacy of the times and receives for it the following rebuke:

Ir duet uns allen schande	*You shame us all*
mit ûren begardien.	*With your beghard[B] behavior.*

A little further in this poem, a virtuous young woman stays back from participation in the lascivious dances planned for the wedding celebration of her more worldly sister; she gets a severe tongue-lashing for her alleged prudery.

Nu was dy brût ein edelwif,	*The bride she was a noble wife*
Hersch unde stolz, dat al ir lif	*Haughty and proud, who all her life*
Zur wereldvroide herze druch;	*Was all for worldly fun;*
Der suster wort sy widersluch,	*She spoke against the pious one,*
Und sprach, vil lyve suster min,	*And said, "Well, darling sister mine,*
Wilt du bi mir begine sin,	*If you must play the beguine[C]*
Ar begardië driven,	*Or be of beghard stripe,*
So ganc zu sulchen wiven	*Then find you women of the type*
Dy des gelusten, dat raden ich;	*That go for that; this I advise;*
Erlaiz der truandien mich,	*Take truand[D] conduct from mine eyes,*
Du solt mir spielen, lachen,	*I'll have you play and laugh and jest*
Und alle vroide machen.	*And merry make with all the rest."*

The following are lines from the medieval poem *The Biography of Saint Lutgard* (*Het Leven van Sinte Lutgard . . . naar een Kopenhaagsch Handschrift* [ed. Van Veerdeghem, Leiden, 1899]). Again we see a person who gets his ears boxed for his attempt at a Christian life-style.

[B]The beghards were originally a reform party within the church; but their criticism of the church's fallenness soon made them operate from outside the church. Then the name came to stand for any "heretic."

[C]The term "beguine" was the female counterpart of beghard. "Beguine" likewise soon became a term of opprobrium and was used to designate a "heretic" of any kind.

[D]*Truand* was another term of reproach applied to those of the rival church; it derives from the fact that the members of the rival church travelled hither and yon as missionaries, people who never were in the place where they were expected to be. Alternative names for Truands were *Läufer* (travellers afoot) and *Schleicher* (persons who enter surreptitiously).

APPENDIX

"Nu comt hier voert, gi papelarde,[E]	"Out in the open, papelarde,
Ghi metten grisen langen barde,	You with the long and flowing beard,[F]
Die al volmaket schinen willet,	Who poses as of men the best,
Ende al benijdt en al beghillet;	Loud criticizing all the rest;
Hort harewart, ghi loese boeven	Your ear this way, you worthless bloke,
Die ommegaet met begardiën!"	Who picks his friends among beghard folk!"

[E] The designation *papelarde* as a smear name for the "heretic" was common; its derivation is uncertain. The most probable explanation is that it consists of a variant of the word *paper* plus the pejorative suffix *ard*; the reference would then be to the "heretic's" way of doting on the "paper" on which the Word of God was written.

[F] Medieval "heretics" were sometimes called *Bartmänner* (men with beards). The wearing of a beard by the men, and of some kind of headdress for the women, was for the member of the rival church a kind of badge indicative of more than ordinary religious rectitude. These badges survive among such groups as the Amish, some Mennonites, and the Hutterites, among whom the wearing of a beard is a religious requirement for the married man.

BIBLIOGRAPHICAL NOTES

Part One

1. Cicero, *Pro Flacco* (Oxford, 1962), Vol. IV, par. 28 (my translation).
2. Hendrik Berkhof, *De Kerk en de Keizer* (Amsterdam, 1946), p. 11.
3. Minucius Felix, *Octavius*, tr. J. H. Freese (London, n.d.), VIII, IX, X.
4. G. C. Berkouwer, *Karl Barth en de Kinderdoop* (Kampen, 1947), p. 112.
5. Emil Brunner, "Die Christusbotschaft und der Staat," *Der Grundriss* (February, 1940), p. 37.

Part Two

1. Oscar Cullmann, *The State in the New Testament* (New York, 1956), p. 20.
2. Quoted in Oscar Cullmann, *Jesus and the Revolutionaries* (New York, 1970), p. 62, n. 11.
3. Martin Hengel, *Die Zeloten* (Leiden, 1961), p. 55.
4. Cullmann, *The State*, p. 15. A. T. Robertson said substantially the same thing earlier in *A Harmony of the Gospels* (New York, 1922), p. 273.
5. Cullmann, *The State*, p. 15.
6. See "Der Zwölfte Apostel," *Vertrage und Aufsätze* (1966), p. 214.
7. For a detailed analysis of *lēstēs* outside and within the NT, see Kittel, *Theological Dictionary of the New Testament* (Grand Rapids, 1967), IV, 257-262.
8. Cullmann, *Jesus and the Revolutionaries*, p. 33.
9. Kittel, *TDNT*, IV, 261-262. Rengstorf's article in Kittel shows clearly how the attempt to stamp Jesus as a Zealot leader is reflected in the language and actions of the Jewish leaders.
10. For a good account of the status of the right of the sword in Jewish affairs at this moment in history, consult Paul Maier, *Pontius Pilate* (Garden City, N.Y., 1968), pp. 129f.
11. Jean Calvin, *Corpus Reformatorum*, ed. Baum *et al.* (Brunsvigae, 1863-1900), Vol. VII, Col. 89.
12. *Ibid.*, Vol. I, Col. 127.

13. Henry Hart Milman, *The History of Christianity from the Birth of Christ to the Abolition of Paganism in the Roman Empire* (London, 1867-1875), II, 287.
14. *Contra Celsum*, VIII, 69.

Part Three

1. *Epistle to Diognetus*, V, *Ante-Nicene Fathers* [hereafter *ANF*] (Grand Rapids, 1973), I, 26-27.
2. Tertullian, *Apologia*, XXXVII, *ANF*, III, 45.
3. James Stevenson (ed.), *A New Eusebius: Documents Illustrative of the History of the Church* (New York, 1957), p. 43.
4. Leo Pfeffer, *Church, State and Freedom* (Boston, 1953), p. 11.
5. W. H. C. Frend, *The Donatist Church* (Oxford, 1952), p. 157, n. 7.
6. A. H. M. Jones, *Constantine and the Conversion of Europe* (New York, 1962), p. 153.
7. Martroye, "Une Tentative de Revolution Sociale en Afrique," *Revue des questions historique*, LXXVI (1904), 365.
8. Jones, *Constantine*, pp. 74f.
9. *Ibid.*, pp. 75f.
10. Justinian, *Codex Theodosianus* (Berlin, 1877), XVI, 5:40. The emperor Justinian revised, enlarged, and rearranged the code of Theodosius and published it in 529.
11. *Nicene and Post-Nicene Fathers* [hereafter *NPF*] (Grand Rapids, 1955), 2nd ser., X, 440-445.
12. Abraham Kuyper, *Pro Rege* (Kampen, 1911-1912), III, 166f.
13. Jacob Burckhardt, *The Age of Constantine* (Garden City, N. Y., 1949), p. 293.
14. Jones, *Constantine*, p. 113.
15. Henry Hart Milman, *loc. cit.*
16. E. Jansen Schoonhoven, "*Corpus Christianum en Zending*," *Christusprediking in de Wereld* (Kampen, 1965), pp. 167f.
17. *Ad Catholicos Epistola*, II, 2, quoted in Frend, p. 255, n. 5.
18. *Contra Epistolam Parmeniani*, II, 2:5, quoted in Frend, p. 167, nn. 1, 2.
19. *NPF*, I, 546-547, Section 10.
20. *Ibid.*, pp. 544f. (This volume also contains the letter to Lady Felicia, No. CCVIII.)
21. *De Correctione Donatistarum*, *NPF*, IV, 642.
22. Sermon LXII on Luke 14:16, *NPF*, VI, 449.
23. Frend, p. 320.
24. *NPF*, I, 385.
25. Letter XCIII to Vincentius, *NPF*, I, 383.
26. *NPF*, IV, 462.
27. Frend, p. 320.
28. *Ibid.*, p. 321.
29. G. R. Beasley-Murray, *Baptism in the New Testament* (Grand Rapids, 1974), p. 104, n. 1.
30. *NPF*, VIII, 217.
31. *NPF*, I, 389.

32. Augustus Neander, *General History of the Christian Religion and Church* (London, 1896), II, 214f.
33. *NPF*, I, 391.
34. *NPF*, I, 558f.
35. *Ibid.*
36. *Monumenta Germanicae Historia* (Hanover, 1829), II, 164, Letter No. 113.
37. Paul Fredericq, *Corpus Documentorum Inquisitionis Haereticae Pravitatis Neerlandicae* [hereafter *Corpus*], 5 vols. (Gent, 1889-1902), I, 143.
38. Thomas Aquinas, *Summa* II, 2, Q. 11, Art. 3.
39. Ludwig Keller, *Die Waldenser und die Deutsche Bibelübersetzungen*, (Leipzig, 1886), p. 43.
40. Frend, p. 322.
41. Cullmann, *The State in the New Testament*, pp. 7, 9.
42. Jones, *Constantine*, pp. 197f.
43. *Cf. Corpus*, under "Hussite," index to Vol. III.
44. Montet, *Histoire Litteraire des Vaudois du Piedmont* (Paris, 1885), p. 137.
45. Von Zeschwitz, *Die Katechismen der Waldenser und Böhmische Brüder* (Erlangen, 1863), p. 179.
46. *Octavius*, p. 43.
47. Ludwig Keller, *Die Reformation und die Ältere Reformparteien* (Leipzig, 1885), p. 76.
48. Herbert Grundmann, *Religiöse Bewegungen im Mittelalter* (Berlin, 1935), p. 20.
49. *Ibid.*, p. 19, n. 10.
50. "*Novel Confort*," quoted in Montet, *Histoire*, p. 140.
51. George Gordon Coulton, *Inquisition and Liberty* (Boston, 1959), p. 189.
52. *Ibid.*, pp. 178-180.
53. Migne, *Pat. Lat.*, XXV, 264.
54. Summarized by Coulton, p. 63.
55. Günther Franz, *Urkundliche Quellen zur hessischen Reformationsgeschichte bearbeitet nach Walter Köhler, Walter Sohm, Theodor Sippell* [hereafter cited as Franz] (Marburg, 1951), IV, 381.
56. *Codex Theodosianus*, XVI, 1:2.
57. Quoted in Grundmann, p. 98, n. 52.
58. Coulton, p. 184.
59. *Corpus*, I, 352.
60. Walter L. Wakefield and Austin P. Evans, *Heresies of the High Middle Ages* [hereafter Wakefield] (New York, 1969), p. 120.
61. *Ibid.*, p. 326.
62. *Ibid.*, p. 328.
63. Adolf von Harnack, "Die Didache und die Waldenser," *Texte und Untersuchungen zur Geschichte der Altchristliche Literatur* (Leipzig, 1866), p. 269.
64. Coulton, p. 198.
65. Krasinski, *Reformation in Poland* (London, 1938), p. 68.
66. A. J. Zieglschmid, *Die älteste Chronik der Hutterischen Brüder* (Ithaca, N.Y., 1943), p. 34.
67. Frend, p. 324.
68. *Ibid.*, p. 332.
69. Ludwig Keller, *Die Reformation und die Ältere Reformparteien* (Leipzig, 1885), p. 396.

Part Four

1. C. A. Cornelius, *Geschichte des Münsterischen Aufruhrs* (Leipzig, 1855), p. 18.
2. *Cf.* Johann Loserth, *Georg Blaurock und die Anfänge des Anabaptismus in Graubündten und Tirol* (Berlin, 1899), p. 11.
3. Cornelius, p. 7.
4. Commentary on Genesis 41:45, *Luthers Sämmtliche Schriften* [hereafter *Schriften*] (St. Louis, 1880), II, Col. 1417.
5. *Cf.* the article on the Böhmische Brüder in Johann Jakob Herzog, *Realencyklopädie für Protestantische Theologie und Kirche* (Leipzig, 1878), p. 663.
6. Details of this meeting of minds, as well as full documentation, are given in Carl Pestalozzi, *Heinrich Bullinger, Leben und Ausgewählte Schriften* (Elberfeld, 1858); also in Rudolph Stähelin, *Huldreich Zwingli: Sein Leben und Werken* (Basel, 1895-1897), II, 223.
7. Guido de Bres, *Racine: Source et Fondement des Anabaptistes*. I have translated from folio 338r of the Dutch translation.
8. *Monatshefte Comenius Gesellschaft*, Heft 9, 10 (1898), p. 308.
9. Jean Crespin, *Histoire des Martyrs* (Toulouse, 1885-89), I, 56.
10. Quoted in Keller, *Die Anfänge der Reformation und die Ketzerschulen* (Berlin, 1897), p. 54.
11. *Schriften*, VII, 200-201.
12. Urbanus Rhegius, *Widderlegung der Münsterischen neuen Valentinianer und Donatisten bekanntnis mit vorrhede Doctor Martin Luthers* (Wittenberg, 1535).
13. Calvin, *Institutes of the Christian Religion* [hereafter *Inst.*], Book IV, 1:13 (Grand Rapids, 1966), II, 292.
14. Luther, *Schriften*, VIII, 4.
15. *Bibliotheca Reformatoria Neerlandica*, eds. S. Cramer and F. Pijper (The Hague, 1903-1914), II, 305.
16. Guy Hershberger, ed., *The Recovery of the Anabaptist Vision* (Scottdale, 1957), p. 137.
17. *Schriften*, VIII, 4.
18. Franz, pp. 102f.
19. *Schriften*, V, 747.
20. Westin-Bergsten, *Quellen zur Geschichte der Täufer, IX Band, Balthasar Hübmaiers Schriften* [hereafter Hübmaier] (Gütersloh, 1962), p. 133.
21. *Mennonite Encyclopedia* (Hillsboro, Kansas, 1955-1959), IV, 429B.
22. *Mennonite Encyclopedia*, III, 473.
23. *Ibid.*, IV, 432, Col. 2.
24. Zwingli, *Hauptschriften*, ed. Fritz Blanke *et al.* (Zürich, 1947), Teil III, pp. 349f.
25. Leonhard von Muralt and Walter Schmid, *Quellen zur Geschichte der Täufer in der Schweiz* [hereafter Muralt] (Zürich, 1952), p. 27.
26. Hübmaier, p. 186.
27. Wm. Hadorn, *Die Reformation in der deutschen Schweiz* (Leipzig, 1928), p. 104.
28. Zwingli, *Hauptschriften*, Teil III, pp. 134f.
29. *Ibid.*, p. 103.
30. *Ibid.*, p. 136.
31. Franz, pp. 226f.

BIBLIOGRAPHICAL NOTES

32. Manfred Krebs and Jean Rott, *Quellen zur Geschichte der Täufer, VII Band, Elsas, Theil 2 (Stadt Strassburg 1522-1532)* [hereafter Krebs] (Gütersloh, 1959).
33. Quoted in Röhrich, *Niedners Zeitschrift für die Historische Theologie* (1860), p. 115.
34. Kittel, *TDNT*, II, 53.
35. Franz, p. 382.
36. *Ibid.*, p. 363.
37. Quoted in William Klassen, *Covenant and Community* (Grand Rapids, 1968), p. 160, n. 64.
38. *Huldrici Zwinglii Opera*, Schuler and Schulthess, eds. (Turici, 1832-42), IV, 58-60.
39. *Huldreich Zwinglis Sämmtliche Werke, Corpus Reformatorum* (Berlin, 1905), XCVI, 464.
40. Zwingli, "Von dem Tauff, Wiedertauff und vom Kindertauff" (Introduction), *Hauptschriften*, II, 12.
41. Rudolph Stähelin, *Huldreich Zwingli: Sein Leben und Werken* (Basel, 1895-1897), II, 482.
42. Ernst Müller, *Geschichte der Bernischen Täufer* (Frauenfeld, 1895). Reference is to the Nieuwkoop reprint (1972), p. 48.
43. *Placcaetboek van Vlaanderen* (Gent, 1639), p. 118.
44. Hübmaier, p. 340.
45. *Complete Writings of Menno Simons*, tr. Leonard Verduin (Scottdale, 1956), p. 506.
46. Luther, *Schriften*, I, 296.
47. *Acta des Gespraechs zwueschenn predicantenn Uund Tauffbruederen Ergangen Inn der Statt Bernn* . . . (In Vol. 80 of *Unnütze Papiere*, in the Staatsarchiv des Kantons Bern; the Mennonite Historical Library at Goshen College, Goshen, Indiana, has a copy of this manuscript.)
48. Franz, pp. 202f.
49. Quoted in John Horsch, *Infant Baptism* (Scottdale, 1917), p. 42.
50. Such sentiments are found throughout Luther's "Von weltlicher Oberkeit," D. *Martin Luthers Werke* [hereafter *Werke*] (Weimar, 1883), XI, 229-281.
51. *Ibid.*, XI, 264.
52. *Schriften*, X, Col. 229.
53. *Werke*, XII, 485f.
54. *Schriften*, XXIa, cd. 571.
55. *Ibid.*, XV, Col. 2572.
56. Zieglschmid, p. 42.
57. Hans J. Hillerbrand, "Ein Täuferbekenntnis aus dem 16. Jahrhundert," *Archiv für Reformationsgeschichte* (1959, Heft 1), 49.
58. *Schriften*, V, 901.
59. "Briefwechsel," in *Werke*, VI, 564.
60. *Ibid.*, XXXI, Band I, 209.
61. *Schriften*, XX, Col. 1718.
62. *Ibid.*, XXII, Col. 1827.
63. *Ibid.*, V, Col. 720f.
64. Manfred Krebs, *Quellen zur Geschichte der Täufer, IV Band, Baden und Pfaltz* (Gütersloh, 1951), p. 150.
65. Franz, p. 42.

66. P. Imbart de la Tour in *Revue de metaphysique et de morale*, XXV (1918), 610.
67. Paul Wernle, *Der Evangelische Glaube* (Tübingen, 1919), III, 56.
68. A. C. McGiffert, "Calvin's Theory of the Church," *Essays in Modern Theology and Related Subjects* (New York, 1911), p. 225.
69. *Inst.*, IV, 20:4.
70. Franz, pp. 421, 444.
71. *Corpus Reformatorum* (Baum *et al.*), VII, 81.
72. Franklin H. Littell, *The Anabaptist View of the Church* (Boston, 1952), p. 7.
73. *Corpus Reformatorum*, VI, 572.
74. *Ibid.*, XII, 283.
75. *Ibid.*, VIII, col. 362.
76. Quoted in Mosheim, *Anderwertiger versuch einer Vollständiger und unparteyischer Ketzergeschichte* (Helmstadt, 1748), pp. 421f.
77. *Archief voor Kerkelijke Geschiedenis* (1842), XIII, 85.
78. Johann Wilhelm Baum, *Theodor Beza nach Handschriftlichen Quellen Dargestellt* (Leipzig, 1843-1851), I, 223.
79. This edict is found in the Knuttel Pamphlets, of which the University of Michigan has a copy in its General Library.
80. Johan Adam Wormser, *De Kinderdoop, Beschouwd met Betrekking tot het Bijzondere, Kerklijke en Maatschappelijke Leven* (Amsterdam, 1864).
81. A. A. Van Schelven, *Uit den Strijd der Geesten* (Amsterdam, 1944), p. 191.
82. *Tolerantie in de Zestiende Eeuw* (published by Comm. Postacademiale Vorming, The Hague).
83. Sweet, *Religion in Colonial America* (New York, 1942), p. 320.
84. *Of the Laws of Ecclesiastical Polity* (Keble ed.: Oxford, 1888), I, 342; III, 1, 7.
85. Roger Williams, *Complete Works* [hereafter *C.W.*] (New York, 1963), III, 351, note.
86. *Tracts on Liberty of Conscience and Persecution*, ed. Edward B. Underhill (New York, 1966), p. 270, n. 3.
87. Calvin, *Commentary on Isaiah* (Grand Rapids, 1947), Introduction, pp. XIX-XXV.
88. Champlin Burrage, *The Early English Dissenters* (New York, 1966), I, 105.
89. *Ibid.*, I, 237.
90. Quoted in J. DeHoop Scheffer, *History of the Free Churchmen Called Brownists* (Ithaca, N. Y., 1922), p. 250.
91. This confession by Helwys is found in Thomas Crosby, *The History of English Baptists from the Reformation to the Beginning of the Reign of King George I* (London, 1738).
92. Quoted in Daniel Neal, *History of the Puritans* (Portsmouth, N.H., 1817), II, 146f.
93. McGiffert, p. 225.
94. Cotton's "Bloudy Tenent Washed . . ." as quoted in *C.W.*, IV, 265.
95. *Massachusetts Bay Colony Records*, II, 85.
96. This early translation of the Belgic Confession, done around the year 1640, is found in the Knuttel Collection.
97. *Mass. Bay Colony Records*, I, 242 (Sept. 6, 1638).
98. From Mather's *Magnalia*, quoted in *C.W.*, VII, 9.

BIBLIOGRAPHICAL NOTES 267

99. *Introduction to the History of the Nineteenth Century* (ET, London, 1853).
100. Quoted in Georg Jellinek, *The Declaration of the Rights of Man and of Citizens* (New York, 1901), p. 77.
101. "Die Toleranzbegriff Lockes und Pufendorfs," *Studien zur Geschichte der Theologie und der Kirche* (Leipzig, 1901), pp. 2, 57.
102. Joachim Beckmann, quoted in Franklin Littell, *Landgraf Philipp und die Toleranz* (Bad Nauheim, 1957), p. 40.
103. *Rhode Island Records*, I, 243.
104. "Die Bedeutung des Protestantismus für die Entstehung der Moderne Welt," *Historische Zeitschrift* (Beiheft, 1924), 63.
105. *Rhode Island Records*, I, 243.
106. Quoted in Keller, *Die Reformation und die Ältere Reformparteien*, p. 65.
107. "State and Church," *The Abiding Word* (Concordia, 1947), II, 510.
108. *Commonweal* (Sept. 6, 1957).
109. "Volkskirche, Freikirche, Bekenntniskirche," *Evangelische Theologie* (1937), 415.
110. *Die Kirchliche Lehre von der Taufe* (Munich, 1947), pp. 39f.
111. *The Church and the World in Idea and in History*, Eight Lectures (London, 1910), pp. IXf.

INDEX

Abba Sikara 65
Abraham 26, 27, 52, 54, 57, 178, 221
Adiaphorists 208
Africa 97, 98, 108, 120, 148, 165, 248
Albigensians 38, 88, 134
Alexander, Pierre 226
Amaziah 39
Ambrose 101
Amos 39
Amsterdam 33, 228
Anabaptists 38, 76, 146, 149, 153, 157, 158, 160-162, 164-171, 174-178, 180, 181, 183, 186-188, 190, 191, 194, 195, 198, 200-208, 210, 214, 217-221, 223, 225-228, 230, 237, 244, 245, 247
Anglicans 215
Ante-Nicene church 251
Anullinus 98, 99
Apostles' Creed 77, 138, 173, 226
Aquinas, Thomas 122, 263
Arian controversy 95
Aristotle 133
Arius 96
Arminianism 102
Athanasius 96
Athenians 16, 17
Athens 16, 17, 19

Augustine 105-111, 113, 118-121, 123, 125, 133, 162, 165-169, 175, 180, 181, 185, 186, 194, 198-200, 204, 210, 216, 236, 251
"Austin Friars" 237

Babylon 12, 27, 45
Bacha 197
Bainton, Roland 167
Barabbas 67, 74
Barjona 65
Barlow, William 218
Barrows 220
Barth, Karl 102, 216, 249-251
Bastian 218
Baum, Johann Wilhelm 261, 266
Baylie, Robert 217, 218
Beasley-Murray, G. R. 117, 262
Beckmann, Joachim 267
Beghards 130, 164, 257-259
Belgic Confession 34-36, 70, 153, 163, 201, 203, 206, 210, 212, 214, 224, 237
Berkhof, Hendrik 12, 261
Berkouwer, G. C. 32, 261
Bernard of Clairvaux 148
Bern Confrontation 196
Berne 183
Beyer, Leonhard 195
Beza 199, 208, 223-225, 266
Blanke, Fritz 264

INDEX 269

Blaurock, George 170, 171
Bloccius, Peter 209
"Bloody Mary" 217, 218
Boanerges 66
Bogerman, Johannes 209f.
Bogomils 134
Bohemian Brethren 130, 206
Boston, General Court in 230, 241
British Isles, Anabaptism in the 218
Browne, Robert 219, 220
Brownists 219, 223
Brunner, Emil 33, 34, 261
Bucer, 176, 183, 184
Bugenhagen 195
Bullinger, Henri 156, 162, 163, 247
Burckhardt, Jacob 262
Burrage, Champlin 266
Burroughs 217
Busher, Mark Leonard 219

Caecilian 97-99
Calamy, Edmund 217
Callinicum 100
Calvin, John 58, 76, 83, 166, 185, 195, 198-211, 217, 223-227, 261, 264, 266
Calvinism 161, 208-214, 218, 222, 240
Cambridge 220
Canaanites 48, 79
Cape Colony 213
Capito 174, 183
Cappel, battle of 182
Carey, William 233
Castellio, Sebastian 208
Castellionists 209, 211
Catabaptists 164
Cathars 133, 134, 136, 137, 165, 166, 168
Catholicism
  and the magisterial reformers 157, 217, 235, 236
  the rival church and 136, 164

Charlemagne 121, 166
Charles V 153
Chaucer 214
Chauncy 229
Chelcicky, Peter 151
Church of England 215, 221
Cicero 11, 261
Circumcelliones 181
Clapham, Henoch 220
Clarke 241
Codes of Justinian 100
Codes of Theodosius 166
Codex Bezae 67
Cogley, John 249
Cologne, 1163 145
Compromis of 1566 159
Constantine 95-104, 111, 127, 150, 151, 155, 166, 192, 193, 234, 235, 248, 249, 251, notes
Constantinian change 95-132, 150, 177, 196, 234, 235, 249
Constantinianism 181, 183, 203, 246, 250, 252
Corinth 81, 82
Cornelius, conversion of 176
Cornelius, C. A. 157, 160, 161, 264
Cotton, John 224, 225, 230-233, 238, 242, 243, 266
Coulton, George Gordon 151, 263
Cramer, S. 264
Crespin, Jean 163, 264
Creutziger 195
Crosby, Thomas 266
Crusades 38
Cullmann, Oscar 63, 66, 126, 261, 263
Czechoslovakia, rival church in 130
Czerwenka 199

Dabszynski 151
Dagon 25
Dalman, G. 65
David 46, 111

David of Augsburg 132
de Bres, Guido 163, 264
Decius 93, 141
de la Forge, Etienne 199
de la Tour, P. Imbart 266
Dewey, John 254, 255
Diana 13
Diego of Osmo 143, 144
Diet of Augsburg 240
Dionysus 18
Dominicans 139, 144
Donatists 97, 98, 106-109, 113, 115, 118, 120, 123, 125, 148, 152, 165-168, 180
Dorchester 228
Dordt 102
Dutch East Indies 213
Dutch Reformed Church 209, 213

Edict of Milan 94
Edict of Toleration 94, 95
Edward VI 240
Eighty Years War 209, 210
Elijah and Elisha 142
Elizabeth I 240
Emser, Jerome 153
Engelbrecht, Anton 194
England 159, 214-222, 237, 239, 240, 242-244
English Puritans 223
Enlightenment 244, 245
Entscheidung 26
Ephesus 13
Erasmus 156
Esau 179
Etienne de Bourbon 139
Europe, rival church in 99, 131, 134, 143, 158, 161, 162, 171, 191, 208, 211, 235, 244, 249
Eusebius 94, 101
Evans, Austin P. 147, 263
Ezra 47-49

Feast of the Booths 28

Ferdinand of Austria 170
First Amendment 140, 243, 246, 247
Flanders 146, 218, 226
Fourth Lateran Council 123
France 159, 164
Franz, Günther 263-266
Frederick IV 240
Frederick of the Palatinate 239, 240
Fredericq, Paul 263
Freese, J. H. 261
French Confession 207
Frend, W. H. C. 115, 124, 152, 262, 263

Gainsborough 220
Geneva 208, 211, 223, 227
German Reformation 198
Germany 159, 218, 245, 248
Gervinus 243
Graaf-Reinet, Classis of 214
Great Commission 107, 113
Grebel, Conrad 155-158, 169, 170, 172, 187, 206, 212, 219
Greenwood 220
Grossmünster, canon of 156
Grundmann, Herbert 133, 263

Hadorn, Wm. 264
Harnack, Adolf von 150, 263
Haug, Conrad 183
Hausman, Nicolas 190
Hebrews (*see* Israelites and sacralism)
Heidelberg Catechism 76, 77, 226, 239, 240, 244
Helwys, Thomas 220, 221, 228, 266
Hengel, Martin 66, 261
Henry VIII 159, 214, 218, 240
Herod 64, 79
Hershberger, Guy 264
Herzog, Johann Jakob 264
Hilary of Poitiers 129

INDEX

Hillerbrand, Hans J. 265
Hisda, Rabbi 216
Hobhouse, Walter 251
Hofmeister, Sebastian 174, 183
Holland 159, 209, 210, 213, 219, 222, 223, 225
Holmes, Obadiah 241, 242
Hooker, Richard 215, 216
Horsch, John 265
Hosea 46, 47, 179
Hosius, Bishop of Cordova 98
Hübmaier, Balthasar 173, 185, 186, 264, 265
Hus, John 156, 187

India 117
Indians 231, 232
Innocent III 123, 139
Ireland, sacralism in 85
Isaac 26, 27, 179
Isaiah 46
Ishmael 179
Israel, modern 85
Israelites and sacralism 25-31, 38-53
Itala 67

Jacob 26, 27, 179
James 66, 176
Jefferson, Thomas 245, 246
Jellinek, Georg 244, 267
Jerusalem 39, 59, 61, 216
Jewish Sanhedrin 68, 69, 72
Jews and Jesus 61-78
Joachim of Fiore 107
Jochanan ben Zakkai 65
John, St. 66, 77, 255
John the Baptist 53-61, 79, 106, 128, 134
Johnson, Francis 220
Jonah 42, 43, 79
Jones, A. H. M. 262, 263
Joris, David 208
Josephus 66
Jud, Leo 156

Judaism 126
Judas Iscariot 66-70
Justinian 100, 166, 262

Kampen 219
Katabaptists 146
Keller, Ludwig 124, 263, 264, 267
Kerioth 66
King Edward 217
King James I 221
Kittel 261
Klassen, William 265
Knipperdollink, Bernard 165, 166
Köhler, Walter 263
Kraemer, Hendrik 251
Krafft, Adam 184
Krasinski 263
Krebs, Manfred 265
Kuchenbäcker, Hans 202
Kuyper, Abraham 33, 101, 102, 262

Lady Felicia 120, 212, 262
Lafayette 244
Lea, Henry C. 137
Lebrman, S. M. 216
"Leonists" 149
Leufer 143
Levites 48
Lezius 244
Liege, 1147 148
Limnat Lake 169
Littell, Franklin H. 266, 267
Lo-ammi 46-48
Lollardim, Lollards 214, 218f.
Lo-ruhamah 46-48
Loserth, Johann 264
Louis VI 240
Lucas of Prague 160
Lucius III 147
Luther, Martin 128, 132, 151, 153, 156, 158-160, 163-168, 186-198, 250, 264, 265

Lutheranism, Lutherans 177, 208, 211, 213, 218, 240, 248
Lynn 241

Maccabeanism, Maccabees 58, 63, 100
Maccabean Wars 51
McGiffert, A. C. 200, 223, 266
Maier, Paul 261
Manes 168
Manicheans 133, 168
Manz, Felix 156, 168-172
Marcion 87, 88, 126
Marcionism 87
Marianus 166
Marpeck, Pilgram 178
Mars Hill 17, 18
Martinist 213
Martroye 97, 262
Mary Tudor 240
Massachusetts Bay Colony 212, 226, 229-231, 240, 243, 244
Massasoit, Chief 233
Mather, Cotton 242, 243, 266
Matthew, St. 69, 209
Maxentius 103
Mayflower 222
Mayflower Compact 223
Meisinger, Karl 183
Melanchthon, Philipp 164, 207, 218
Melchizedek 161
Meliton of Sardis 94
Metz, Bishop of 139
Meyer, J. 257
Meyer, Theodore 248
Middelburg 220
Migne 263
Milan 94
Milman, Henry Hart 262
Minucius Felix 14, 261
Missouri Synod 248
Moneta of Cremona 149
Montanists 88
Montet 263
Moravians 213

Moses 94, 120, 231
Mosheim 266
Müller, Ernst 265
Münsterites 181
Müntzer, Thomas 206
Muralt 172, 173

Naaman the Syrian 142
Navajo Indians 13, 20
Nazarites 28, 29
Nazis 245, 249
Neal, Daniel 266
Neander, Augustus 119, 263
Nebuchadnezzar 12, 101, 109, 110, 184
Nederduits Gereformeerde Kerk 213
Nehemiah 47, 48
Nero 38
New Jerusalem 35
Newport 241
New Spain 20
Nicodemitism, Nicodemites 141, 142, 145, 197, 205
Nicodemus 141
Niemoeller 246
Nieuw Amsterdam 213
Nijenhuis, W. 211
Nineveh 12, 13, 42, 43
Ninevites 42
North Africa, churches of 97
Norwich 220
Novatian 89, 118
Novatianism 89

Oecolampadius 174
Olivetan 199
Oracle at Delphi 22
Origen 90, 94

Palatinate 240
Palfrey 241
Papists 208
Paris 144
Parliament, British 217, 218, 220
Passover 28
Patmos 255

INDEX

Paul, St.   17, 18, 20, 39, 40, 48, 67, 77, 81-83, 87, 110, 186-188, 195, 196, 204, 231
Paulicians   87
Peasant War   153
Pestalozzi, Carl   264
Peter, St.   63-65, 68, 100, 111, 138, 204
Peters, Hugh   228
Petilian   109
Pfeffer, Leo   262
Philip of Hesse   177, 187, 188, 195, 197
Philips, Dirck   186
Philistines   25
"Picard Bible"   192
Picardism, Picards   130, 160, 164, 191, 194, 199
Piedmont   130
Pijper, F.   264
Pilgrims   222, 223
Pilichdorf   151
Plato   23, 83, 93, 99, 178, 196, 205
Plymouth colony   228, 229, 233
Poland   151
Pontius Pilate   67, 70-76
Pope Pelagius   112
Predikheeren   144
Providence, R. I.   226, 236, 243
Puritan   220

"Quakers"   226

Raleigh, Sir Walter   220
"Ranters"   226
"Rebaptizers"   149
Reformation,
  rival church in the   155-212
  and the hybrid   155-212
Reformed Church   34, 35, 37, 163, 210, 212, 213, 223, 252
Reformed Presbyterian Church   37
Rengstorf   261
Rhegius, Urbanus   165, 166, 264
Rhode Island   212, 243, 247

Richter, Michel   177
Rinck, Melchior   198
Rival church   130n., *passim*
Robertson, A. T.   261
Robinson, John   220, 223
Röhrich   265
Roman Catholic view of church and state   37, 120, 249, 250
Romans   14, 15, 18, 35, 50, 51, 58, 62-68, 70, 71, 74, 75, 81, 90
Roman Empire   115, 152
Rome   11, 12, 14-17, 38, 88, 94, 97, 114, 215
Rott, Jean   265

Sacconi   135
Sacramentarian   144, 149, 160, 191
Salem   230, 233, 238, 239
Samaritans   79, 80
Samuel   30
Saracens   215, 248
Sattler, Michael   170, 171
Saul   30, 32, 33, 37-39, 101, 104, 127
Saxons   121
Scheffer, J. DeHoop   266
Schippers   213
Schleicher   142-144
Schleitheim   200
Schleitheim confession   201-206
Schmid, Walter   264
Schoonhoven, E. Jansen   262
Schwarzhaus   177
Scrooby   220
Secession of 1834   213
Sejanus   70
Seneca   199, 202, 204
Sermon on the Mount   35
Servetus   38, 206-208, 210, 211, 224
Shear-jashub   46
"Shipletter"   236, 237
Simon the Cananean   66
Simon Zelotes   66
Simons, Menno   186, 265

Sippell, Theodore 263
Smyth, John 220, 221, 228
Sneek 210
Sohm, Walter 263
Sol Invictus 96, 97, 104
South Africa 37, 49, 213, 214, 216, 252
Stähelin, Rudolph 264, 265
Spalatin 191
Stephen's sermon 78
Stevenson, James 262
Stockenström 214
Strasbourg 177, 183, 184, 194, 199
Stuyvesant, Pieter 213
Swabia 161
Sweet, William Warren 211, 266
Switzerland 156, 157, 208, 218
Sylvestre (Pope) 151
Synod of Dordt 120, 209
Synod of Jerusalem 176
Synod of Terracona 123
Synod of Toulouse 123

Talmud 65
Tarshish 43
Tarsus 39
Tertullian 92, 262
Tesch, Peter 218
Theodosius 100, 102, 138, 141, 166, 207, 262
Tobiah the Ammonite 47
Treaty of 1555 240
Troeltsch, Ernst 247
Tyrol 171

Underhill, Edward B. 266
Uzziah 31-33, 37, 38, 101

Vadian 157
van Brugge, Jan 208
Van der Eeke 146
van Haemstede, Adrian 195
van Prinsterer, Groen 210
Van Schelven, A. A. 210-212, 214, 266
Van Veerdegham 258

Vincentius 110, 262
Virginia 229, 244
Volkskirche 59, 102, 171, 174, 213-215, 249, 250
von Muralt, Leonhard 264
von Usingen, Bartholomäus 164
Von Zeschwitz 263
Vulgate 115, 192

Wakefield, Walter L. 147, 263
Waldensians 38, 88, 129, 130, 135, 149, 151, 160, 162, 163, 199, 225, 247, 257, 258
Waldo, Peter 129, 149
Wartburg 191
Watt, Joachim 157
Wernle, Paul 200, 266
Westin-Bergsten 264
Westminster Assembly 217
Westminster Confession 131
William of Newburgh 137, 138
Williams, Roger 212, 214, 217, 218, 223-244, 247, 266
Winckler 141
Winslow 230
Winthrop, Governor 225
Wittenberg 162, 192
Worms 156
Wormser, John 210, 266
Wyclif 187

Zealotism, Zealots 58, 59, 63-69, 73, 74, 100
Zell, Katharina 187
Zieglschmid, A. J. 263, 265
Zollikon 156
Zuni Indians 14, 20
Zürich 155, 156, 161, 168, 172, 181-184, 189, 212, 219, 229, 247
Zwickau 195
Zwingli 156, 157, 162, 163, 169, 171-175, 178-183, 186-188, 191-194, 196, 247, 264, 265
Zwinglians 208, 211